DON'T SLAP YOUR WIFE

DON'T SLAP YOUR WIFE BUT DON'T GET SLAPPED EITHER

DR SUNIL VAID

EBURY PRESS

An imprint of Penguin Random House

EBURY PRESS

USA | Canada | UK | Ireland | Australia
New Zealand | India | South Africa | China | Singapore

Ebury Press is part of the Penguin Random House group of companies whose addresses can be found at global.penguinrandomhouse.com

Published by Penguin Random House India Pvt. Ltd
4th Floor, Capital Tower 1, MG Road,
Gurugram 122 002, Haryana, India

Penguin
Random House
India

First published by Random House India 2013

10 9 8 7 6 5 4 3 2

ISBN 9788184003840

Typeset in Elegant Garamond BT by R. Ajith Kumar

Printed at Repro India Limited

www.penguin.co.in

FSC www.fsc.org MIX Paper from responsible sources FSC® C047271

This is a legitimate digitally printed version of the book and therefore might not have certain extra finishing on the cover.

For my mom, Shahni,

perhaps the first mother ever to say to her only son
a day before his wedding, 'From now on,
your wife's word should mean more to you than ours.'

To answer the question she knew this raised
in her son's mind, she added, 'I will be happy
ONLY if you keep her happy.'

Contents

PART IV

A DIRECT WORD OF ADVICE

Preface

I know, I know, I know . . .

I know the portrayal of marriage that I'm setting out to draw, where the wife is the perpetrator of injustice, is true of only two out of ten urban homes in India. I also know that in more than double that number of homes, it is the wife who is suppressed, manipulated or tortured by the husband.

But two out of ten is approximately 20 million men, in India alone. Their Western counterparts are not faring much better. Many of these men are suave, urban and well-read. This is the segment in which the malady of the exploitation of husbands is catching on faster than the lure of the smartphone. The problem is compounded by the silence around the subject, just as female exploitation festers when the fear of speaking out against it keeps women silent.

The reason men keep it all bottled up is the ignominy of being considered 'not man enough'. This book is the voice of these men and advice to other men who are thinking about marriage.

Why this book?

One question at the top of the minds of most bachelors (after sex, of course), is—will his 'would-be wife' be compatible with him and his family?

For those of you who are already married: have you ever caught yourself wondering, 'Do I have a good marriage?'

If you have never pondered over this question—that is great! You have as close to a 'perfect' marriage as is possible. You and your spouse have accepted each other as unquestionable parts of your lives. Congrats! However, if you have frequently wondered or, worse, worried about the state of your relationship and about its future, then you are part of the majority of couples who have compatibility issues.

While talking to many of my long-standing male patients who've got married recently or are planning to get married, I learned that most of them were desperately seeking advice on marriage. Some, seeing the plight of others who were suffering the consequences, were afraid to bite the unforbidden apple. Others had bitten it already but were nibbling at it noncommittally, not sure whether they liked the taste. And a large number had bitten more than they could chew and were now literally choking on what had first seemed a delicious, rejuvenating elixir. As one of my patients, Abhishek, put it, 'I never realized that the wife I took home as the solution to all the problems of my life would turn out to be the cause of all of them.'

Abhishek, like most men of his ilk, won't go to a counsellor because he is shy/ashamed/scared/prejudiced/afraid of social stigma—'What kind of a man is he, if he can't even manage his wife?' Men like him also somehow feel that though the apple is bitter, it is not YET rotten enough to require a marriage counsellor.

'Why don't you refer to a good book on marriage, then?' I asked Abhishek.

'Which book?' he asked.

'Any good book—I'm sure there must be more books on marriage than there are matrimonial advertisements in a Sunday newspaper,' I offered in my know-it-all voice.

> My wife suggested I read a book to improve our relationship. It is titled *Women Are from Venus and Men Are Wrong*.

'There are books,' replied the burly Haryana lad , 'but they are all so politically correct that you feel they stop well short of addressing the main issue, leave alone tackling it. They all tell you what *should* be done ideally—not what can be done in real life. And most address issues purely from a female perspective. They don't have any advice for the decent, non-tormenting husband, about how to cope with a demanding wife.'

This seemed unlikely, so I decided to check it for myself. In the end, I was surprised at the veracity of the young man's comment. Even some of my favourite authors who had written extensively about the male–female equation preferred to steer clear of the advice that would have befitted today's changing paradigms of the husband–wife relationship . Their books, though interesting and conceptually spot on, just didn't address the issues foremost in the minds of disillusioned urban males, especially regarding how to balance their modern wives' aspirations vis-à-vis their own perceived mindsets or, worse, their conservative family's expectations.

So, dear friends, here are my two bits of advice—consider them and keep it at the back of your mind even if you disagree with some of them. It might prove to be a marriage-saver. For, if the source of a person's greatest happiness and biggest pain is one and the same thing—marriage—then it makes sense to invest in it to make it blissful.

Let the journey begin.

~

This book is dedicated to you, dear reader, for you are the reason for my existence.

I'm grateful to you from the core of my heart and assure you that any feedback or communication from your side, whether by mail, e-mail, a bouquet or a slipper thrown at my head, will be given due attention, even if I don't agree with you.

Dr Sunil Vaid

1

The Story of the First Night

> While creating women, God promised men that they would find 'good and ideal' wives in every corner of the earth. He then made the earth round.

'To phir, kal billi kisne mari?' (So then, who came out tops on the wedding night?)

The statement pulverized the veneer of courtesy between the three newlyweds. All their 'Helloji, what-a-nice-day, lovely-evening'-type statements were suddenly pointless.

They had met the day before at Mumbai airport, which was flooded because of the early rains. Flights had been cancelled. What had brought the group together was that they were spending their respective honeymoons in the same resort in Goa and had travelled together from Mumbai in the mini-bus that the travel agency had arranged. Now, they were meeting after their respective 'first nights' as they ventured out to the beach.

The reclining chairs in the shack opposite the resort were inviting and Saloni was the first to settle down under the netting strung up on poles by the shack owner to keep the leaves and the occasional coconut from landing on the guests. Except for a single bearded person sitting at the makeshift bar, the shack was totally deserted. The beach and the sea formed an idyllic backdrop and the solitude and rhythmic whoosh of the waves had lulled Saloni to near-slumber. Parminder and Savitri spotted her and joined her to chit-chat.

There was a momentary hush because of the brashness of the question, followed by blushes on the faces of other two ladies. This was something they had all wanted to know but didn't know who to compare notes with.

Registering their predicament, Parminder, a buxom, tall, Punjabi lady in a stylish, white chiffon top and see-through capris, who had asked the question, decided to take it forward.

Brushing her fashionably styled shoulder-length tresses, she said, curling her painstakingly painted, blood-red lips, 'In our case, I made it clear who the boss is in this marriage and who will always be!' To emphasize her statement, she snapped her carefully manicured fingers and raised her index finger as a mark of triumph.

The other two took a collective deep breath of disbelief.

'Yes! I refused to cow down to his sexual demands.'

'Really?' Savitri was aghast and her face seemed to have absorbed the crimson colour of her salwar-kameez. Her widely parted eyelids and dilated pupils pointed to her small-town simplicity. Thick, coarse mehndi applied by untrained hands to the tips of her fingers and toes and a large circle made in the centre of her palms suggested a village background. Her garish attire and bejewelled golden sandals confirmed this picture. But her darting eye movements and complementary rapid hand-gesturing indicated an effervescent personality.

'Yes,' continued Parminder, 'The poor fellow went up the long ladder and when he reached the peak, I pulled the ladder. I know he ended up masturbating in the toilet—a small price to pay for lifelong dominance. Now he will be eternally obliged whenever I decide to give in to his amorous advances.'

Having spilled such intimate information before a couple of complete strangers, Parminder felt lightheaded. The anonymity was a boon. The plan devised by the 'Libber Cats', her liberated women's group, had worked perfectly. But she was feeling as physically unsatiated and frustrated if not worse than her 'prey'—the word used by the Libber Cats for new acquisitions, whether husband or boyfriend. This aspect surprisingly had never featured in their advice.

She shook her head to get rid of the feeling of sympathy for her husband that was creeping into her heart; the Cats had strictly forbidden empathizing with the enemy. Instead, she cooed, 'I felt in complete control and that feeling was just great. You know, I won all three rounds of our ganna-playing.'

Parminder recalled her first day in her in-laws' house. Just as they crossed the portals, the newlywed couple was made to sit in the living room, surrounded by the relatives. His aunt brought forth a shallow bowl, filled with milk and water along with some rose petals, grass and coins. She took some sacred red thread, mauli, and tied it to the groom's ring to make the ganna. Then she invited the couple to play the ganna game of finding the ring—a common ritual in most north Indian families.

Parminder smiled, remembering how she was determined not to let him win, for it is believed that whoever finds the ring the most number of times will have the upper hand in the marriage for life.

Parminder added with an impish smile, 'Initially, he actually found the ring, but I dug my nail into his hand so fiercely that he winced and let go. The next two times he hardly tried.'

'Even I won the first two rounds,' said Savitri, coming into her element. 'But then I let him win the third round, lest he feel that he has married a ladaki billi.' She rolled her eyes and gestured with two claw-like hands.

'And what did you do yesterday?' Parminder winked at Savitri.

'Nothing as radical as you. I have to be careful not to antagonize my husband while trying to get the upper hand. My husband is a conservative person—he didn't ask what I wanted. I just gave in and let him do what he wanted. My granny says, "The husband behaves best when he gets out of bed feeling like the cat that got the cream. Then he will agree to all you say." True enough. Though he was pretty rough, he promised a shopping expedition to make up for it. "Buy what you want, my malika," he said in the morning.'

'So you did extract your pound of flesh,' said Parminder, nodding in appreciation. 'What about you?' she turned to the third lady, who was listening in awe.

Saloni, who seemed a bit reserved by nature, was obviously

uncomfortable but was obliged to do her bit as she had heard their side of the story—the cloak of anonymity did help lower her inhibitions. 'Actually, I felt no need to do anything out of the ordinary. He was so considerate and it all happened so naturally that it was pure bliss.' She blushed. 'He even asked me if I was comfortable doing it on the very first night. He had already made me feel completely at home by talking about his people, his job, his aspirations, and even his girlfriends. He invited me to tell him more about myself and my dreams and heard me very interestedly.'

Though she was not as fair-complexioned as the other two, her make-up-free face and delicate henna work on her hands and feet bestowed a sophisticated touch to her personality. Her beach flip-flops and cotton polka-dot top and jeans signalled that she was modern and dressed for comfort. Her oval face seemed innocent, almost child-like. However, her deep jet-black eyes looked very sure of themselves, almost resolute.

'He must have asked about your ex-boyfriends. I know that is what they really want to know when they ask you to tell them about yourself,' Parminder said.

'No, nothing of that sort—he never asked about my boyfriends.'

'He will. He will. They all eventually do that. But never tell them anything. They are all hypocrites. They may have slept with a dozen different women, and may even tell you all about them, but they all expect their wives to be angelic virgins.'

Savitri nodded vigorously. 'My cousin made that mistake, of talking about her relationship with a boy in school—there was no physical relationship even. But her husband sent her back to her parents' house for good. He took her back after five years and that, too, because his sister was getting married and he didn't want to make it known that the daughter-in-law of the house had been turned out. To this day, he taunts and tortures her for that confession, though more than a decade has passed. These men are . . .'

'Susheel is not that type,' Saloni said hastily, freezing Savitri's gesticulating arms, mid-sentence.

'They are all sugar and honey when they are courting you, to have sex. Once they've had their fill, they show their true colours, which are different shades of black,' Parminder said urgently. 'If I were you,' she continued, looking into Saloni's eyes, 'I would ask him to tell you more about his ex-girlfriends. They can be caught off-guard in the beginning to divulge their secrets. This will come in handy later as the ammunition to tame them with—and also to extract the most in case things don't work out and you separate.'

Saloni shook her head and said, 'Isn't it counter-productive to discuss the negative side right at the start of a new relationship?'

'Don't be naïve,' countered Parminder as she lit a cigarette. She blew out a smoke ring. 'Smart women go into marriage fully secure with watertight prenuptial agreements so that they are not left high and dry if there's a divorce. In any case, in India the dowry law is the ace up our sleeves. Any hanky-panky and I can throw the whole family behind bars with one false complaint of harassment.'

She took another puff. 'I've even decided what I'll demand if things go sour.'

'What?' asked Savitri who was listening wide-eyed.

'A red Pajero. He gives it to me and I absolve him of using my body.' Another smoke ring curled up in the air.

'Pajero? What is that?'

'A very fancy car,' answered Saloni briskly.

'Wow!' Savitri was impressed. 'Sadly, I can't do anything of the sort in our setting. If I'm difficult, he will simply send me back to the village to serve his parents and brothers. And it could affect the marriage prospects of my sisters. I have to make sure my husband is happy with me and if possible, stays in my mutthi. There is no option.'

'I know the plight of us poor women,' Parminder breathed, as she drew the last long puff of her cigarette.

'Doesn't he mind your smoking?' asked Savitri.

'Mind? He'll have a heart attack if he comes to know of it. We are Gursikhs and smoking is prohibited for us. But I can't focus until I have had a fag. I'll make sure though that he never comes to know.' She sprayed her mouth with a mint mouth-freshener and tossed a cardamom pod in her mouth.

Saloni was not really enthused by the talk. Though, she had to admit, listening to these two made cleared her mind about what she wanted from her marriage and how. She got up and said, 'Okay, girls, let's go now before our hubbies come looking for us.' They all reluctantly got up from the reclining chairs and headed towards the Royal Goan Palm Resort, across the road.

'They won't,' assured Parminder. 'They are at the bar and I bet they will be boasting about their feats in bed. Even my hero will be detailing how severely he tortured me, despite not having laid a finger on me. Otherwise the other guys will think he is not macho enough.' She laughed out loud. 'I'm going to play along till he makes a false move. Then all I have to do is utter the 'I' word and he will do anything to keep me quiet—anything!'

Realizing that the other two had not figured what the 'I' word is, Parminder gave a sigh and enlightened them.

'Impotent! That's the ultimate weapon . . .'

~

Parminder could not have imagined how far off the mark she was. Contrary to her assumptions, the husbands, gathered together at the poolside bar in front of the giant screen showing a T-20 match, discussed everything under the sun, from the Indian cricket 20-20 victory to Obama's economic policies, but they didn't squeal a word about last night. It's true that most men boast about and display their trophy girlfriends, or brag about the wildcat under the bedsheet, but when it comes to their wives, it is a different ball game altogether.

Some may later discuss details or problems of their sex lives with their closest buddies, but I personally doubt men are ever totally honest about their fears—the size of their penis, and their ability to satisfy their wives. These details are stored deeper in their subconscious than the number of their Swiss bank accounts; even a narco-analysis test may not reveal the truth. Men would have been affronted by their wives talking about their sex lives—if they ever came to know, that is. Fortunately or unfortunately, they are generally naïve enough never to come to know about wives' talk and remain smug in their perceived dominance.

Ignorance truly is bliss.

~

The ladies were unaware of a pair of ears straining hard to catch their words above the swoosh of the ocean waves. Durjan Singh, the owner of the shack outside the five-star resort, was sitting across the counter, his back to the women. But his ears strained, like that of a dog, to catch what was being said. He was fuming at the men married to these so-called 'modern' girls.

'Bloody impotents! They are bringing disgrace to the male breed,' he thought. 'They are even worse than my son, Joginder. If only he could hear these tarts, he would come to his senses and learn how he should treat that wife of his. Tulsidas was right when he said, "Dhol, gawar, shudra aur naari—sab hain taran ke adhikari"' (The drum, the illiterate, the low-caste and the female—all deserve to be beaten).

He was transported to thirty years earlier—to his own wedding night. His friends had primed him to believe that whoever dominated the first night would always do so. Durjan was not the one to suffer the ignominy of being a wimp. He had entered the flower-bedecked hut, determined, for his wedding night. His eyes glistened with a resolve—to establish once and for all who was the lord and master of the house. A couple of very large Patiala pegs had propped up the resolve.

A delicate figure in a red sari sat huddled at the farthest corner of the bed. A huge ghoonghat covered her face. Durjan had not seen his bride yet. He didn't know how to initiate the conversation, because he had never talked to a woman other than his mother and sister in his twenty years.

He sat down on the bed and, as he had been tutored by his friends, summoned his bride in a rough tone.

The girl hardly moved.

He called her once again; again the girl did not obey. He moved towards her and said sternly, 'Don't you listen?'

Then, with one flick, he lifted her ghoonghat and for a moment was spellbound by her beauty. He had never seen anything so alluring.

He was on the verge of melting and saying something complimentary, when his best friend's words resounded in his ears. 'All these girls are cheaters. They bewitch you and enslave you for life.'

He shook his head to clear it of his sentiment and gruffly announced, 'Remember, I want all I say obeyed instantly or else!'

The girl looked up and there were tears in her eyes that would certainly have melted his heart had he not been prepared by his friends for this contingency.

'Don't try this drama with me!' he snarled, 'Get me a glass of water, pronto.' He remembered his dialogues well. She got up and fumbled around, looking for a glass.

'What is taking you so long?' he shouted.

'I can't find a . . . glass,' she whispered.

'Stupid woman! Go look in the kitchen.'

She was going towards a small adjoining door when he shouted, 'Why are you going to the toilet? Bewakoof!'

'I don't know where . . .,' she was shaking with nervousness.

Confident that he had succeeded in sending out the right message, he hissed, 'Leave it. It is beyond you.' Then he pulled her towards him.

The alcohol level had peaked by now. As he pulled her veil away, she resisted shyly.

'What is it?' he asked sternly.

'Nothing—it is just that I feel unwell.' She'd caught the flu two days ago and on top of that and fever she was exhausted by the day-long travel followed by all the wedding ceremonies.

'Shut up and stop this acting. Come here!' He pulled her roughly and removed the long dupatta that was covering her face and head. As he went for the buttons of her blouse, she instantly covered herself with her hands.

This infuriated him. He hit her on her face with the back of his hand. 'Stop me again and I'll thrash you.'

As the sobbing girl tried to pull away from him, he slapped her again before forcing himself onto her. He repeated this a few more times before he, satiated physically and mentally, went to sleep, snoring and leaving the poor girl to weep the rest of the night in pain.

'She has behaved immaculately since that day,' thought Durjan with some satisfaction. 'Had these husbands of today done the same on their wedding nights, they wouldn't have been in such pitiable states today.' His attention shifted back to the three ladies who were winding up their discussion. 'Joginder must hear them,' he thought. 'That is the only way to make him realize what charlatans women are. Their shameful talk would ensure that he follows my advice and stops being a joru ka gulaam.'

He suddenly got up and gingerly approached the ladies. 'You from Delhi?' he asked in halting English.

The three women nodded in unison.

'My son runs a restaurant there, named Rendezvous, for the Gagar group. Please visit it at least once. He will be pleased to welcome you. They make excellent south Indian food.'

Seeing the ladies dither, he reluctantly said something he had never said before, 'Let your first visit be on me—complimentary.'

As he walked back to the counter, the girls looked at the card. 'Not a bad idea. We should meet and share our thoughts in Delhi also, just as we have done here. What do you think?' asked Parminder.

The other two nodded.

'Where do you live?' Savitri asked Parminder. Parminder, however, had an agenda.

'I think we should keep these details—names, addresses—out of the picture', she said. 'Without our anonymity, inhibitions will creep in. Let us just be our aliases—and remain unknown and thus frank as only strangers can be. We hold such meetings in our Libber Cats organization regularly. It has great therapeutic value for troubled minds. We can also have meetings like this. Call me Pammi, and tell me what your nicknames will be. We will contact each other only through our mobiles. Okay?'

Savitri and Saloni nodded.

'Call me Savvy,' said Savitri.

Saloni reluctantly became Sally though she didn't like the sound of the word the moment she uttered it.

'Okay then, let us meet some two weeks later, say on a Tuesday,' proposed Pammi.

'Make it Wednesday. I go to the temple on Tuesdays,' said Savvy.

'Okay—it's Wednesday then, 11 a.m.' volunteered Saloni.

'11 a.m. it is.'

The meeting dispersed; and the bearded writer jotted the date and time on the thick notepad on which he had been recording the conversation. It seemed like he had hit a jackpot of information for his forthcoming book, *Romance Your Wife: It Could Be Your Marriage-Saver*. He was not going to let go of such a fantastic opportunity. He lifted his large frame from the stool and gulped the last sip of his coffee. Raising his arms to stretch his back, he was an imposing figure, over six feet tall. His soft brown eyes, however, were benevolent-looking. He kept the thick notepad in his denim shoulderbag and slung the bag and the camera over his shoulder.

On his way out, he asked the bewildered shack-owner for a card of his son's restaurant in Delhi.

He would be there . . .

~

'What is catharsis of the soul?' I asked Shri Harbanslal, my grandfather's younger brother, regarded as one of the wisest men of our community of Mohyals. He asked me to prop him up on the bed as the chemotherapy he was being treated with left him with little energy. Mohyal Brahmins had long ago given up working as priests, their traditional occupation, preferring now to serve in the armed forces, in line with their ancestors like Guru Dronacharya, but their brahminical penchant for discourses had not dimmed.

After deep thought, he said, 'Uninhibitedly getting rid of your thoughts is cleansing.'

'But how can we rid ourselves of thoughts without inhibition?' I asked.

'Your grandfather, whom I consider my true guru, once told me, "I never stay in hotels or posh guesthouses while travelling alone. I always stay in dharamshalas, where people mingle under banyan trees, sharing thoughts and experiences. Not only do you learn worthwhile lessons but you can clear the clutter from your mind; the anonymity allows you to speak freely." He considered going through these motions akin to a confessional and it made his heart feel unburdened.'

I regularly witness such therapeutic cleansing in my clinic. Women who accompany their children for check-ups pour their hearts out to strangers in the waiting room, even at the cost of foregoing their appointments for which they might have waited for over an hour. Most women get together in their homes or socialize under the guise of kitty parties to communicate their innermost thoughts to their friends and colleagues, often after their husbands leave for office, and get their worries off their chests.

Most men are, unfortunately, extremely poor at communicating concerns regarding their personal or sexual lives—it goes against the image of male self-sufficiency and strength, an image ingrained in them from birth. Their thoughts fester in their minds, raising their BP and stress levels. If men were better at getting their worries off their chests it would reduce the strain in their marriages considerably and also reduce the incidence of heart attacks. Much of the stress of our marriages can be removed if only we can see that stress exists in others' lives too.

Many people are now trying such catharsis, by way of anonymous blogging and online chatting. So, fellow males, let us have an anonymous catharsis and get the stress out of our lives and marriages. You can share your concerns with me and others at:

www.dontslapyourwife.in

PART I

THE STATUS REPORT

Son to father: 'Dad, I want to get married and be happy.'
Father: 'Pick one, Sonny.'

A Word from the Author

'Why don't you get married?' I once asked my cousin Rattoo, who was in his forties. Rattoo is a self-proclaimed happy bachelor, who likes to remind us 'poor married souls' (his definition) of the fact that he is a 'bachelor by choice'—that is he has understood and accepted the futility of marriage.

I asked him, 'How did you get to this conclusion—without ever having been married?'

'Simple!' he replied. 'By reading about it.'

When on the instigation of his mother, who is desperate to see him married, I probed further, he countered with this logic:

'Remember, Bhaiya, every evening, we used to sit around the fire on mats and our elders used to read us stories. If you can recall, we were once told the story of a wazir who would sniff swords to test their sharpness. The wazir never passed a sword without a hefty bribe, and a blacksmith decided to teach him a lesson. He applied some snuff to the edge of his sword. The moment the wazir sniffed the sword, it induced a sneeze so violent that his nose was severed from its base, thus also proving the sharpness of its blade.'

'Now, the wazir was faced with the predicament of becoming the butt of everybody's jokes. To counter this, the smart wazir thought of a plan. He announced that by getting his nose severed, he was able to see God. A few gullible persons under his influence agreed to get their noses amputated so they could also see God. When they still saw no God, the wazir convinced them that the only way out of social ridicule was to make everyone noseless. The noseless convinced those with noses to join them, with even the king falling for the hoax. The king decreed that everyone must get their noses severed.'

I was wondering what Ratoo's point was, when he continued, 'Something similar is happening in the kingdom of marriage. The nose in our culture symbolizes dignity. Those who lose their noses, that is, their dignity, through marriage, convince others that they have achieved bliss. They, pulling off the same hoax, trap others. Some well-meaning souls from the noseless group try to warn others from the group who still have their noses that there is no bliss at the end of the tunnel. But the young souls are so naïve that when warned they think, "He has attained bliss and does not want us to attain ours." And they jump onto the bandwagon and become 'nak-kate' (noseless, or shorn of dignity). I'm the rare exception who has taken such sage advice seriously. So when I toot my thumb at you noseless people, I remind you of what you could have been had you not . . . married. To absolve yourselves of guilt, you all try even harder to woo me to lose my nose.

'So, sorry to disappoint you, big brother, but I have learnt from others' experience that marriage is just not worth the risk.'

~

This, in nutshell, is the dilemma many young men face.

I had no arguments left in my quiver to convince a die-hard sceptic like my cousin. But to other young men with open minds, I would like to say this: 'True, married life is no bed of roses but it can be a very fulfilling and enjoyable experience if only you enter it with a fair attitude and a level head on your shoulders. The fair attitude is mandatory, because only when you are fair yourself can you expect a fair and honourable response. A level head is vital to overcome early infatuation, for the female of the species—she can make you lose your head so badly that you end up hitting your foot with an axe so many times that you have no foot left to take a stand in your marriage. Though I firmly believe that marriage is not a game of winning or losing, hitting so many self-goals can never make you a winner.'

So let us evaluate the institution of marriage. Is it really doomed or do we have a ray of hope?

2

An Institution under Siege

> Wife: If men had some common sense, many divorces would have been prevented.
>
> Husband: Sure, all marriages would have too.

'Why do men get married in the first place if all they want is sex? There are other ways for them to satisfy their libido,' fumed Pammi, as she settled down in the chair adjacent to the window in Rendezvous restaurant. This south Indian restaurant had by now become their fortnightly meeting point, as it was equidistant from everybody's home.

Savvy looked up, perplexed, at Pammi. 'What happened?' This looked promising.

'Haven't you seen today's newspaper?'

'Newspaper?' Oh my God, had her story already reached the media? wondered Savvy.

Pammi took the newspaper out of her bag. It carried the story of the gruesome murder of a woman who had been hacked to pieces by her husband. Before the husband was arrested, he had carried the dismembered body in a suitcase for the entire day.

While Pammi and Savvy pored over the newspaper, Sally joined them, saying, 'I am sorry, I got stuck in the traffic jam.'

'Bloody men,' muttered Pammi.

Seeing the photograph of the couple in the newspaper, Sally became pensive. 'Well, I knew this couple. They lived in the same complex as my uncle in Noida. The husband seemed like a decent man, liked by everybody. In fact, it was always the wife's behaviour that was obnoxious; his was rather exemplary.'

'Wow, look at you! What warrants being hacked to death like this?' fumed Pammi.

'That's not the point. Nothing can condone this. But when angered beyond a point, even a decent person loses his sense of perspective and can act irrationally. This is what seems to have happened. I am not defending him—all I'm saying is that there are always two sides of a coin.'

'As far as I'm concerned, in the husband–wife or rather, in-laws–bride relationship, there is only one facet. They exploit, she endures.' Pammi was so sure of her opinion, there was no room in her mind for an alternate thought.

'I agree,' interjected Savvy, who was until now quietly sipping her cold coffee. 'Women are usually the ones being exploited. Look at me living in this house with four men—and the onus is on me to keep myself covered, lest any of them get a peep at my cleavage or calves. My husband scolds me for the smallest slip of my dupatta. First of all, no one's looking and if anyone does, shouldn't he be castigated for ogling at me. He doesn't say a word to them; they are his brothers after all, his blood, and who am I? An outsider.'

Pammi and Sally clucked their tongues in sympathy, Pammi more forcefully than Sally.

'You poor thing!' Pammi chipped in.

'He wants me to cook and wash for his two brothers and one distant cousin— but if I talk to any of them smilingly or chat with them alone, he gets upset and scowls. He also told me that had I not been a virgin on the wedding night, he would have sent me back to my parents' house.'

'I used red ink on the wedding night—in fact the third night, for I had sent him off panting the first two nights,' Pammi said. 'I knew how men boil if they believe their wives are not virgins on the wedding night, even if they've had affairs themselves.'

~

'I would have beaten her black and blue had she not been a virgin, and my dad would have disgraced her whole family publicly, while throwing her back at their doorstep,' thought Joginder, the restaurant-owner, who, as instructed by his dad, was eavesdropping on the ladies' conversation. He was a lean man, like his father, but there the similarities ended. Unlike his dad, he was immaculately dressed and extremely courteous. Under that polished exterior, however, there existed a fierce, tough-as-nails personality, which occasionally peeped out from his suave exterior when one of his workers rubbed him the wrong way. Then he was not averse to resorting to using his hands.

Unknown to the ladies, there were other uninvited guests like Joginder, riding the ebb and flow of their conversation. Their choora, the bangles worn by new Punjabi brides, had attracted the attention of a young marketing executive, Shravan, sitting at a table close to their cabin. A wheatish-complexioned young man of medium height and build, Shravan had ostensibly plugged in his earphones to listen to music but a closer observation showed that the earplug was almost out of the right ear, which faced the ladies' cabin, and his mobile was off.

He was eavesdropping, hoping to get some clues that would help him make up his mind about his marriage. He had been torn between the conflict of choosing between his beautiful heart-throb and the traditional girl selected by his family. He had recently almost reached the final decision, but a small doubt was still holding him back. 'Would the suave, convent-educated girl he was in love with be able to adjust with his parents?'

On the other table, the bearded gentleman had already consumed six cups of coffee while scribbling furiously on his thick notebook in sync with the ladies' conversation. After the ladies had arrived, he had moved to the table behind their cabin, where their conversation was clearly audible. But a disappointed look was replacing his early-morning enthusiasm. He had come to the restaurant expecting the soft, romantic babble of newlyweds. Instead, he was being made to taste the bitter castor-oil of the hard facts of life. In just six weeks of their honeymoon, the women seemed to have forgotten all about honey and the moon. Still, he was an optimistic soul and knew that ultimately, romance would win over the harsh realities because he was convinced that romance was the true saviour of marriage.

~

'What is your set-up like?' Savvy asked Pammi.

'Well, so far there is not much of a problem because I hardly set foot outside my room when my husband is at work. I cook up one excuse or another to stay in my room and sleep. I know my mother-in-law wants me to take charge of the kitchen. But I've told her that I plan on rejoining my PhD studies soon and I will not really be available for kitchen work. In any case, there is not much work with a full-time servant and two maids. Still she cribs that she can't get all the work done alone.'

'That sounds like fun! Just like Pallavi in the serial *Sautan*,' thought Savvy. 'Dramatic!'

'Won't it bring you down a few notches in your husband's eyes? I mean your bunking off to avoid household work,' asked Sally. 'Work never finishes in a home, irrespective of the number of helpers.'

'Yes, he does sometimes complain. But I am not bothered. I know that once you allow men to dictate terms, they get the wrong signal. Being saddled with an male chauvinistic pig is the last thing I want. I've found the ideal escape route.'

'I wish I could find something that would get me out of the house regularly,' sighed Savvy wistfully. 'Maybe a job or something, like the smart vamps in the serials,' she said.

'Have you ever worked before?' enquired Sally.

'No. Why?'

'Then let me assure you, it is no bed of roses. It's one thing to have a hobby or do a course, but if you are out to earn your livelihood, it is a tough, mean world out there. After working for five years in the cut-throat IT industry, I'm lucky an opportunity to set up an office at home presented itself. The hardest life always is that of the working woman's. All the glitter of going out of the house is dissipated within a week and then it's just grinding on, right to the end.'

'Absolutely.' For once Pammi agreed with Sally. 'At our club "Libber Cats", we discuss the plight of the working women in great detail. Tell me, Sally, how is your life?'

'Pretty good—somewhere between your two extremes.'

'What about your in-laws?'

'They live with us. My mother-in-law is pretty strict and maintains the schedule of the house with an iron hand. She has to be informed of everything on a prior basis.'

'Being so regulated is awful, isn't it?'

'Well, to be honest, my mother was as strict, if not more. So it is no big deal. In any case, my mother-in-law doesn't refuse anything. She just wants to know everything in advance. That is more than my mother ever granted. My father-in-law is a thorough gentleman—he doesn't interfere with my mother-in-law's orders.'

'Isn't that suffocating?' asked Pammi. 'My mom was very strict also—that was one of the reasons I wanted to get married, for the freedom to do what I want. I am not prepared to be saddled with the same regimentation after marriage too. No way. I plan to live life on my own terms and that is exactly what I'm doing, everything else be damned.'

Savvy's face lit up. The seed of an idea had been planted. She wondered how she could do something similar, something akin to a TV serial, in her own life.

Pammi's stand had also struck a chord with Sally. She, too, was in her own way planning to make her married life smoother.

~

'I hope my would-be wife is not like Pammi, or I'm dead,' thought sales executive, Shravan. 'The problem is women look so sweet and soft from far.'

'Dad was right,' thought Joginder. 'Girls nowadays are really clever. They plan and scheme about how to hoodwink their husbands and in-laws. That white-pant lady, however, is very decent and that capri one is obnoxious. I will have to handle my wife carefully or she'll also become like them.' His father's plan seemed to be working.

The bearded writer sitting behind the chamber had a vacant look. He had filled thirty pages without a word of what he wanted—romance. 'Where are we headed? And where is romance in all this fragmentation and strain? Maybe it will start after they settle down.' He decided to wait.

In his notebook, he wrote, 'Marriage in the Time of Strife: The institution of marriage is under siege…'

~

Marriage in the time of strife

How do we stay happily married in the age of strife?

I occasionally visit an acharyaji, whose predictions are vouched for by many of my family members and friends. Despite being an incorrigible rationalist who doesn't believe in the mumbo-jumbo of astrology, I go to him because of his uncanny witticisms and common sense that make him an interesting future-gazer.

About two decades ago, one of his favourite games was guessing how many kids a couple would be blessed with.

But he's now dropped the kids' section, his rationale being that with family-planning measures, this has ceased to be exclusively in God's hands. Hingeing a prediction on something that was human-controlled was hazardous for his career.

I noticed another prediction slowly vanishing from his repertoire: marital prospects. When I asked specifically about my son, who was thinking of going abroad, 'Will he get married there or here in India?' he eluded the issue thus: 'Arre, let these things be—I'm telling you, he will be happy in his personal life. That should be enough!'

My wife, used to hearing a spade called a spade, was worried, fearing that the acharya with his verbal jugglery was pushing impending trouble under the carpet.

'Will you please explain in detail what you envision?'

Now the acharya launched into his philosophy of life.

'See, Doctor Sahib,' he said, turning to me in the hope that I would understand his logic better. 'The word "marriage" needs to be redefined. Formerly, too, there would be a ritualistic marriage that was more of an "intention to marry", and it could occur as early as in infancy. Then there was the conjugal marriage—gauna, in which the girl moved to the groom's house and the marriage was consummated. We used to say we cannot predict the ritual marriage, that is, intention to marry—only the real marriage, when marriage was consummated, sexual initiation. Today, how can you put a date on sexual initiation? Young people may have many "marriages" before the official one. More often than not, after the honeymoon, stresses and strife pile up so that these youth become more celibate then they were ever before. So, if we're pressed, we gauge when turbulence in the marriageable age shows up and predict marriage a few months before that. This is fairly accurate.'

My nodding brought a smile on the acharya's face, 'Also, some new terms have crept into the marriage arena. The other day, I predicted the exact date of the marriage of a client's son, studying in the US. The date was accurate but my client is very unhappy with me. The reason: he doesn't know whether his son is the husband or a wife in his same-sex marriage.'

IN A NUTSHELL

These days, quarrelling and conflict seem to have become integral to married life. The lack of devotion in this generation of fast-food eaters has brought the institution of marriage under siege. Thus, we have downgraded our social system as follows: community living→joint family→unit family→live-in relationship→what next—unit living? Individuals living alone? (As is already happening in many Western countries.)

Scary thought, isn't it?

3

The Story So Far—
the Very Poor Track Record of Men

The husband comes home and is greeted by his wife dressed in a sexy negligee.

The wife says in a seductive tone, 'Blindfold and tie me up and you can do whatever you want.'

The husband ties her up and goes off to play golf.

'Our honeymoon is over,' moaned Pammi, even before she settled down in her favourite chair at the Rendezvous restaurant. 'Now life is going to be one long trudge of squabbles and complaints.'

She drew the curtains of their cabin, thus providing visual privacy, though the sound waves were free to go outside. The restaurant was beautifully designed like a south Indian marriage hall, complete with ornate mahogany wood carvings and wooden idols. All the furniture was in the same shade of dark mahogany and at the rear end, there were three family cabins for those who wanted privacy. The air was thick with the fragrance of sandalwood agarbati and the soft strains of classical Carnatic music could be heard in the background.

'What happened?' asked Savvy, sympathetically. She was keen to hear the sordid details because so far Pammi's life was causing her stabbing pangs of jealousy. She hated that she was busy all day slaving in the kitchen, cooking to satisfy the insatiable appetites of four hefty young men and occasionally for their old landlord, while Pammi read novels in an AC room.

'My husband told me to make chapattis for my mother-in-law because she is unwell. She must have told him to get me to make them. It was so difficult,' she continued.

'I know. Cooking is tough and in summer it is nothing short of murder.'

'My mother used to cook for a family of sixteen and on an angeethi,' thought Joginder. 'One complaint and she was belaboured by my abusive father. He remembered his father's words on his wedding day, "Son, the only way to keep these fillies in check is to slap them frequently; or you'll be tossed like unwanted garbage".'

'You mean I should hit my wife?' he had asked innocently.

'A true male definitely should. See how well we have lived our married life—hassle-free. It is all because of the slap; these so-called modern men consider it below their dignity to wield the slap—see how tension-filled their marriages are.'

Joginder had serious doubts about whether his parents really had a happy married life, but he had been pretty vicious with his wife on his wedding night and was torn between sympathy for the poor girl and his father's stern advice. He frequently vacillated between arrogance and appeasement and even argued with his dad when the older man had jeered at his appeasement. As a result, he was hardly on talking terms with his dad. Now, listening to Pammi, he felt a revulsion for women in general. 'Maybe Dad was right, maybe we do need to slap them to keep them in line.'

Durjan's son was now beginning to follow in the inglorious footsteps of his ancestors.

~

My grandma talked to me often and of all the subjects she discussed, the most frequent was about my grandpa. She eulogized him—his love for children, his generosity and compliance as a husband, his giving her a free hand in household expenditure. Why did she consider him so wonderful? None of what he did is unusual today.

VOTING RIGHTS FOR WOMEN IN THE US

Women got the right to vote half a century after African-Americans. The Fifteenth Amendment to the United States Constitution, which was ratified in 1870, prohibits denying the right to vote 'based on race, color or previous condition of servitude'.

The Nineteenth Amendment that prohibits any citizen of the US from being denied the right to vote based on sex was ratified on 18 August 1920.

In the 1920s, it was rare for men to indulge their families and my grandpa was considered eccentric for doing so. He would shut down his printing and publishing business for two months every year to take his family on a vacation. How many men in those days did that?

The fact is that for centuries, most men have lived pretty self-centred lives, with little sensitivity towards their wives' or families' needs. In rural and semi-literate urban areas, this mistreatment of women is prevalent even today.

A driver in my uncle's employment in Dehradun told me that he beat his wife regularly, and quite unnecessarily, just to keep her in line. When she actually made a mistake or disobeyed him, he even branded her with a hot iron rod. He lamented that the modern generation has become soft and stupid. 'Education has spoiled their heads' was his explanation.

The track record of men has not been so different over the ages. With their superior physical strength, men constructed a world where might was right, and took this rule home to minimize the significance of the women in their families. Through history, men have treated women like commodities or members akin to the pets and livestock in their households. Witch hunting in Christian history and female infanticide in northern Asia was another form of subjugation.

Has the so-called modern male changed his attitude? I am afraid not. The sword may have been replaced by a BlackBerry but the code of conduct remains the same, with a bit of tweaking for the tweeting generation. Despite education, the modern male has started accepting the role and significance of women in society rather recently, and reluctantly. In the

SOME TALIBAN RESTRICTIONS ON WOMEN INCLUDE:

- A complete ban on activity outside the home unless accompanied by a mahram (close male relative—father, brother or husband)
- A ban on dealing with male shopkeepers, doctors, teachers, drivers, etc
- A ban on studying in schools, universities or other educational institutions
- The whipping of women in public, for having their ankles exposed
- The public stoning of women accused of adultery
- A ban on the use of cosmetics (Many women with painted nails have had their fingers cut off.)
- A ban on wearing high-heels which make a sound while walking (A man must not hear a woman's footsteps lest it excite him.)
- A ban on wearing brightly coloured clothes
- The compulsory painting of windows so that women cannot be seen from outside their homes

Western world too, male–female parity has come about after centuries, though they are not there yet. The anti-West lobby, the Islamic clerics and their foot-soldiers, the Taliban, are bent upon bringing back women's rights to that of the age of the cave-dwellers (see box).

This subjugation over the ages has had the effect of sowing the seeds of revolt in the minds of women who have manifested their ire with bitterness. And an angry reaction, my dear friends, is never balanced or rational.

Before we go into the alley of the reaction of women, we must stop and look back at the highway of our past and ponder 'how' and more importantly 'why' women ended up as the oppressed and men the oppressor—universally.

IN A NUTSHELL

The bitterness with which the woman of today is manifesting her ire has been borne out of a reaction to male oppression over the ages.

4

Historical Perspective: Why Have Women Been Universally Oppressed?

A woman worries about the future till she gets a husband.

A man never worries about the future—until he gets a wife.

Pammi walked in and settled down in her favourite chair facing the window. The group of three had staked a permanent claim to the partially covered family enclosure at the far end of the Rendezvous restaurant and Pammi had taken up the reins of the unofficial honorary president of what the bearded writer called the ANC—Abla Nari Club ('The Helpless Women's Club'). The other two had accepted Pammi's status without putting up any competition, either because of the three she was the most dominating or because she would drop them in her car at the metro station, from where Savvy took the metro and Sally took an auto.

Pammi's attempt to become the financer of the group had been thwarted by Sally, who insisted that they go dutch, each paying for themselves. Pammi would have liked to become the 'dictator for life' of the congregation, just as Jassi had become at Libber Cats.

She pulled out a golden-coloured diary, opened it and announced, 'I've made some new year resolutions.'

'But the new year is many months away,' interjected Sally.

'Well, these are for the year that has gone by. I was so starry-eyed about my marriage and honeymoon that I forgot all about my cause.'

'Cause?' Savvy asked wide-eyed.

'Yes! As a life member of Libber Cats, I had pledged to withstand and thwart male oppression. Seeing the modern face of my sweet husband, I was lulled into believing that men have changed. But now his true colours are showing. The MIL, that old bag, is poisoning his ears and he lists new chores for me to do every day. Though he is polite, coercion is coercion. Yesterday, he even scolded me when I talked back to my mother-in-law. She is the real villain.'

'But your mother-in-law is a woman and . . .'

'I know. But men have oppressed us for so long that even some of our own tribe have imbibed their behaviour. Come to think of it, be it in Africa, Asia or Europe, we have been oppressed universally.'

~

Daiv , the bearded writer, who had been following the women's conversation since their honeymoon, had a bright idea. He started scribbling furiously, 'Status of females in our society—the historical perspective'.

~

So why is it that in at least five independently evolving civilizations of the world, men gained dominance over women? Even if you discount the law of averages, at least in one cradle of civilization, women should have become the dominant partner in the family or society.

The Hindu scriptures include female deity worship and women are shown as the source of power (Shakti). This, as far as I know, is the height of the veneration of the female. Yet the trinity of Hinduism—Brahma (the god of creation), Vishnu (the god of nurturing) and Mahesh (the god of annihilation)—remains resolutely male.

Why?

The theological answer is that God, or nature, in their wisdom, chose not to make males and females similar or equal. Men and women were crafted differently, so that different roles were designated to them. Man was made physically strong to enable him to hunt and thus provide for and protect the family. Women, on the other hand, were designed to carry on child-bearing and child-rearing, and as an outcome of this, she got saddled with the hearth. As compared to the male's power of physical strength, she was given superior observation, perception and analytical powers.

Unfortunately, the superior physical power of the male made him the ruler and the perpetrator of rules. Thus empowered, men framed norms and rules for society that suited their ends. In his zeal to imprint his superiority in the battle of the sexes, the male neglected the superior sensory and intuitive powers of the female and propogated instead, a false notion of female inferiority. It was decreed that more brawn automatically meant more brain.

The female came to accept this inferiority and it was so strongly ingrained into their psyche that women themselves became perpetrators of oppression and suppression of other females. Thus, they rejoiced when a male was born and submitted to the system of a girl going to the boy's house after marriage. This crushing of women by women contributed to females becoming the 'inferior' sex. The more females accepted this inferior status, the more they lost out on their otherwise superior intellect. The smart ones ruled by proxy, from behind the puppet thrones of men.

This concept of the male–female difference is not just physical but manifest in evolution also. It is reflected in our brains, females on an average showing less hemispheric specialization than males (research of O'Boyle and Gill 1998). Thus, while on the one hand they seem more emotional, vulnerable, soft and sensitive, on the other hand they can also be more determined, haughty and manipulative. This reminds me of the popular Punjabi saying, 'Dine daran parchavayan; rati nadi charen', meaning, 'she who is afraid of even shadows in the daytime is ready in the middle of the night to swim across a river'. The reference is to the legendary Soni, who would cross a swollen river on a pitcher to meet her lover in the dead of night. This facet of a woman, the steely resolve to achieve what she desires, come what may, remained concealed for a long period because of male predominance and oppression. Now, with the opening up of societies the world over, it is becoming evident and is construed as perseverance on the positive side and manipulativeness on the negative, depending on the perspective. Add to this the pent-up vindictiveness for the past and prevailing injustices perpetrated on women, and the combination is lethal.

History will bear testimony to the fact that a manipulative and revengeful female is to be feared.

It is the 'reversal of the historical perspective' with a vengeance—the call of liberation. And remember: the female of the species is deadlier than the male.

IN A NUTSHELL

The male's superior physical strength made him the dominant partner. But he misused his power to downgrade the female's superior powers of observation and analysis, thus creating the myth of female inferiority.

5

The Libber's Call

A woman would rather have beauty than brains, because she knows that a man can see better than he can think.

Pammi suddenly said, 'You know what—I've made a video of our lovemaking.'

Sally and Savvy (and the onlookers) were aghast.

'What did you make?' asked Savvy in her trademark wide-eyed, bewildered tone.

'Oh, just a film of me and my husband having sex. Want to see?' She giggled. 'I've a clip of it in MMS format in my cell phone.'

'Your husband knows?' Savvy's eyeballs were now bulging out of their sockets.

'I don't think so.'

'What if he comes to know?'

'No big deal. I made a couple of them in college. Husbands never come to know.'

'If I did such a thing and my husband discovered it, he would certainly kill me,' said Savvy. What she thought but didn't say was: If he comes to know that I've friends who do this, he will lock me up at home for good.

'This is dangerous, Pammi,' cautioned Sally. 'In my school, a girl and boy foolishly did the same thing and, as luck would have it, the MMS landed in the wrong hands, and was sold to anyone willing to buy it. The boy was expelled but the girl, unable to bear the shame, committed suicide.'

'What a shame. This all is so narrow-minded. If you have a great body, where is the harm in flaunting it? Don't you want your beauty appreciated?'

'That is different. Why do you have to take everything to the very extreme? To get appreciation, we wear attractive clothes; we do not run naked in front of strangers.'

Seeing that the discussion was getting heated, Savvy changed the topic, 'Forget it.' She turned to Pammi. 'I thought you were taking us to some club today.'

'I sure am. I am just waiting for my friend and guide, Jasbeer. She has her office nearby. You'll be thrilled to meet her. She is a true libber, who lives life on her own terms. After her second divorce, she had refused to move in with her conservative parents and started living alone. Now, she has a flourishing event management business and lives alone in a sprawling bungalow with her three dogs, each with its own air-conditioned kennel. Occasionally, she acquires a boyfriend but keeps him in control with a collar and tight leash. What a woman!'

'No wonder all my boyfriends run away. You describe me so unflatteringly,' said a husky and authoritarian voice from behind them.

Pammi jumped to her feet. She gave a warm hug to the latecomer. 'Ladies, meet my friend and mentor, Jassi.' Jassi was a tall, wheatish-complexioned lady, wearing a denim top with jeans tucked into denim boots. Not a beauty in conventional terms, she exuded an earthy sexiness which she projected with supreme confidence. No wonder heads turned towards her wherever she went.

'Are they ready to join our club?'

'Not yet, but they are interested. So, I thought, why not show them our hideout and our philosophy.'

'Oh, the philosophy is simple. A world without the pricks—I mean men,' smiled Jassi mischievously, as she settled down in a vacant chair.

'But . . . but . . . how is that possible?' stuttered Sally.

'Why not? What do we need them for? Just procreation! For that we can store a billion sperms of the brightest minds and have a world not only dominated but cohabitated exclusively by females. That would not even be unnatural. In nature there are many instances—in the insect world, either the male dies naturally or is killed by workers, or even by the female, once the queen is impregnated. You know, the female praying mantis starts devouring the male even while the sex act is going on. To make him complete his act of consummating her, she starts eating him head first.' She waited for the gasps to die down before adding, 'Why can't we have a similar male-free world?'

'Isn't that a utopian idea? I mean what do you intend doing with all the men? Surely you can't simply wish them away.'

'The point is not to annihilate men. It is just to understand and get into every female's psyche that we can live without men. We can do whatever men do and we can do it better than them. We don't need them—they need us. We can procreate with frozen sperm but men can't give birth all on their own, try as they might. The female is not only superior but also self-sufficient. The only good thing males do can be done better with a good-quality vibrator. It is more satisfying,' Jassi winked, even as Sally winced.

'Wow!' exclaimed Savvy, not quite registering the last statement. 'What you say might not be true but is good to hear because I've always been told that males are superior in every way.'

'That is because there is a well-planned male conspiracy to make you believe that. Haven't you read the *Da Vinci Code* or more pertinently *The Holy Grail*, on which the *Da Vinci Code* is believed to be based?'

As Pammi, Savvy and Sally shook their heads in silent wonderment, Jassi continued with a renewed vigour. 'These researches clearly state that Christ firmly believed that only females could perform miracles—the biggest miracle being giving birth. He considered females to be superior and the more intelligent beings. It was much later, when the Roman emperor Constantine embraced Christianity to save his throne, that he inducted the idea of male superiority into the Bible, so that only men could become the custodians of religion and as a corollary the harbingers of knowledge. The murderous pogroms that followed burnt or killed millions of well-read, intelligent women under the pretext that a well-informed woman was a witch. From then on, we women have learned to hide our intelligence and let the belief prevail that males are superior beings. Even when women realize that most men are dumbos, they know that in this male-dominated world, they need the thumb impression of a male to further their cause and quest. We at Libber Cats believe that if you really do need a rubber-stamp impression of the male to survive, then just cut the thumb and put it in your pocket along with any other thumb-shaped organ of theirs, if you've taken a fancy to it.'

Pammi interjected, knowing that this hard-nosed philosophy didn't go down too well with Sally, who was looking visibly upset. 'Okay, let's wind up this discussion and go over to our den, otherwise we'll be late.'

They all got up and left, leaving behind three listeners who, if allowed to comment, would have shouted, 'Bloody shrews!' in unison. And they all would have given anything to follow them out, but couldn't because . . .

~

'Dogs and men not allowed' was the signboard at the entrance of the club. Underneath, a witty male (presumably) had scribbled, 'Only bitches welcome!' The door, which was less than six feet high, was followed by a tunnel-like passage that was even shorter, making it pretty uncomfortable for a man of average height or a tall woman to walk through. The entrance to the hall was guarded by a huge gate, which was padlocked, and a stern-looking woman, occupying all of the tunnel's height and most of its width, stood guard.

As the four women squeezed past her, she saluted smartly and opened a sub-door within the door. That sub-door was barely three feet high and everybody had to bend their heads to enter. As they lifted their heads after passing through, they were greeted by a large golden board with huge words emblazoned in blood red: 'You are bowing to Women Power—Libber Cats'. It had been ostensibly placed there for the occasional male visitor.

Just next to the proclamation was a bright-red poster saying: 'A male-free world'. Underneath, a banner-like poster said: 'Grab their jobs'. Below that was a woman in a short skirt manning a large drill and saying: 'That is the only way to beat THEM.' Similar punch-lines adorned other posters. One in particular caught Savvy's attention: 'God has given you a beautiful tool—your vagina; make good use of it and you can rule the world.' Sally stifled a smile at the skewed thinking. The smile was not lost on Jassi.

They all were led to a large room with the nameplate 'Indo Room' on the door. This was the room for indoctrination into the Libber Cat ethos. The room was adorned with thermocol question marks on each of which there was the poser question: 'Unfair—why dowry for brides only?', 'Why only females are burnt?' 'Why less wages for woman workers?'. . .

In the end there was the brightest '?', 'Why should only females produce children?—Unfair!' Underneath was another caption in blood red: 'Men exploit us by making us pregnant—Tell them to produce their own kids'. Next to it was another nugget: 'Men exploit us right from conception to marriage—our only chance to exploit them is during divorce. Plan your divorce beforehand. Ensure a favourable prenuptial bond—come to Libber Cats before marriage.'

Sally could not stifle her smile this time. Jassi noticed that too. 'You find this funny?' Everybody looked her way.

'Hilarious!'

'This is the fact of a woman's life. Not a word said here is untrue.' This was Jassi's style. She started the process of indoctrination with a discussion so it seemed much more authentic, unlike an orchestrated speech.

'Indeed, but it just shows only one facet of life. That in itself makes it a half-truth.'

'Isn't it true that women have always been oppressed? She still bears the brunt of male atrocities in conservative societies the world over.' She reeled off examples of many countries. 'Men use women as a humping toy to vent their lust.'

'It is indeed true.'

'Then what is wrong in fighting oppression by males?'

'Nothing, but from your messages, you seem more inclined to fight God or, rather, God's system rather than the male suppression.'

'God didn't say that women should be shackled with menial household tasks and men should get the title of the 'Boss—the Almighty Provider'. Why shouldn't men then take up the household chores and let women be providers for a change?'

'According to you, women can get equality only by doing a man's job and the only way she can redeem herself and the female fraternity is by breaking her marriage. Wow! Instead of promoting harmonious relationships, the hallmark of the strength of a fulfilled woman, you are advocating that she become the wrecker-in-chief of her marriage and then extract a profit from the wreckage of a sunk marriage. It is like breaking up a flourishing industry to profit from the garage sale of its parts—funny logic. Isn't it?'

Everybody was stunned by the outburst of the mostly quiet Sally—most of all Jassi. Even the most vocal opponent had not been able to snub her this way. She didn't realize that, unwittingly, she had stepped on the core beliefs and ideals of Sally.

'You don't seem to understand the problem. You indulge in such rhetoric because it is still early days in your marriage. Soon your husband's MCP-type behaviour will show and he'll also start sleeping around. Then I'll ask the same question. I'm sure your answers would be much less charitable. I would know—I have faced the music during both my marriages. Once the infatuation with a brand-new body peters out, a husband loses interest and stops caring about you. Either he starts womanizing or hits the bottle. Either way, you are left high and dry. The only things that can come to your rescue then are either a well-prepared prenuptial agreement or manipulation of this dowry law that, thankfully, is heavily loaded in our favour. Once these bastards realize how easily we can send their whole family to jail with a single FIR, they shove their malehood between their legs and agree to all that you say.'

Jassi pointed towards the last poster on the wall: 'Bahut kar liya in Ramon ne Ahilya ka uddhaar laat mar kar...' (a reference to the mythological story in which Lord Rama gave life to Ahilya, who had been turned to stone by a sage, by touching her with his foot). 'Now the time has come for us to do their "uddhaar" by kicking their asses.' This was Jassi's favourite poster as she had coined the slogan.

'Yes! The time has come to pin these guys down. Now we'll indulge ourselves in every way we want. We'll have extramarital affairs. We will command the world and if they as much as squeak, we will throw the law book at them with such force, they won't know what hit them. My second husband and his family languished in prison for six months for crimes they had never committed. That is the way to bring them to their senses. True liberation is to realize our hidden power, our sexuality. This is one thing that, if used properly, can make men go weak in their knees. This is what I did when my second husband started giving me trouble—I started flirting with his best friend openly. When he yelled at me in front of a whole party, I shouted back that he was impotent, and that is why I have to go to another man. After that he never squeaked, till I got my divorce. Even now I keep my boyfriends on a tight leash, as Pammi puts it. I use them to have a good time, get expensive gifts from them in return for the good time I give them and then I just discard them like used condoms when I'm bored with them. Most often they continue to salivate all through their lives for me but I never look back.'

Jassi looked triumphantly at Sally. Sally, however, was unimpressed by the rhetoric and was getting more and more disenchanted by the lopsided concept of avenging the past by spoiling their's and their families' future.

The concept, however, had found fertile ground in Savvy's mind. Though she had touched her ears a couple of times, to ward off the evil effect of being disrespectful to Lord Rama, her mind was being sown with the subversive thoughts flying about and she was devising ways to implement her newfound wisdom. A seed was buried deep in her mind, a seed that would bear fruit soon—bitter or sweet, only time would tell.

~

Daiv's jottings: The women libbers, who bravely took up their fight on behalf of women, have also inadvertently aided and abetted the MCP's stance. While trying to correct injustices perpetrated, they went overboard with male-required-only-for-sperms-type of rhetoric. They lost sight of their goal of female upliftment and started doing what run-of-the-mill men have been doing for ages—downgrading the dignity of female-designated chores and chasing male-designated tasks. Moreover, they fought for the equality of men and women; this brought females more trouble because this ideology pitted them against the males in those fields, which by nature suit the male physique and capabilities.

Thus, the libbers unintentionally pushed the female into an unequal competition with the male, in the field of his strength. This often resulted in her being burdened with the roles of both provider as well as homemaker, further frustrating her.

The additional problem for her is that even when she succeeds against all odds in this unequal battle, she gets burdened with testosterone, the hormone that is required to achieve the drive to accomplish male-designated jobs. Testosterone, which relieves the male mind, tends to depress and stress the female mind, while her own protective and fulfilling hormone, oxytocin, gets depleted by these jobs. (See box)

CORTISOL vs TESTOSTERONE vs OXYTOCIN

Cortisol is the stress hormone produced by the adrenal gland in response to stress. It results in:

- Mild depression→loss of passion
- A sense of urgency and distress→reduces foreplay
- Decreased testosterone→low energy and libido
- Reduces Oxytocin in female→low interest in relationship + frustration

Testosterone is the primary male hormone.

- It increases as a result of goal-setting, problem-solving, success in tasks, power, appreciation and money
- In males it produces satisfaction, confidence, relaxation and mood elevation→lowers stress
- In females it produces aggression and low oxytocin→ stress

Oxytocin is the social, feel-good, female hormone.

- It causes relaxation, sexual arousal, lower stress→ feeling of well-being
- It increases as a result of nurturing children, sharing, talking, beauty, teamwork, compliments and cooperation
- It reduces as a result of aggression, stress, loneliness and competition

Raised levels of stress are the cause of much of the female agony and tension in the modern world, leading to broken and strained marital relationships. This indirectly leads to reactionary male tension, which too is going to be washed up the woman's shore. The 'women's libber' needs to see that the only way to a lasting and respectful male–female relationship lies in upgrading the female-designated tasks! True female upliftment can only occur by giving the deserved importance and respect to the tasks of homebuilding and child-rearing. Rather than eulogizing the role of women as homemakers and family-binders, libbers downgrade these tasks as menial and akin to bonded labour.

Why can't they glorify the field in which women not only excel but are naturally superior, like that of homemaker, family-binder or a multi-tasking team manager. This is the only way women across the globe can gain.

What good are ideas such as males-only-as-sperm-donors or males-giving-birth-to-children that cannot even be comprehended by 99 per cent of women in the world, let alone executed. Wake up to the reality!

~

A CATCH-22 SITUATION

According to women libbers, women want to become more like men and want men to become more like women (and do all the household chores). Men will either oblige or they will not. Let us see what happens in either case:

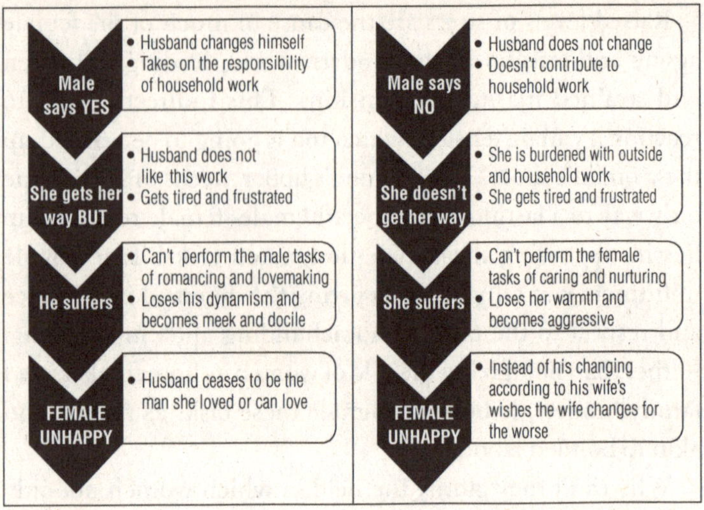

Inference: Her efforts to change him to become like her results in her suffering.

IN A NUTSHELL

Advice to men: In this game of women's lib, you both will suffer. You are doomed if you change according to her wishes and you are doomed if you don't. So hold on to your identity and hope that 'this too shall pass' when she finally sees the insanity of it all.

PART II

THE PROBLEM

> The only gamble your preacher approves of is the one that can be the most devastating—marriage

A Word from the Author

'Why does Mamiji fight with Mamaji all the time?' I asked my mom a long time ago.

For a change, my mom was at a loss for words. Then she smiled and said, 'Remember that joke I told you about two boys, Munna and Tunna, who couldn't hear?'

'Yes, yes,' I replied eagerly and to show that I really did, I narrated the joke. 'Munna says, "Are you going to the market?" Tunna replies, "No, I am going to the market." Munna reacts, saying "Oh! I thought you were going to the market." But how does that relate to Mamaji–Mamiji's fights?'

'Now imagine if these two boys could hear and still had the same conversation. Then?'

'Then . . .' I hesitated. '. . . I guess they would call each other stupid and maybe ... fight.'

'Right! That is the reason your Mama and Mami fight. One doesn't listen to what the other is saying.'

'How come? Mamaji is neither deaf nor stupid; he is so intelligent. Why doesn't he catch hold of Mami's neck and make her understand, like you do with me?' I persisted.

'Son, there are issues that are not so simple. You can't make someone understand unless he wants to understand.'

'Why won't she like to understand when she is wrong?'

'No! She is not wrong.'

'Then, is Mamaji wrong?'

'No, he is also not wrong.'

'If they are both right, why do they fight?'

'Because his "right" is different from her "right".' Mom never lost patience, despite my persistent questioning.

'Mom, now you are talking in riddles,' I said with exasperation.

'Marriage is one big riddle.' She exhaled deeply, as her forehead was etched with furrows of worry.

'Don't worry, Mom. I'll solve it. I am very good at riddles.' With the conviction of a five-year-old child, I made a tall claim. A VERY TALL ONE …

Now, fifty years later, I am still trying to solve the same riddle, with the help of all the world's psychologists, scientists and philosophers. This chapter is my best attempt to understand: 'Why do men and women fight?'

6

Why Is Marriage under Siege?

> To be happy with a man: You must understand him a lot and love him a little.
>
> To be happy with a woman: You must love her a lot and not try to understand her at all.

'I'm a widow,' Pammi said with a dramatic sigh.

The hush that fell at the comment was not restricted to that cabin alone. People outside the cabin also gasped and looked up, a vada dropped to the plate, a pen slumped onto the notebook, the counting of currency notes in a wad got garbled.

'... for twenty days in a month. My husband is hardly home for ten days a month.' Pammi completed her lament.

Savvy and Sally heaved a sigh of relief even as the vada was picked up, the pen was put to use again, and the counting of notes was resumed.

'Shh . . . Don't say such an inauspicious thing,' Savvy said, covering Pammi's mouth with her palm. 'My elder brother died in an accident. Though he was a very harsh man, I can tell you, nothing compares with what his wife has to go through as a widow. Humiliation is too mild a word to describe her ordeal. This is when my parents are not exactly the conservative, torturing types.'

Sally nodded, 'Yes! That is true and the worst thing is that everyone looks at you as if you are unclaimed baggage and seeks sexual gratification from you. A close friend, despite being a senior bank executive, is facing this dilemma.'

'You two are talking like my mother-in-law,' Pammi scoffed. 'She also says "Don't say that word—widow." See, I don't think my husband is going to die just because I say it. So chill, yaar. I'm just pointing to the fact that the biggest strain on my marriage is his incessant travelling. I'm sure that such continuous tours can only do one thing—make him adulterous. If I feel so sexually deprived, won't he? Plus, he has all the opportunity in the world. A well-off single male in a swanky hotel can have many wham-bam-thank-you-ma'am opportunities. He thinks, "What'll the poor wife know?" and goes right ahead.'

'Aren't you being too suspicious and phobic?' commented Sally.

'Maybe! But let me tell you, this staying apart because of the husband's constant travelling is the biggest tormentor of marriage.'

'Here, I don't agree with you,' replied Savvy. 'I believe the biggest tormentor is lack of privacy. The walls in my house are paper-thin. Actually, my house is a hall divided into two bedrooms and a dining room with thin tile partitions. Every sound we make can be heard across the partitions. Even the wall between our bedroom and the landlord's bedroom is just a single brick wall. That old lecher keeps listening to all we say or do and my husband hates this. He abhors being heard, especially when he comes near me at night. Thus, he keeps saying "shh . . . shh . . ." during our . . . you know . . . love. Even then our bed's joints are a bit squeaky and the sound gets across and I'm certain that old man does HP later, as we can clearly hear his grunting while he gets a release.'

'You mean he masturbates?' asked Pammi.

Savvy nodded, getting crimson by the moment. 'I suspect my cousin brother-in-law does something similar, for I have seen him rushing off to toilet, many a times after our ... love. My husband is so irritated, I'm afraid he will become celibate soon. The biggest strain of my marriage is these thin walls. I don't mind it as much as my husband does. A couple of times, during the act, he just . . .' she blushed.

'He what? Went limp?' chided Pammi.

'Yes,' giggled Savvy. 'And all because of that landlord. The old man is hard of hearing and sometimes asks his servant, Bahadur, in a loud whisper, "What are they saying now?" When my husband hears him pulling the chair to be able to put his ear to the small ventilator, he clams up mid-stream.'

'Yes! That is true. Men don't have the capacity to multi-task,' added Pammi. 'Even my hubby loses steam midway if his mobile rings. That is why I put his mobile on silent at night. This mobile is another big destroyer of marriages.'

'Maybe it is! I was thinking about our marriage the other day,' said Sally softly.

Everybody strained their ears towards her, for she spoke rarely and generally kept to the point. Joginder even shouted to Chhottu, 'Oi, turn down the volume of the TV.'

'. . . and I realized that the strain is coming from small little things that we both have learnt to do differently over the years. The bigger issues, like job demands or housing problems or in-laws' attitudes, though much larger, are mandatory problems that we have to compromise with because we all realize there is no way out; the husband can't change his job, the house can't be changed pronto, the in-laws' attitude will take ages to change. We, however, get infuriated about little things that each of us believes our spouse can easily change but doesn't. We think, why doesn't our spouse see things our way, or why doesn't he put in the small effort required. His stinking socks, his shoes lying in the passage, his dirty hanky lying in his pocket, his not putting the toilet seat down—they're all small things that add up. As we come out of our honeymoon stupor, these are the sights that greet us, leaving us sour and bitter.' She waved a hand in the air, as if she was clearing away these negative thoughts. 'It is here that we start trying to change each other, the cause of post-honeymoon blues. This is what I've been indulging in these past couple of months, and it frustrates me to find that he does not respond. I'm sure he is feeling the same way and facing the same strain.'

'Can such inconsequential things damage relationships?' queried Savvy.

'I think they can because these things are considered too

trifling to warrant a serious dialogue. So they remain bottled up and fester so much that even small disagreements result in fighting. Without these irritants, we would resolve those issues harmoniously. So issues like your husband's travel or lack of privacy that we would have otherwise adjusted to become contentious.'

'Come to think of it, you might have a point,' nodded Pammi. 'His going away, in fact, gives me a sense of relief. It is his brushing my complaints away lightly that really galls me. His smile when I'm on the verge of tears especially infuriates me.'

'I also think my husband is more irritated by my openly talking to all the men in the house than just the lack of privacy,' thought Savvy.

~

Joginder's thoughts took him to his wife, 'If she didn't smell that awful and didn't pick her nose continuously, I would have had no quarrels with her. Maybe a deodorant and hanky set can take care of the problem.'

The writer, looking for romance, also remembered the first year of his marriage, 'We might not have got separated, had her farts not killed all the romance.' He scribbled, 'Why is marriage under siege?'

~

Marriage is the beginning of REAL life, life after the euphoria of college and turmoil of career-planning are over. This is meant to be the steady phase of your life, the phase of maximum growth and biggest successes, one where, after a hard day's work, one comes back to the tranquillity of the home to recoup for fresh battles the next day.

This is why marriage is the beginning of real life. However, if there is any strain in a marriage, it can be the end of life—I mean the life in your life, the romance in your life, the happiness in your life.

So, let us have a look at why and how this strain creeps into our marriages. Why? Because life goes in a 'sine curve' and the pendulum always swings.

If previously it was men who by their belligerence and stubborn dominance brought this institution under strain, now it is the women, who are bent upon upsetting the apple cart with their unwarranted aggression. Rather than making the homemakers' role more respectful, the itchy-bitchy libber brigade has downgraded that most important task by advocating that the path to female progress lies only outside the home.

The government hasn't helped matters by making stringent but ineffective laws that do little for genuine grievances, as there is no system of implementation and execution. As a result, the real sufferers continue to get victimized by males, as they fear courts' procedures and society's wrath. On the other hand, devious urban females have found a great tool to flog husbands and their families with if they don't crawl when told to.

Will such injustice balance out the other injustice of a bygone era? History doesn't bear out that belief.

Let us look at the other issues that together have put cumulative pressure on the marital bond.

THE DEVIL OF SMALL LITTLE THINGS

Strain in marriages arises from day-to-day matters which in themselves seem innocuous but early in a marriage become so important that they can bury the romance in a marriage. For instancc:

- Her body odour after she cooks
- Her shouting at the kids
- Her haggling with vegetable vendors over petty amounts
- Her bad breath in the morning

or

- His smelly feet
- His habit of not keeping shoes, clothes, etc. in their proper places
- His speaking loudly
- His eating sloppily
- His hygiene

Any of these can cause minor blips in relationships, but when many such blips combine, they cause the marital relations to heave. Generally, these small irritants do not cause disruption in themselves but they can certainly exacerbate any potential incompatibility that would have got patched up without their added interference.

MAIN REASONS FOR SEPARATION/DIVORCE:

THE WEEK–C-Voter took respondents' views regarding what might cause marital strain:

- Anger/short temper: 46.3 per cent
- Staying out of town for long periods: 45.7 per cent
- Financial/housing troubles: 44.1 per cent
- Ego/attitudinal problems: 41.1 per cent

All you have to do to keep these small things at bay is to be observant of the initial reaction of your spouse to these things and remove the blips yourself before they are vociferously pointed out and become an issue.

Making war when love can't be made in privacy

Ego is the biggest undoing of romance and to opening up, vital for a new couple trying to discover each other. The problem compounds when there is an omnipresent audience. Then it becomes the fiefdom of ego. Neither partner wants to concede to anything that will make him/her look inferior in the eyes of the audience. On the other hand, seclusion makes each other more caring and accommodating.

In conservative families, it is the relatives that play spoilsport. In modern, urban settings, their prying eyes have been replaced by an arena full of strangers. High-rises, with paper-thin walls, are not very different from the Mumbai chawls where everyone eavesdrops on everyone else, with couples always feeling exposed.

A lack of privacy often becomes the first loose cog in the wheel. It is bound to disturb the balance in many adjoining cogs.

An unprofitable business

This gives moolah but takes away marriage. In the US, some statisticians believe there is a direct correlation between the rise in travelling sales jobs and the rise in divorce cases. Being away from home tends to take you very far away from your spouse, not only physically but also from her mind. The longer the interval between visits home, the higher is the chance of marital discord. The wife of my cousin, who works on a cruise ship, put it thus: 'When my husband comes home after six months, my daughter and I are in a predicament about how to reconcile to his presence. We have created a lifestyle for ourselves and he feels like a guest. I shudder to think what will happen when he decides to leave his job and stay here permanently.'

Even worse is the situation in which husband and wife, though together, are not really together because they have different work schedules, as in a situation in which one partner works in a call centre—the husband works nights and the wife works days or vice versa. On the extreme end of this spectrum are the 'two-executive families', with both partners in management positions that leave them inaccessible to each other.

> A travelling salesman came home only on Sundays.
>
> His son introduced him to his teacher during a parent–teacher meet saying, 'Madam, this is my Sunday dad.'
>
> When I read this joke in school, it sounded funny. Now I know it is a sad fact for many kids.

Similar situations are also seen in business families (typically in conservative bania families), where the husband remains busy in his business circle, plans his recreation with his male friends and relatives, and spends very little time with the wife.

These jobs and businesses might be the realities of today that can't be wished away but some solution will have to be found, or your fat pay packets will buy you nothing but misery.

Don't loan your life in lieu of that loan

Loans are a burden that weigh heavy on the marital bond. These are taken either just before the wedding or immediately after, for wedding expenses, or the desire to buy a home, vehicle or other material comforts of life. These purchases are usually undertaken by the male, ostensibly to show off his status to the new entrant in his life and at that point of time, these may seem absolutely necessary to start a good life.

Starting a marriage with a huge loan is like starting your maiden cricket match on the last over, requiring six 'boundaries' to win—one miss and all is lost because more often than not these loans are repaid either by forfeiting one of the salaries or, worse, by slicing off a major part in the case of a single earner.

When you have effectively mortgaged a part of your life to a loan, any job change or lay-off is bound to strain the marriage fabric irrevocably.

LATER—ALWAYS LATER, ESPECIALLY LOVE, ROMANCE, SEX

In your busy schedules, there are always small fires to be doused. These routine things, like filing returns, paying bills or school fees, or maintaining your rolodex, all take priority over more important aspects of marriage. You postpone your moments together—an anniversary candlelit dinner, a weekend vacation or an evening out for the movies that the two of you planned. These marriage rejuvenators somehow get pushed to 'later', when you presume you will be free, which might be never. This is bound to strangle the romance and passion in your life. As Dr Tushar Guha, psychologist and MD of Nrityanjali hospital, confirms, 'Recession is affecting the sex life of couples... sometimes it is as infrequent as once in two months and the worry about money and jobs is making it worse.'

I believe it is better to say 'no' to a plan rather than saying 'later' because that way you would at least remember the fact that you have dropped something important. By procrastinating, you deny that your 'later' is really 'never' in your marriage, till it is too late.

NEXT—THE SCOURGE OF GEN-NEXT MARRIAGES

The young live life in a fast lane and love it. Good for them—it heralds success and achievements. But this speed makes them insatiable materialists. Everything becomes changeable and only the new and instant is coveted: instant fad-foods, recently launched mobiles, the latest feature-rich TV, the fastest laptop, the loaded tablet, the latest model car, a brand-new home. Everything should change yearly or maybe every alternate year.

When everything old is considered 'oh so boring!', how can the same old spouse be good enough?

The idea of settling down is daunting to the single youth. Added now is their fickle commitment that makes them even less devoted to family life. As a result, they enter marriage sceptically, testing the waters rather than taking the plunge, and hang on to the support that can pull them out at the first sign of chill in the water. No wonder the time they give to try out things has shrunk for decades, as in our parents' case, to years, in my generation, to weeks for the generation of today. It is not unusual to find a marriage solemnized after six years of courtship and showing cracks by the end of six weeks.

Add to this the lack of moral grounding, which leads to an increasing incidence of infidelity and the slackening of the marital bond very early in marriage. Infidelity also tends to rise due to work schedules that pair you for long hours with colleagues of the opposite sex, who invariably become confidants/es. All this does not augur well for the tottering institution of marriage.

KIDS—THE MISSING GLUE

Children bind marriages. They reduce stress and tension in relationships. They are the investments that you make towards your marriage. The small difficulties and the resultant sacrifices that having children brings are the very factors that bind marriages and help couples sail through the most turbulent early years.

Doing something for and accepting a lot for the sake of your child teaches you to do more for your spouse and be more accepting, which is the hallmark of a strong relationship.

THE REEL DRAMA

Adding to all these factors that promote incompatibility is the sour icing on the cake, the TV soap drama and reality shows that have caught the imagination of our generation, as well as of the gen-next. To garner the all-important TRPs, these programmes tend to spice up serials in such a way that they project an extremely distorted picture of families and the lives of celebrities. The masses addicted to these shows emulate the soap characters or reality-show divas, taking their histrionics as something to aspire for.

Often, women watching these shows start looking within their own marriages for plots to oust them from their households. They formulate strategies to counter impending attacks by the in-laws. The primed wife confronts her husband the moment he enters the house and shows him a negative facet of his parents or siblings, the likes of which he may not have seen in the last twenty-five years. This leaves the husband dumbfounded and fuming—he is at his wits' end trying to understand what is going on. He would have recognized his wife's new avatar had he seen the face of the MIL shown in the afternoon saas-bahu serial. But in all likelihood, he wouldn't have seen the soap and is bound to get stressed. This stress will accumulate and he will explode either at his mother or his wife, depending upon whose version he accepts. If the former, there will be strained relations between the mother-in-law and the daughter-in-law; if the latter, a direct strain results in the marriage.

These contributing factors would still have got sorted out had they not got another dollop of fuel in the form of advice of 'well-meaning' friends and peers that acts as the proverbial last straw by affecting the thought process.

Let us see how...

IN A NUTSHELL

Many compulsions of modern life threaten the very foundation of the institution of marriage, and we can do very little about this. But there are innumerable small things which we can correct with an understanding attitude. More often than not, these small factors become the irritants that make the bigger things unbearable.

7

Birth, Propagation and the Boom of Discontent

When you marry the right woman—you are complete.

When you marry the wrong one—you are finished.

'You know, Jassi Didi was absolutely right,' Savvy said, thumping the table for emphasis. 'These males, really, are suppressing us females.'

Savvy fired her salvo even before sitting down. Despite the strong words, she didn't seem too perturbed. Her tone had the joyful bounce of a new crusader.

This was pure music to Pammi's ears. 'Jassi, you're great!' she thought, sensing another convert. 'What happened?

'That husband of mine doesn't care two hoots about me. We

only share food, sex and snoring.' Savvy used Jassi's words, and even her tone, for normally she avoided using words like 'sex'. 'On top of that, he wants me not only to take care of his three brothers but also ensure that they don't see me with those dirty eyes—if they do, it is my fault.'

'Has he changed recently or has he been like that from the beginning?' asked Sally.

This made Savvy pause and think. 'Maybe he has been like that, but now I am becoming more aware of his MCP nonsense.'

Thanks to Jassi, thought Sally.

'Now, I've also found a way to avenge myself.' She rolled her eyes and chewed her lips, which made her listeners sit up expectantly. 'You see, my husband is actually ill at ease with his cousin, Rahul, who is staying with us. For one, he is tall and fair, unlike my short and wheatish-complexioned husband. Second, he has a very happy-go-lucky style, akin to Aamir Khan in that movie *Fanaa*. In fact, now that he has also started taking tourists in his Innova, he has kept the alias Rehaan, after the character in *Fanaa*. My husband is especially bothered if I laugh and talk to him.

'One day, when my husband scolded me and went to office in a huff, I started sobbing loudly. Rehaan was home—he usually plies his taxi in the evenings. He came over to sympathize. I cried on his shoulder about the maltreatment my husband is subjecting me to, just like Kamolika did in that saas–bahu, mother-in-law—daughter-in-law serial. He was all sugar and honey and I could feel that he was trying to hold me close to his body. I even felt his maleness . . . you know . . .' she giggled.

'You mean his erection,' completed Pammi.

Savvy nodded.

'Then what did you do?' enquired Pammi excitedly.

'Nothing! I just freed myself coyly.'

'Oh no! You should have gone forward and . . .' Pammi winked and nodded suggestively.

Savvy's fair face turned a crimson red at the suggestion. 'Ever since, he brings me sweets or a savoury snack every day after my husband has gone to office. I know now that he is under my control and will do exactly as I will bid him to. He even took me shopping and sightseeing one day.'

'Yes! That is a conquest. Keep it up. This may be the route to your emancipation from drudgery.' Pammi was encouraging.

'Isn't that dangerous? What if your husband gets a whiff of it?' Sally asked cautiously.

'Actually, Rehaan is also scared of him, so he takes utmost care to keep it all hush-hush. And, if anything goes amiss, I can always say that my innocence has been taken advantage of. In any case, my husband thinks I am pretty naïve.'

'Still, it is like playing with fire. Anybody might notice and report it to your husband.'

'In fact, that wretched landlord did see me with Rehaan once but instead of squealing, he did an odd thing. He called me to his room and told me to get something from his bathroom as his servant had gone out.

'In his toilet, I saw a beautiful Parker pen in the WC. I fished it out, cleaned it up with soap and kept it.'

'Then?' asked Sally.

'Then, when I came out, I saw the old lecher smiling at me

mischievously as if he knew what I had done. To avoid being accused of theft, I decided to hand it back to him. He said, "Keep it. You have earned it." Then he said a funny thing. He said, "Whenever you need something extra, you can always come to me and ask for it." I replied, "How can I take anything from you?" He said, "Then in return you can do something for me . . . something to help me or make me happy." I couldn't understand what he really meant.'

'I think he was making a pass at you,' replied Pammi.

'It is far worse,' said Sally. 'With that pen, he was checking how desperate you are for materialistic things. By offering goodies in exchange for pleasing him, he was offering to buy you, or rather, sexual gratification from you. You should shun him like plague and should complain to your husband so that he can look for alternative accommodation.' Sally was forthright as ever.

'But what if he tells my husband he saw me with Rehaan in his vehicle. And you don't know my husband. He will blame me for everything. He has already told me many times that I invite ogling by wearing all this make-up, even when I am sitting at home. Now tell me, Pammiji, do I put on heavy make-up?'

Pammi shook her head, 'No, no, you hardly wear any make-up.' Sally could hear the sarcasm in the remark but Savvy carried on, oblivious.

'I know. The ladies in all these serials wear such elaborate make-up and have complicated hairdos, even while sleeping. But he thinks that my wearing a bit of lipstick, kajal and nail polish is seductive and inviting. How backward of him, no?

Rehaan, on the other hand, appreciates my getting decked up and encourages me to get manicures, pedicures and even waxing. So, I have decided to say nothing to my husband, who in any case will never understand me.'

'I also believe that is correct,' supported Pammi. 'In any case what is the harm in taking a few gifts? These are little privileges of our femininity. When we accept the burden of our sex, why deny ourselves the privileges. Jassi always says, "Use these bastards and empty their pockets—give little in return." I, too, have had many boyfriends in my college days. I, too, enjoyed movies, fine dining and getting gifts. All the boys wanted was to touch my arms or thighs. So I let them and then left them to drool. What is the harm?'

'For a movie and dinner, a touch may not be too harmful. But then what about the more expensive gift next time? Won't he expect a full return? And what will that reduce us to—proverbial whores, isn't it?' Sally uncharacteristically raised her voice.

The other two had no answers but their defiant shrugs indicated what they thought of Sally's cautious approach.

Had Sally looked around, she would have seen three heads nodding their assent.

~

Joginder's brows furrowed with disgust. Though he was sickened by the ladies' talk, another thought was simultaneously rocking his brain. 'Roshni is not like these ladies but then I, too, complain all the time and blame her for everything. Am

I pushing her inadvertently into someone else's arms because of my callousness? I think I should pay more attention to her. What is wrong if she wants to deck up a bit? All ladies want that. I'll take some cosmetics and perfumes for her today.'

Shravan was thinking, 'Maya, too, could have used her femininity to get gifts.' He wanted to shout a resounding, 'No way!', but all he could manage was, 'I hope not . . .' Then could she have slept with . . ., he was thinking. A vigorous shake of his head brought him back from his reverie but the question mark had formed in his mind.

Daiv was getting more insight into the female mind. He turned to a new page in his notebook and wrote: 'The formation of the mindset of women'.

~

Men are often baffled at women's mindset, especially at how it gets altered, sometimes so irrationally. How do women end up emulating someone whose ideas they had never agreed with?

The formation of the mindset

This occurs in four steps:

1. Sowing the seed of an idea: This is done by people around you, deliberately or unconsciously. For example, repeated inputs regarding torture of women by husbands or in-laws plants the seed of rebellion against them. Such seeding is much easier in a virgin, fertile mind that is still immature.
2. Appreciation of a role model: Witnessing dominating

behaviour of family members, friends or even characters from TV serials makes one want to behave similarly.

3. Internalizing behaviour: Over time, one starts subconsciously acting in the same way.
4. Self-concept: After the internalizing period, one acts as if these thoughts and actions are one's very own.

While emulating the mindset of a role model, one overlooks how different another's life and circumstances are. There is a saying in Punjabi: 'Dusre ke laal gaal dekhke, apne gallon ko thapad maar kar thora hi laal karna hai (If someone has naturally rosy cheeks, you don't slap your face to make your own cheeks red). Something similar is happening in the world today. Most people are slapping their faces and their lives to make them as rosy as the ones they are emulating.

IN A NUTSHELL

Planting an illusionary idea about a perfect life is a dangerous thing because it leads to the formation of a mindset which perceives that one's present life is wretched. One who dreams about a perfect life is bound to be disgruntled with her real life.

8

Expectations and Assumptions—the Bane of Marriage

> A woman marries, expecting her husband to change but he doesn't.
>
> A man marries, expecting his wife not to change but she does.

'In less than a year, all my dreams have been shattered…' Pammi lamented.

'My dream of living life exclusively on my own terms without restrictions of any kind—the dream of ruling my world as the unbridled ruler—all have been quashed.'

'Your career dreams?' enquired Sally, even as Savvy blinked, unable to grasp what Pammi was saying. 'Dreams… unbridled ruler… my own terms… what is she talking about?' she thought.

'No! My life dreams—the dream of living uninhibitedly after marriage. The dream of ruling my household . . .'

'How did you assume that these things would be possible after marriage?' questioned Sally. 'I thought that was possible only for professional spinsters who are financially independent.'

'It is possible. It's what has been happening in my parents' house for years. My dad severed relations with his parents, brothers and sisters when my mom couldn't get along with them. In fact, my hubby also projected similar images before marriage but his true colours became apparent immediately after our honeymoon. He started suggesting how close he was to his sister and parents and would never like to stay separately. Even then I tolerated his attitude, but yesterday he crossed all the limits.'

She looked at the expectant faces of her friends and continued. 'Yesterday, my sister-in-law and her husband visited us. My in-laws have a fetish that come what may, the son-in-law should be pampered like a prince. So I was ordered to do this and that and arrange the living room and what not. I got really bugged. Why all this special treatment for the son-in-law but not for me—their daughter-in-law. The moment I got a chance, I slunk away to my room, on the pretext of being unwell, and didn't show up till lunchtime. As luck would have it, my own friends had arranged a get-together in the evening and I got ready to join them. My in-laws made such a fuss: "If you could go to a party so far off, couldn't you have come down and sat with jawai sahib for half an hour?" They even complained to my hubby and he scolded me.' Pammi was furious.

'That mother-in-law is a so-called social worker in an NGO and is supposed to work for the upliftment of wronged women and look what she does to her own daughter-in-law. If she does not mend her ways, I'll teach her a lesson she won't forget in a hurry.'

'Relax, relax, Pammi,' said Sally. 'I don't think it is such a big deal at all. Most families in India do pamper their sons-in-law and expect their daughters-in-law to show proper courtesy to him. I think you are making an issue of a non-issue. Calm down.'

For once Savvy nodded, for she agreed with Sally, though she didn't voice her agreement lest Pammi get annoyed. She believed that for a similar offence, her mother-in-law would not only have made her life miserable but would also have given her a tight slap on her face.

Pammi, however, was undeterred by this argument. 'I don't know. In my Nani's house, such pampering was unheard of. My dad, despite being an army officer, was treated just like another family member, nothing more. Why all this hypocrisy?'

'I think what you are cribbing about is more the norm than exception and you are being unrealistic if you can't adjust to this minor infringement on your sovereignty,' said Sally

'I am basically very practical, not unrealistic at all,' countered Pammi indignantly. 'It is just that during our prolonged courtship, my hubby dear projected such a rosy picture of married life that I assumed that my life after marriage would be better than the best setting in any TV serial—a rosy financial picture, a modern, understanding family, do-what-you-want-to type of attitude all around, with no interfering kith or kin.

Compared to my parents' status, my in-laws always looked so modest, pliable and down to earth, as if they would do anything I ask them to do. They had frequently said, "We are so lucky to have a tie up with a family like yours" and "Your daughter will be accorded a princess's welcome and given the same comfort and freedom that she is used to in your house." But what I find is that the father-in-law is a religious fanatic, who believes that the daughter-in-law should always have some cloth or chunni on her head, especially when he is present. Just imagine that! My mom always wore spaghetti straps, irrespective of who was present, and I am told to wear chunnis. So I hardly come out of my room when my father-in-law is around. For that they label me a shirker, who doesn't contribute to the household.' Pammi was fuming, so Sally let her get it all off her chest.

'See, Pammi, these things happen in all households—it's bound to when two sets of people come together. As for premarital projections, these are always a bit exaggerated because both the partners are trying to impress the other. Don't we women wear the best make-up and dresses while going out with our fiancés or boyfriends? Don't we behave our best and reveal only our best qualities to the male? Then why do we assume he won't do the same? Of course, he too is bound to profess exaggerated strength and finances. We can hold him culpable if he is a manual worker and postures as a manager but not for minor bolstering of his assets or future projections. I think, partially, we are also at fault. We make lofty assumptions based on a bit of what he says. Then our expectations go sky high. Amongst the three of us, you are the best off and have the most freedom. Still, you feel the most frustrated. This is because your expectations were the highest. What you have got is simply not able to fit into that large frame.'

~

Shravan's mind was buzzing with a zillion questions. 'What are Maya's expectations from me? She has already hinted that she would never be able to stay with my parents. Today, she is willing to send some money back home for my sisters' marriage. I don't know what she believes I earn. She might consider what I get after tax deduction and EMI deduction for the loan that I've taken insufficient even for us. Will I be able to send anything home at all then? If not, what about our mortgaged land? What about the marriage of my younger sisters? What about my parents?'

He decided to discuss everything with Maya. 'I hope she understands,' he thought, which brought out another question: 'Will she?'

Daiv's coffee turned cold for he had forgotten all about it as he jotted down points in his notebook: 'Assumptions—the bane of marriage…'

~

Assumptions, assumptions

Both men and women cross the threshold of marriage with a huge baggage of assumptions. These assumptions are about all the negative things that can happen to your relationship and how you plan to ward them off. Also, you have assumptions about what positive things could happen to you. These assumptions are based on what has happened to others in the past, fuelled and spiced by folklore and fantasy abundantly available in the saas-bahu serials.

This last factor has singlehandedly done more damage to the institution of marriage in India than all others put together. For the sake of TRPs, the saas–bahu serials have introduced a factor unheard of until now—a strategic conspiracy within the household. Most brides and many grooms now believe that after marriage they will enter the treacherous ground of a conspiracy-ridden household and face chess-like manoeuvres hitherto reserved for the 'dirty-politics department' of palaces.

ASSUMPTIONS OF NRIS:

Home Grown, a BBC radio documentary presented by Yasmeen Khan, depicts a crisis in the British Asian community. The men disliked British Asian women because 'the girls are too outspoken and want too much equality'. They wanted to bring back wives from their home country because they felt they were more 'virginal and innocent'.

They discounted that a gap of one generation made the 'home girls' more independent. Their assumptions about these girls fall flat once they meet them in real life, leading to troubled marriages.

Thus, every rope is envisioned as a snake and every sniffle as a hidden message to start a sinister trick.

Complicating this scenario is the male mindset that has an equal and often diametrically opposite set of assumptions based on hearsay and the well-meaning or nefarious advice of friends and relatives, who advise them to exert their dominance and control over the newlywed wife or else all hell will break loose.

The flashpoint occurs because neither partner is aware of the assumptions of the other half. If the two of you can sit down before or immediately after marriage, and open your hearts, lay down your assumptions and accept that the other may have assumptions in variance to your own, it may be the single most effective solution to your marriage woes.

The dilemma of lofty premarital projections

Both men and women glorify their personal qualities and future prospects when they interact before marriage, showing off not only their best clothes and behaviour but also the best projections for the future.

Women certainly project a rosy image but their projections are more emotional, that is, they project a coy, soft, shy image that in any case is expected to change after the honeymoon.

Men's projections are more concrete, as they relate to their status, career prospects, financial status and role in the future household. This is something that you will be held accountable for and which you cannot alter without looking like a charlatan. These projections raise very high expectations from the life ahead in the minds of the women. Saying things that you actually 'can't/

don't do' will later lead to charges of being a 'promise breaker'; ditto for trying to be something that you are not.

What lands you most in trouble is appeasement. You tend to go head over heels in your endeavour to impress your fiancé with grandiose claims. The same happens during the honeymoon and post-honeymoon bliss. You are so grateful to your wife for relieving you of your overflowing semen, especially if you are an Indian virgin male deprived of a regular dose of sexual gratification, that you agree to do anything to show your obligation. These are the formative years of your marital relationship, when the two of you are trying to find your respective levels of duties and responsibilities. Instead of intelligently negotiating this period, you nod your head, with stars in your eyes.

The problem is that patterns set in this phase will need to be maintained for a long, long time, if not forever. The result of these lofty promises is naïve expectations from marriage—the wife sets her goals and priorities accordingly. Added to this is the treatment meted to her during the wedding, when she is dressed in clothes and jewellery befitting a queen. Then comes the honeymoon, when all the wife's wishes are your commands and you behave as if the only reason for your existence is to please her in every way possible. Now, after the honeymoon,

Remember:

She is your would-be wife for keeps—not a date to be impressed with false, lofty projections.

when this dreamy queen is told to set foot on the hard real earth and take up her duties, she is dismayed. How can she even imagine that she would be required to cook and take care of the family?

Most women believe they are going to a household where everyone will not only accept her as the uncrowned queen but that her fiefdom will also extend to the other kith of the husband. She finds to her shock that not only does the husband have a spine but also an ego that forces him to take the moral high ground whenever there is a clash of interests. Adding to this is the propriety of her in-laws, who expect conventional behaviour from their daughter-in-law.

This is contrary to her assumptions and expectations, and all the castles she had planned to rule come tumbling down. She now realizes that, unlike in her parents' house, where the male may have been just the master of the house in name and was ready to lie prostrate before the wife at the slightest provocation, her in-laws will go this far and no further when it comes to cetain issues. She also realizes to her chagrin that unlike her father, her husband is not ready to sever all his relations if ordered by his wife. No wonder she revolts.

Woman1: Men are like ceramic tiles.

Woman 2: How so?

Woman 1: Fix them properly once and for all, and then you can walk all over them forever!

Where does the fault lie?

- The husband's parents are not at fault; they try their best to accommodate the daughter-in-law's wishes and on their part they've done more than is their wont to accommodate her. They realize that the more they succumb, the more demanding their daughter-in-law becomes. Their only fault, if you want to call it that, is the humility that projected the image of pliable in-laws.
- The girl is also not at fault—in her own maternal house, she may have seen total subjugation of the male. The image of her in-laws, in keeping with her premarital exposure, was of a soft, spineless husband and family. Naturally, she acts accordingly and is shocked to find an unbending attitude. Had she seen the reality upfront, she might have retracted her steps, but chances are that she would have readjusted her expectations and aimed only to become the feudal lord of her room and not Queen Victoria. Perhaps this would have been allowed by her in-laws.
- The major mistake lies in the husband's exaggerated projections that lead the wife to assuming a near-impossible future.

A husband contributes to the pendulum shift by doing some very naïve things in the premarital period that make his role in the future unenviable. Toning down projections about what he is, what he has, what he earns, how well he will provide for his wife, and what role she will have to play in real life, will make it much easier to for him to fulfil them and his wife is less likely to feel let down.

Proverb: Intelligence is in accepting that when frogs start croaking during the rains, it is better for the koel to keep quiet.

Caution: Keep quiet but never let the frogs think that they sing better than the koel—a mistake most husbands make.

Marriage and its success are all about 'respect and love'. The problem is that neither of these things can be bought (with gifts) nor can they be demanded (with authority) nor begged for (with appeasement and flattery) and definitely not procured with elevated claims. They can only be earned with an astute and caring attitude. Yes, you should let the wife feel important but never make the mistake of letting her believe that she is superior to you and your family, if your parents and siblings play a large part in your life. All this should be sorted out before getting married.

Think it over. It is a small thought that can bring a catharsis and save you and your marriage from the wrath of a woman who firmly assumes that she has been wronged. And feminine wrath can be quite terrible.

Want to feel its pangs?

IN A NUTSHELL

The husband's tendency to fall head over heels while wooing his future wife becomes the proverbial millstone around his neck when he gets down to dividing responsibilities, duties and powers in a household. So, pamper your would-be wife wisely and don't project lofty dreams.

EXPECTATIONS OF TODAY'S WIFE

Jai Siya Ram, Jai Jai Siya Ram
Aisa pati mujhe do bhagwan
Subah uth ke voh chai banaye
Chai bana kar mujhe uthaye
Aur bole—peele meri jaan, peele meri jaan.

Jai Siya Ram, Jai Jai Siya Ram
Aisa pati mujhe do bhagwan
Mujhe nashta khila kar daftar jaye
Daftar mein khoob paise kamaye
Paise kama kar seedha mere paas aaye
Aur bole—udaa meri jaan, udaa meri jaan.

Jai Siya Ram, Jai Jai Siya Ram
Aisa pati mujhe do bhagwan
Shaam ko phir woh ghar per aaye
Aa kar woh chulah jalaye
Chuleh par phir who khana pakaye
Aur bole—kha meri jaan, kha le meri jaan.

Jai Siya Ram, Jai Jai Siya Ram
Aisa pati mujhe do bhagwan
Raat ko phir mere bistar par aye
Bistar par baith kar mere paon dabaye
Aur bole—pyaar karun meri jaan? pyaar karun meri jaan?

—Punjabi folk song sung at weddings

9

The Empire Strikes Back

A woman has the last word in any argument.

Anything a man says after that is the beginning of another argument.

'That old bag is always backbiting to my husband that I don't work and that I bad-mouthed her. She's made a mountain of a molehill. All I had told her was to mind her own business. She was trying to force me into the kitchen by saying, "Please make some chapattis, I am not feeling well." All she had was a mild cold. What is the big deal? If you can't make it, order from outside. No! That is against her religion. "I don't eat from outside"—bloody hypocrite. My masseur-maid told me she had seen her eating gol-gappas one day. She must be doing that every day. How else could she have got that sore throat? How come I never get a sore throat? Then she says, "Why do you lie around all day? It is not good for your health." I told her to mind her own business and the shrew complained to my hubby—which led to our first-ever fight. Imagine, I had been planning to celebrate the whole of the twelfth month of our marriage as a romantic anniversary-month and my hubby scolds me on the very first day. He and my mother-in-law are trying to snatch away my freedom and shackle me to the kitchen even before my one year is over in the house.'

Having spewed out all that was bothering her, Pammi settled down comfortably. Such had been the force of her desolation that not only did Savvy and Sally stay mum but a hush descended over all the others in the restaurant too.

Pammi called the waiter, 'Get me a double cheese sandwich and an uttapam—very crisp. I'm famished.' Then, turning back, she said, 'You see, I've declared anshan and given up eating or even having water. Now all I eat is what I can grab when I'm out and have to drink water from the bathroom tap.'

'Hasn't your husband tried to dissuade you from going without food?' asked Sally in a sombre tone.

'He has. In fact, to coax me to give up my fast unto death, he has also not had dinner or breakfast for last two days. He must be eating at the office and blackmailing me so I give up my protest. I think he is doing this as he is scared—because I threatened in the heat of moment that I would complain to the dowry cell that he and my in-laws are torturing me.'

'Wasn't that a bit extreme for such a trivial issue?' Sally eventually opened her mouth. Even Savvy felt that way but she kept mum for she wanted to see if Pammi could achieve her objective this way. If she succeeded, maybe she, too, could use this method in future. 'Why would they bow to such a frivolous threat if they have never asked for dowry?' countered Sally.

'First of all, this threat is a serious business for all in-laws. They know that, even without an iota of proof, I can make their lives miserable and even put them behind bars with one complaint. In my case, the real threat, which would send them scurrying for cover, is loss of reputation. Imagine the headline: "A social reformer, who fights for wronged women, harasses her own daughter-in-law." It would negate the in-laws' life-long crusade and standing in the society. That is why I know they would all succumb to my demands. Don't tell me you don't indulge in similar gamesmanship when required.'

'In my case, I have to do everything in a covert manner,' said Savvy. 'One wrong word and I will be shunted back to my in-laws in the village. You know, when my hubby came to Delhi for the first time after marriage, he left me in the village to look after his parents, most likely on their insistence. When I said that he would need homemade food as the outside food is bad for his health, they scolded me. So, the next time he came visiting us in the village, I mixed jamal-ghota (a very strong laxative) in the laddoos his mother had prepared for him. Every time he ate one, he got the loosies. After four bouts a day and losing seven days of work, my mother-in-law finally sent me to Delhi to take care of her son. So I got my objective without any confrontation. Isn't this better?'

Pammi shrugged her shoulders, indicating that she need not indulge in these stealth tactics.

Sally, however, nodded. 'Yes! These techniques though

ethically wrong are much better than confrontations and threats. In fact, these have been used by Indian women since time immemorial and were termed triya charitra, meaning ulterior or wicked methods to achieve one's goals. These techniques, of using emotions or mannerisms, have been women's traditional strength and all of us have used these to manipulate situations. Only the other day, my husband got together four of his friends at the last minute for dinner. Both my mother-in-law and I were dead tired after a major bout of house cleaning that day and we didn't like the unannounced visitors. My mother-in-law had once mentioned that Sunny, one of my husband's friends, was a great expert in cooking non-veg. I told him, with fluttering eyes, that we would love to taste his cooking. The plan worked. Immediately, one of the friends went scurrying to get mutton, a second one to get some cream and other ingredients, while the other two got busy with the kitchen. And when the food was finally ready, I made chapattis for everyone in fifteen minutes and had a great feast. Now, that is smartness and it worked without confrontation. My mother-in-law is strict but not unjust. I listen to her occasional harsh words because I know she would be equally harsh on my husband or for that matter on my father-in-law if they made the same mistake. I believe women have always been smarter than men, for they always knew how to take advantage without confrontation. The new dimension they have added is that they have started hitting back deliberately, even where a subtler approach could have worked. I don't know whether this is good or bad for women but attacking where it is not required at all is naïveté.'

'You might think so but a majority of us are increasingly taking up cudgels for our freedom and independence. My dad, Colonel Ahluwalia . . . oops . . . sorry, no names.' Pammi had forgotten their pact for anonymity in the heat of the moment. 'Anyway, he always said, "It is better for a young woman to divorce than compromise." He always advised me to hit men who take advantage of us where it hurts the most.'

'The point, my dear friend, ' interjected Sally, 'is this: are our husbands really taking advantage of us or are we fighting shadows in our own minds?'

~

Shravan was reminded of another retired army officer, Major Singh, Maya's father. According to his plan, he had told Maya that he wanted to talk to her about finances and how they would manage them after marriage. She told him to come over and they would go to a restaurant and discuss it but the moment he reached their house, Major Singh caught hold of him and started chattering about his job and salary. This was very unusual because Major Singh had never said anything to him before beyond a casual 'hello'. Now he craftily veered the topic towards his daughter's interests and expenses. Before Shravan could catch the drift of his conversation, the Major dropped a bombshell by pronouncing that the only way Shravan could marry Maya was if he could provide her with the kind of lifestyle she was used to.

Though Maya kept saying, 'Leave it, Dad, we will discuss it later,' Shravan felt that this ambush had been planned by her. That much wisdom he had gained from his visits to the Rendezvous restaurant. He excused himself from going out with her on the pretext of not feeling well. Maya, surprisingly, didn't press for going out. Maybe she wanted to give him time to think about what her dad had told him.

~

Joginder was lost in thoughts of the happy moments that Roshni had provided him in return for a packet of cosmetics. The gastronomic delights she was showering on him had made his life, otherwise full of drudgery, one of bliss. She is good. Thank God she is not rebellious like these women, or at least like her, he thought, looking at Pammi with contempt.

Daiv wrote, 'The female uprising—the pendulum shifts . . .'

~

Why the female uprising?

The male single-point focus has made him a better skilled worker. But with changing paradigms, the top jobs have become multi-tasking ones: managers, planners, team-builders. These require a multi-focused approach more suited to females. In China, which has a conservative, patriarchal society like India, most shop-owners or office managers are women. Men there do more labour-intensive tasks or run errands. The multi-focused woman probably adapted better to the changing scenario of individual business houses now starting up in China. This is taking women upwards not only in monetary terms but also in terms of status. Add to this the female zeal to prove herself in a male-dominated society and the scenario is clear: women are surging ahead very rapidly. This is a very positive trend, except that the change is too rapid for males to adjust to.

Moreover, the choice of professions also has a bearing on this equation. Women are increasingly migrating into either public relations jobs, which demand unabashed assertivness, or into teaching, and research or administrative jobs that make them dominating and more demanding. Men, on the other hand, are increasingly shifting to sales and business profiles, where they need to be more accommodating and compromising. This has led to a sort of behaviour reversal; males are becoming softer and more understanding, whereas females are becoming more self-confident and aggressive.

In their endeavour to take on men's jobs, women have also started to adopt a 'male attitude'; this is part and parcel of the job. To be equal, they counter male aggression by being more aggressive. In the process, they are letting go of their real strength, that of a shrewd motivator and a team manager. As a result, where they dominated as the real power behind the throne of the master of the house, now they want to be declared 'the lord and master of the house'. The reconciliatory and persuasive approach has been replaced with a confrontationist approach, which was for long a negative male hallmark.

This aggression is fuelled by provocative statements from peers, parents or relatives who advocate female aggression because it appears progressive-sounding in social circles.It may also be because of the mistaken belief that they are helping the female cause.

On this combination of a provocative seed and fertile mind, the media acts as a superphosphate fertilizer. Every injustice done on women is highlighted by eulogizing the roles of women who have done away with conventional female roles. The result is the development of a militant attitude in the minds of young women. They expect their in-laws to mistreat them, so they strategize the counter-attack in advance, often without any real provocation.

The female empire is striking back with a vengeance. The only problem is that in many cases they are attacking a hostility which does not exist, except in their own minds. They enter their new homes full of suspicion. Whatever the case may be, this attitude is sure to shake the foundation of their marriage and cause stress not only to their husbands and in-laws but to themselves and their parents too.

And then the last straw is . . .

IN A NUTSHELL

Women are hitting out at the conventional mindset, forcing a paradigm shift. The danger is that they might end up fighting shadows that exist only in their mind.

10

False Sense of Competition and Its Consequences

Wife: I have changed my mind.

Husband: Thank God! I hope the new one works.

'Today I won on every front over my hubby dear,' Pammi said, chuckling.

'Interestingly, I was about to say the same thing,' Savvy, too, was jubilant.

'Are you two playing games at your homes?' asked Sally tersely, though she had an idea what the two must be hinting at.

'Sort of! Have you heard the Hindi song, "I'm playing the game of love . . ."? Well, we are playing the game of marriage. It is more intriguing than even chess, and much more rewarding if you win,' Pammi raised her eyebrows mischievously.

'Yes, very rewarding!' echoed Savvy.

'What did you win?' Sally asked Savvy because she felt that she was parroting Pammi's words mindlessly.

'You know, I won a movie and dinner out and a rose. And what's more, this will be repeated every time I keep my mouth shut.' Sally realized that Savvy meant what she was saying.

'I won much more.' Pammy tucked her hair behind her ears and showed off sparkling diamond earrings. 'Plus a final consent to my joining the PhD programme. Of course, I had to play a prolonged game of cat and mouse with my husband.'

'How, how?' Savvy was literally jumping out of her chair, for this was sounding more and more like a TV serial.

'As you know, I was fasting for being reprimanded. After a lot of persuasion, I gave up my fast because it was becoming impossible to sneak out every time I was hungry. But I continued to sulk and had stopped talking to him. He continued to ignore my sulk and went about life, as if my not speaking to him was having no effect at all. In fact, he talked to me normally, whether I replied or not. The same "good morning", "bye-byes" and all. He even said, "this kutti [keeping mum] is childish" and that he was far too mature for it. He must have been advised by his mom to say so. For many days he kept winning but I didn't give up.' Pammi smiled.

'Then there was this party thrown for his uncle's family that had come from America. I made it clear that I would have no part in it, nor would I pretend everything was normal in front of them. Now he was in a fix, as he wanted to leave a favourable impression on his influential relatives; I had him by his balls. He tried every argument, even cajoling, and later he even begged me to behave responsibly. But he didn't agree to my demand for not doing any kitchen work. So on the day of the party, I used my last ace. I feigned depression and put some glycerine in my eyes that ensured a bountiful supply of tears and red eyes. During dinner, everybody asked me about my red eyes. I magnanimously lifted the blame off his shoulders and told them that I am allergic to cooking fumes. The US aunty scolded my mother-in-law, asking her why she made me cook when I have this allergy. Then I dropped the bombshell and announced that it was not my mother-in-law who made me cook. I did it on my own, as I've started enjoying cooking, especially now, when I know my PhD would keep me away from the kitchen for a long time. This was the move that checkmated the family. There was no way they could refute my statement without losing face and seeming petty. The cherry on the cake was that my hubby got me these diamond danglers for saving his reputation by attending the dinner. Now that's a complete victory, isn't it?'

'Yes!' agreed Sally, adding, 'You murder the husband and then get compensated handsomely because you are a widow. Wow!'

~

Shravan had come here seeking some hard answers but instead he was being bombarded by new and painful questions. Or were these questions pointing towards a probable answer. He wasn't sure. Of late, he had started dreading coming to this restaurant. Every time he heard these women talking, he was painfully reminded of a facet of Maya's personality that left a hole in the rosy picture of life that he had envisioned for himself with her. Like today, when he was reminded of his engagement party last week. Maya had said that she wanted a hush-hush engagement at home, with no guests, and that too, immediately as she would be out of town after that for a few months. As a result, he could invite no relatives of his and went for the engagement with just one friend. But he was shocked to see that more than a hundred of Maya's relatives and friends had gathered in the gala party tent outside Maya's home. When he expressed his displeasure, Maya shut him up with a kiss and the lame bail-out, 'Dad just didn't agree to my hush-hush thing and arranged everything yesterday,' she claimed. Though every cell of his brain was screaming that such arrangements could not have been done without at least a fortnight's planning, he had gone ahead with the ceremony. Even the fact that Maya never left town afterwards never raised an alarm, except now. He was thinking, 'Maya was trying to show me who the superior partner in our relationship is. She also felt that my family was not good enough to be presented to her relatives. I am such a sucker.'

He was seething.

~

Savvy clapped her hands excitedly, snapping everyone out of their reverie. 'It is straight out of that TV serial, *Sasural*.'

Pammi smiled back and asked, 'What about you? How did you achieve your win?'

Savvy was now ready to spill the beans. 'Things for me are not as dramatic but still there is a significant change. I told you that my husband abhors it if anybody hears any sound when he comes to me . . . you understand . . . I mean at night. He prefers to come and have his fill—he doesn't say a word and then snores away to glory. I realized that if I moan or say something aloud, he goes . . . you know . . . limp. So I decided for once to do his bidding and hinted to him that if he treats me well I wouldn't utter a word when he wants me. The treat he is giving me is for this.'

'Oh! So, you have started using your femininity?'

'Well, you can say that! One thing I wanted to ask. Why don't I feel satisfied after the act? He has a mighty release and I hardly feel anything. In the beginning there used to be some excitement but now, even that has fizzled off. Why so?'

'You see, Savvy, not all women achieve the classic release orgasm that males experience,' replied Sally.

'It is not that—I do have orgasms. It is just that it's not with him.'

'You mean you had sex with somebody else also!' exclaimed Pammi, for Savvy definitely looked very restrained.

'Oh, no! It is . . . how should I put it . . . I get orgasm while doing HP.'

'HP?'

'Yes, what do you call it when you stimulate yourself with your own hands? I read in some magazine that boys call it HP.'

'You mean 'hand-practice' for boys, masturbation . . . you insert an object in the vagina and . . .'

'Not exactly. I hold my thighs together tightly and just rub them and . . . and think of somebody and I achieve it.'

'Okay! So who do you think of?'

'Actually different persons but nowadays, mostly my Rehaan,' she blushed. 'I am trying to follow Jassi Didi's advice—use sex as a weapon and achieve what you want, and then get gratification elsewhere, everybody is happy.'

'Now that you have said it, I too believe that sex is a very potent, well . . . I'm not saying a weapon but definitely a potent tool,' said Sally, and coming from her it was a revelation. 'You know what, my poor husband has severe job-related stress because of the recession. Many of his colleagues in the IT industry are getting fired. As a result, he has a lot on his mind and you know what, twice in the last week he could not perform. He was very embarrassed but I supported him and said it is a natural thing and, you know what, he was so indebted that he has been showering me with praise even to the extent of defying my mother-in-law when she said something harsh. He said, "Mom! She is working so hard, you should be careful about her health." Also, he has been bringing me presents on a regular basis; that is his way to show his gratitude. He has also promised me a vacation once things in the office settle down.'

~

Joginder had the first smile on his face for the day. He had been disturbed all morning for the rebuke that he had given to Roshni. Emboldened by his showering of gifts on her, she had tried to start a game of one-upmanship with him. When he came into the kitchen, she said, 'I haven't cooked anything. I can't cook in such heat. Why don't we get food from your restaurant? You can eat there and bring me a tiffin.' He had lost his cool and shouted, "Over my dead body" and left the house.

Now, he was glad he had done that. He was realizing that in marriage, one has to walk the middle path, being neither too demanding nor too compliant. It is a tightrope walk, where your resolve is constantly tested.

~

Daiv started scribbling:

A false sense of competition: Marriage is a game played by two players who are supposed to be on the same side of the fence. Then where is the opposition team? It is the world. Couples who don't understand this end up on the opposite sides of the fence, fending each other off.

Consider our ganna rasm, the ritual of playing 'find the ring'. To a slightly immature mind, this competition and idea of vanquishing the spouse can be appealing, but where does it lead to? In its benign form, this false sense of competition gets converted into winning brownie points by slighting the spouse in front of an audience. When this idea gets perpetuated and escalated it can turn malignant and in its worst form, it can take the shape of winning a legal battle in front of the court.

Interestingly, the whole process of marriage is made to look like a competition between the bride and groom and their respective families. Take for instance:

- Lifting up of the men in the groom's side by those in the bride's during the milni is an all-out effort to show the other side down; the milni is supposed to be the ritual of the relatives of both sides introducing and greeting each other, when the baraat arrives at the bride's place—not an opportunity for one-upmanship
- Telling the groom to stand on his toes so that the bride can't put the garland around his neck during the jaimala
- Not letting the groom get off the horse until the flower-line is broken
- Worst of all is playing 'ganna' (finding the ring)

Adding fuel to fire is the advice of friends who tutor the couple with nuggets like:

- Whoever wins the first round dominates for life
- If the first instance of sex is weak, you lose dominance forever
- Don't be too friendly or succumb to her charms or she will make you her slave

Though all these things do lend colour to the marriage ceremony, they also encompass a sense of competition. Are you monkeys out to entertain people with a mock fight? Hankering for winning praise by defeating the partner in front of an audience is a harbinger of disastrous one-upmanship.

Analyse what you are doing to win this praise: you are putting down your spouse, that is, you are lowering her image in front of others. After marriage, the world sees you two as a joint entity. By lowering the spouse's image, you are inadvertently lowering the image of your entity, a thing that you will very soon repent.

~

Financial competition

One facet which leads to strain in a marriage is financial competition. The person earning, or at least earning more, usually assumes the dominant position and is the one who will decide how money will be spent. This problem of competition occurs more in unit families where the wife earns a sizeable portion of the household income or is the main earner. The husband in such cases is unwilling to relinquish his dominance and the right to decide how the money is spent, resulting in a severe power struggle.

As in all husband–wife tussles, the solution is not a formula but lies in suggestions that will reaffirm that they are a single unit, a team.

1. The ideal system is one in which the couple have a democratic joint account. All significant purchases are decided jointly. A study by the Tata Institute of Social Sciences states that such joint pooling brings togetherness, trust and equality, which are the pillars of a happy marriage.
2. Split your authority with mutual consent. The wife decides all home-related expenses, including children's expenses, groceries and domestic servants' salaries, and the husband takes care of all the external costs, like car purchases, holiday expenses and taxes. These roles can be reversed, too, with each others' consent.

3. If any one partner has to work extra to be able to provide additional income, it should be done as a gift and not as a sacrifice for which repayment is expected.
4. If only one partner is working, to avoid the other partner's guilt for spending money, a fixed figure for how much each partner should spend be agreed on.
5. When money is tight, it is a good idea to form separate debit accounts so that each person can spend this much and no more. Also, work out the budget of the amount spent together.

Outcome of this competition

Let us see the effect of this competition on marital relationships.

1. Man dominant→female endures→marriage sustains (with more work for the male and more endurance for the female).
2. Female dominant (as in some Khasi tribes in Assam)→male endures→marriage sustains (with more responsibility on the female and more endurance for the male).
3. Both dominate or try to dominate→nobody wants to endure→power struggle→marriage under strain.

This is the situation today. The old paradigms of division of labour with set roles for the husband and wife are showing cracks and new paradigms are taking root. The husband has not yet given up his reins of dominance, and may never give them up completely, but the wife has staked the claim for the throne without truly realizing the perils associated with it.

THE 16:8 RULE

Nature works in a 16:8 ratio. After sixteen hours of work, a person requires eight hours of rest. If he/she does a mentally stressful job for eight hours a day, he/she needs four waking hours of de-stressing at home. If he/she returns to more family-related stress, it is a sure-shot recipe for clogged coronary arteries.

Women now are openly competing for the position of control. This has far-reaching consequences and means that in each household, every couple will have to find their own specific equilibrium of dominance through open or covert competition. The resultant tug-of-war or power struggle is bound to compromise the couple as well as their families.

The effect of this strain of competition on the couple

Nature/God made every system into a sine curve. There is work followed by sleep. There is winter followed by summer. Even at the cellular level, there is hectic activity during division followed by relaxing, the 'interphase' to recoup. Similarly, we humans have our stress cycles. Intense stress and strain of work, say lasting eight to twelve hours, require the peace and quiet of the home, say five to six waking hours, to recoup.

With both spouses working, the stress cycle which previously got dissipated at home, is glaringly present. It is as if the work-stress cycle is followed by a home competition-stress cycle, especially if the couple hasn't come to an understanding of each others' needs and wants. The result is there for all to see: the lowering age of heart attacks, thirty-five-year-old burnouts and, worse, even women falling prey to diseases like hypertension, strokes and myocardial infarctions, which were hitherto considered the male domain. For women, parity has been achieved, but at a cost.

Perpetual competition to win points takes a heavy toll on mental attitude and family life. Warmth is diluted (why should I bother when he doesn't?); scepticism increases (is he/she trying to pull a fast one on me?); kids suffer (if they are even conceived in this hostile environment); tolerance evaporates (every mistake of the other's family is a chance to score a point, so why tolerate it?); and fault-finding becomes the route to supremacy (just as in office politics).

The effect of strain on the family

Your happiness depends not just on how successful you are perceived to be by your colleagues but also by how your family looks up to you. As is often said about one of the most successful presidents of the US, Abraham Lincoln, the public reverence he enjoyed lost much of its sheen because of the humiliation he suffered at the hands of his wife.

Try and visualize the impression a perpetually squabbling couple would have on their children and relatives. Do you see any chance of the couple's earning their children's respect? By the time they reach their equilibrium of dominance, if at all, they lose the respect and moral high ground required to rein in their children who by now will defy them with impunity. This makes the rest of their lives further stressful.

Strain begets strain and stress begets stress. Stress and strain have the habit of self-escalation.

The effect of strain on society

Strain related to a power struggle is a recent phenomenon in Indian (and Asian) society but has been prevalent for longer in the West, where its effect can be seen in their tottering family system. The number of unwed mothers/single parents, school drop-outs and divorce cases are all rising alarmingly due to this.

Some more serious side-effects, though noticeable, cannot be that easily calculated, as there are no pre-set indices for them. These fester under the surface but damage future generations. Our children's sense of respect, their belief in relationships, their faith in human beings, our own urge to rear and protect the next generation, our virtues of tolerance and commitment, are all linked to harmony at home. When these start their downward slide, we should prepare for strong reactions.

IN A NUTSHELL

When partners start playing against each other rather than playing as a team, the false sense of competition takes a heavy toll on the family's health, mental well-being and happiness.

11

Reactions, Reactions—the Huge Consequences of Inconsequential Reactions

> Question: What should a husband do after winning an argument with his wife?
>
> Answer: Apologize.

'Today the treat is on me.'

Everybody looked, startled, at Savvy. This was the first time she had offered to pay. She usually cribbed about inflation and read the menu from right to left, ordering the least expensive items.

'Something very good must have happened for you to be so exuberant?' Pammi winked.

'My mother-in-law died last week in the village.'

'Oh, I'm sorry!' Pammi muttered.

'Don't be. I'm celebrating.' Savvy gestured with a dancing pose. 'You can't imagine how difficult it was to keep my joy under wraps when we went to our village to mourn. Thank God my hubby didn't get a hint of my feelings otherwise he would have killed me. He reacted so sharply when I just said, "She was a strict person." Everyone knows that she was a terror who fought with everyone in the village. Still, he told me to shut up and not use such words for the deceased.'

Pammi jumped onto the wagon, 'You're so right. My husband, too, reacted as if stung by a scorpion when I said something as simple as, "She looks like Lalita Pawar." He himself teases her often by calling her Lalita aunty, because one of her eyes is slightly smaller, just like the actress. But when I said the same thing, it was blasphemy. He reacted so scathingly, as if I had abused his mother. How come he can say so much about her but reacts when I say even a little something about her?'

Sally rationalized the situation. 'You know what, I believe this happens because we don't want to hear anything derogatory about someone we consider close, even though in our heart of hearts we know what has been said is true. Somehow we consider it our privilege to say what we feel about someone, but feel that another person, even our spouse, has not earned that privilege, not yet anyway. For example, you have said many things about your dad that are not very charitable but if your husband said the same about him, you may not like it. If, God forbid, he says it during a tiff, it will elicit a huge reaction from you, won't it?'

Pammi nodded, realizing the truth of Sally's words.

'These seemingly inconsequential comebacks are ever-escalating chain reactions that can do more damage to our relationships than major issues.'

~

Daiv was startled that such inconsequential reactions could have such huge consequences.

~

There are four kinds of maladies that can affect your marital relationship:

1. Divine acts, which you cannot help. A challenged child, for example, which puts a huge strain on marriage, or an accident that leaves one partner crippled.
2. Dissatisfactions: For example, you strongly dislike something about your spouse—his utter disorganization, her shabby appearance or unkempt clothes, his habit of perpetually snacking or her quarrelsome nature.
3. Your reactions to his/her dissatisfactions: Your reaction to something he or someone from his family says or does.
4. Virtual reaction: You think somebody said or will say something and act or react in anticipation. This is the worst and most common malady, especially for housewives. It is a Catch-22 situation because the commonest grouse is overwork and the only solution is to keep busy. An idle brain is the workshop for TV serials.

The most common problem then is actually your reaction to an act or words. The more inconsequential the action to which you react, the worse are the results. By that measure, the absolutely worst results are when you react to an action which has been perpetuated only in your mind.

The huge consequences of inconsequential reactions

Imagine that a couple is discussing an innocuous topic one Sunday morning.

She asks: 'Remember who taught the kids to eat with a fork and knife?'

This was something that may have happened a decade or more ago. How does it matter who taught them? Does it make any difference now?

Consider how the responses can change the course of the day or even a week and in some cases, whole lives.

1. You say: 'Of course, you taught them darling.'→Happy wife→she hugs you→you get a great breakfast→great outing→maybe great lovemaking→a strong bond added to your marriage.
2. You say: 'I don't remember.' She reacts, 'You never remember anything I have done. I keep doing all the right things in your life and you don't even acknowledge them.'→An average sort of day and that too, only if you don't further react to her comment.
3. You say: 'Me, of course'—the 'intelligent one in the house' is implied. She reacts, 'Hmph, bloody MCP, always taking credit for things.'→She remains sullen all day.

4. You say: 'My intelligent mother' (whom your wife despises).→Brace yourself for a bad, bad day.
5. You say: 'Your ultra-smart friend, Sangeeta.'→Reaction of instant jealousy→Very foul day, with wife fuming.
6. You say: 'Meeta, my ex-flame.'→I can't describe the reaction, for it will be censored→severe tension in marriage for a long time.

All for an inconsequential question.

THE WORST FORM—REACTION TO ACCUSATIONS

When you accuse your wife of something, you have to remember a few things:

1. Women are not always rational when reacting to an accusation. They get on the defensive and lose whatever little rationality they possess. So the answer to your 'very rational accusation' can be very irrational: 'Yes, I'm always wrong'→start of a sulk, or 'You think I'm a dumbo'→ start of a fight.
2. The effect of an accusation on a relationship is always negative, that is, it brings in a negative flow of thought. Any chance of finding a solution evaporates. All that is left is more reactions, leading to more accusations.
3. The reaction to an accusation is always an aggressive and exaggerated counter-accusation that will not only take you away from the solution but will actually worsen the existing situation so that it becomes unsolvable.

The solution

How can you counter this chain of reactions? The solution has to be:

A. Lack of reaction

If you don't react to something that your wife has said or done that is unarguably wrong, she will feel most guilty after she accuses you of something that you haven't done. Let her have her say, then make her realize her error. This is when a remorseful wife will be most amenable to your suggestions about how to solve future disagreements. This is the time to suggest changes on issues on which she has not, so far, been amenable.

B. Mirror of truth

Instead of reacting, you look into this mirror and reflect on what you can do that is positive when she is making accusations or reacting to something you have said or done. This self-reflective thinking should be on the lines of: what should I do that will make her happy/less angry/less frustrated? Reflection and patience will dissipate a potentially flammable situation.

IN A NUTSHELL

No reaction or, better, a positive response to the wife's reaction, even if it was unjustified, is the only way to transform her perception of things.

12

Transformation of Perceptions

'You eye specialists have destroyed the balance of nature.'

Everybody at the party was stunned at the old man's off-the-cuff remark.

'How is that?' asked the host.

'You see, nature perfectly balanced reality with expectations. As the wife ages, nature accordingly dulls the husband's ability to appreciate beauty by dimming his vision. Meaning every wrinkle on the wife's face is proportionate to the increase in the husband's myopia. So, in his head he always sees her as she was in her youth.

He paused. 'But now you have upset God's balance by giving man the artificial power to see wrinkles. So he now hankers after a new wrinkle-free face.

Pammi, as usual, started the conversation with a bang. 'Yesterday's dream thrilled and saddened me at the same time,' she said.

On being prodded, she continued, 'I dreamt of my teenage fantasy. Ever since high school, I have dreamt of marrying a dashing and powerful man, before whom the whole world bows. But when he'd come home, he'd surrender to my charms and behave like a lovelorn puppy. Alas! Nothing of this kind happened in real life.'

'As the CEO of a multinational company, your husband is powerful . . .' commented Sally. 'And he does give in to you at home. So, why do you sound so disgruntled?'

'It may look like that but only I know the truth. He is no knight in shining armour. At the workplace, he is shit scared of the company owners and at home, he tries to force me to follow his mom's diktats. Moreover, there is no romance in his mannerisms at all. He is the opposite of my fantasy.'

Savvy interjected at this point. 'My fantasy has gone the same way. I daydreamed that, like in films, one day the prince of my dreams will come and take me away on a horse to a palace full of servants who'd be at my beck and call; two maids to bathe me, two to cook and a foreign masseur to give me erotic massages to prepare me for the night with my prince. What life dished out is just the opposite. I work like a maid all day, and my prince hardly even looks at me till the lights are switched off. Then he satiates himself, goes off to sleep and snores. Wow, as far as romance is concerned, it seems he doesn't know even the meaning of the word! The only bit of romance I get is from that occasional outing with Rehaan.'

Pammi knew that if allowed to carry on, Savvy would go on and on with her Rehaan stories, so she turned to Sally instead. 'What were your fantasies about married life?' she asked.

Sally thought for a moment, 'You know what my fantasy was—a well-organized home and a satisfying professional career. And I wanted a husband and in-laws who are appreciative of my efforts. I envisioned a busy but well-balanced life. From that standpoint, my real life matches seventy per cent with my dream. What I haven't got, I'm trying to get, if possible.'

'You sound like my mom,' Pammi said. 'She used to say that the only way to achieve your fantasy was to keep it as realistic as possible, but then what is the fun of having a fantasy? I like to follow Jassi in this regard. She always says, "Don't compromise—fantasize queen-size and seize it whenever possible." You know what her fantasy is? A very smart husband who submits to all her whims and fancies. Terrorized in-laws, who dare not open their mouths when she is around. She fantasizes about having sex with her husband in bondage, that is, she ties him with ropes and whips his arse with a leather hunter before making love to him. Unfortunately, neither her husbands nor her boyfriends have met her expectations. But she doesn't give up.'

Joginder shook his head to clear it. He could not even dream of becoming the man these women were fantasizing about. The only fantasy he understood was Sally's. The rest, according to him, were simply fabrications of perverted minds. 'That way, Roshni is very good,' he thought. 'She praises me lavishly, even though I don't treat her all that well. I should take better care of her needs.'

~

Shravan was getting more and more disillusioned listening to these ladies. As a boy in the Government Boys' Higher Secondary School, he had coveted smart, English-speaking jean-clad girls and believed that they could bring a fresh perspective and sense of purpose to one's life. In school and even in college, he would virtually have given his proverbial right hand to befriend such a smart girl. Even a casual hello from such a girl puffed up his chest and enhanced his status in the eyes of his peer group.

No wonder he fell head over heels when he was introduced to Maya. He couldn't believe that a girl of Maya's class would even talk to him. When she later turned her attention towards him as a friend, he wondered why the gods had bestowed such largesse on him. They grew closer, and he became completely smitten by Maya. So much so that he stalled ongoing talks about his marriage, which were close to being finalized with a girl chosen by his parents. That was more than a year ago.

But since he had started listening to these women, he had

decoded some new facets of her personality that were not quite to his liking. Had he objectively analysed this, he would have realized that none of these characteristics was new but, somehow, he had never given much thought to them. Now, even her happy-go-lucky attitude and her habit of calling a spade a spade, characteristics that he had admired in the beginning of their relationship, seemed untenable for a wife, especially while dealing with his conservative family.

Today a new worry had been added. 'What if she, too, has fantasies like these? I am neither a prince in shining armour nor a dashing CEO and I am not capable of becoming a henpecked husband for life. She will find my real persona disgusting.' He shuddered at the thought of what his life would be reduced to.

I need to have a heart-to-heart talk with her soon, he thought.

~

Daiv, too, was a bit pensive. He was hearing none of the things that he wanted to hear and write about. Where was the romance? Still, he was furiously writing, long after the ladies' meeting was over. He wanted to pen down his new attitude that had been built up as a result of what the ladies had said. This new stance was not charitable at all. In fact, it was downright antagonistic towards marriage.

He wrote: 'After marriage the male seems to undergo a . . .

~

REVERSE METAMORPHOSIS: FROM A BUTTERFLY BACK TO A CATERPILLAR, THAT IS FROM A SMART BOYFRIEND TO A TIMID HUSBAND

How does that young, dashing, dynamic, carefree boyfriend become an irresponsible, even careless, show-off caterpillar that neither deserves a second look from the wife nor a word of appreciation for any of his qualities? How does the most eligible bachelor on the entire block, chosen after detailed deliberations, get transformed after marriage into this utterly useless and despicable creature? Does he really get transformed or has just the perception of his persona changed?

This transformation in perception occurs mainly in the eyes of the wife; other women may still find the husband handsome and desirable. For older generations, this change used to evolve over decades and was attributed to the 'familiarity breeding contempt' syndrome. Now, as the speed of life increases, with fast food, fast vehicles and fast-track careers, the plumetting

SPOUSES CAUSE MORE STRESS THAN BOSSES

Electronics and healthcare manufacturer Philips conducted a poll that found that 58 per cent of respondents felt that their spouses put them most under pressure as compared to 43 per cent who felt that their managers did this. The poll also found that women worry more about their weight than their earnings.

of the husband's stature in the wife's eyes has also become superfast. Or, maybe the expectations of the present-day woman have galloped too fast for the male to saddle them.

It is not uncommon to see an eligible bachelor, selected after rigorous scrutiny and prolonged courtship and touted as the best bet, suddenly getting cast aside after marriage as a good-for-nothing. Traits that were initially applauded—forthrightness, conscientiousness, uprightness and a dashing personality—become mutated into brash, demanding, unyielding, stubborn and aggressive. And traits like civility, understanding, carefulness and diplomacy get altered to timid, spineless, scared and pretentious. Seen in perspective, the traits remain the same; the change is in what they are being used to describe. When the husband defends his wife from comments of his relatives, he is chivalrous and conscientious but if he tells her not to make similar comments about his mother, he is domineering and ultra-conservative. The attempt, thus, is to cut the husband's stature to a size that can fit into a lifestyle coveted by the wife.

On the flip side, this nosediving in the man's stature is one of the main reasons men seek more flattering company that can boost their ego. When women feel unappreciated for their looks and efforts, they too do the same. For men, however, this tendency may be more pronounced because their centuries-old mindset calls for a dominant role for them. Social pressures also weigh on his mind—he does not want to be written off as henpecked. There is also the constant pressure for him to perform in his professional life.

These pulls and pushes crush romance and result in extreme

mental strain for the husband. This is bound to take a toll on the mental and physical well-being of the couple, more so on the husband's.

No wonder heart attacks for men under the age of forty are no longer a rarity.

~

So what should you do?

The only permanent thing is change—accept it. Girlfriend→lover→fiancée→newlywed wife→family's bride→mother of your kids and so on, till she becomes your retirement partner. And vice versa. Hankering for and, worse, cribbing about how your wife used to be and what she has become, is as futile as pining for the lustrous hair of your college days. Your balding pate won't reverse to those swirling curls, nor will your wife go back to the state in which she was as your girlfriend. All you can do is: preserve what you have and adapt as well as you can.

What is really in your hands is to change yourself, not your spouse and definitely not the world. Do what is possible, with a cool mind. Rushing off into the soothing arms and fulsome words of another female is at best a stop-gap arrangement and will last just as long as familiarity doesn't set in. Then you have to pay a very heavy price for that infidelity.

How heavy? Let's find out.

IN A NUTSHELL

Familiarity breeds contempt and the spouse who seemed ideal starts looking like a pale shadow of your expectations. Learn to accept reality and be happy rather than hankering after what you don't have.

13

Infidelity, the Marriage Breaker

A fact:

After sex, 60 per cent men roll over and sleep.

Forty per cent get up and go home.

Pammi entered the restaurant and was greeted by a chorus of 'Happy Anniversary!'

Pammi, Sally and Savvy were meeting after a month; Pammi had returned from south India, where she was on a 'second honeymoon' for two weeks. She had started from Goa, been on a three-night backwater cruise in Kerala and then spent a week in the idyllic environs of the hill-station of Munnar.

Going by Sally's small get-together to celebrate her anniversary and the half-kilogram of sweets brought by Savvy's husband, Pammi's celebrations were grand. But she didn't seem all that thrilled.

'Happy Anniversary to you too, but . . .' she said to no one in particular, '...were your anniversaries really happy?'

The other two looked at her quizzically. Sally nodded, remembering with satisfaction the movie and dinner. Savvy, too, shook her head nonchalantly, in the characteristic way she made her head bend from side to side, indicating a mixture of aye and nay.

'Well, mine was a disaster!'

'You couldn't go on that cruise?' enquired Sally.

Pammi shook her head, 'I did but...'

'Did the hill-station tour get cancelled?' asked Savvy, who was enamoured of hill-stations.

'No, not that. We went everywhere but were sullen and fighting.' Two amazed looks propelled her to go on. 'Actually, my husband seems to be cheating on me and that became the agenda for the whole trip. You can understand how happy we were with the perpetual shouting and crying.'

'Cheating—are you sure? Or are you jumping to your own conclusions?' Sally was wary of Pammi's suspicions.

'No, no. I am pretty sure of his infidelity. I may not have the caught-red-handed type of proof but then you can't expect to have photographs of them naked in bed. They do their nefarious activities locked in a room and the best one can have is circumstantial evidence that adds up to a plausible picture. Let me tell you what I know.'

Pammi took a couple of mouthfuls of her uttapam and gulped her coffee before continuing. 'Before marriage, in a mood of boastful exuberance, my hubby told me that many girls had crushes on him. He named Leena as one of the smarter ones. Later, when I asked him about Leena, he said she got married and had left his office. A couple of times, I caught the occasional lipstick smudge and unexplained restaurant bill or my hubby becoming untraceable. The last straw was on my wedding anniversary party when I met Leena. She told me that neither was she married nor had she ever left the office. Worst of all, she related an incident about her trip to Singapore in May where my husband had told me he had gone alone. When I enquired from his secretary, who was there in that party, she told me that only these two had gone and had stayed in the same hotel in adjacent rooms. Now tell me, what should I make of all this? It is screaming infidelity from every angle.'

Sally could have found a dozen flaws in her reasoning but decided against it, for Pammi did not seem to be in any mood to listen. 'Did you confront your husband?' she asked.

'You bet I did. I confronted him every single day of our trip but he has become so perfect at lying that be never admitted to any transgressions. Though he had no answer when I caught his lies. He says he had fabricated the stories so that I wouldn't get upset. When we came back home, my mother-in-law also parroted the same line—"You are making a mountain out of a molehill. It is all in your mind." Blah-blah . . . But now I am bent on proving that I am right. I've hired a private detective and told him to tail my hubby. We will soon know the truth and have the proof too.'

Her declarations were so vehement that nobody dared to suggest the contrary. In a sombre mood, the three dispersed early that day.

~

Joginder's thoughts took him to the day when his mother had confronted his father for the first time for his openly going to a prostitute. Joginder had been just ten years old then but he still could feel the vibration of that slap that left his mother's lip swollen and eye bruised. He could never fathom how his mother had acquired the guts to stand up to his father that day. He also remembered the noises coming from his parents' room that day. His mother, seemingly, had refused to have sex with his father, who had then forced himself on her.

As a child, Joginder was appalled by the injustice and had hated his father for his infidelity, more so because his loving mother then went into a shell of depression. She came out of it many years later, only to periodically go into hysterical convulsions, in which she used to dance in a trance with her hair and clothes dishevelled. Many tantriks and aghoras (ghost-fighters) were called upon, but to no avail. When Joginder studied psychology in college, he learnt that hysteria was a manifestation of prolonged suppressed feelings.

His hatred for his father had gone up a few notches and he had decided that, come what may, he would never commit the same mistake.

'Am I being just to my wife?' he thought for the first time.

~

Daiv had a pensive look on his face. 'Could it have been my occasional fling that cost me my marriage? Why do we males indulge in infidelity?' He started writing . . .

~

The seven-year itch replaced by a three-year glitch

A survey of 2000 British adults in steady relationships revealed that it takes less than three years for couples to start taking each other for granted and to begin to grow apart. At the three-year mark, these couples fought an average of 2.7 hours a week and their passion had dimmed, with just 16 per cent having sex three times a week as compared to 52 per cent in the beginning of the relationship.

WHY?

Because marriage kills passion . . .

A survey in Britain has found that one out of five couples do not kiss for a whole week or more, and when they do, it is usually quick, lasting no more than five seconds. As actor Eva Mendes says, 'Marriage is a very old-fashioned, archaic thing . . . Husband and wife is just very unsexy.'

Esher Perel, while talking about her book *Love in Captivity,* says, 'Marriage works well, except for people who want to have sex.' That is because the very things that make marriage so desirable are the arch nemeses of passion—emotional intimacy inhibits erotic expression. So, in a nutshell, marriage kills sexual desire and there is a reason for it. Love requires closeness, intimacy and familiarity to flourish; desire needs distance, insecurity and surprise.

The big 'passion killers' after marriage are:

- Weight gain

- Snoring
- Stinginess
- Personal hygiene
- Alcohol abuse
- Longer working hours
- Financial issues

Cause of infidelity

Passion and infatuation work chemically, like drug addiction. According to a poll, 85 per cent of the women and 58 per cent of the men polled felt the addiction. Scientist Larry Young, who has researched the connection between genes, the brain and behaviour, studied the brain to understand what goes on in the minds of people in love. In humans, there are four tiny areas that form the circle of love. The hottest spot of these is the Ventral Tegmental Area—VTA—which lights up in MRIs when a person in love is shown photos of his/her beloved. The emotions flow chemically as the VTA produces dopamine when stimulated.

'When you are trying to win the world's greatest prize, a mating partner,' says Dr Helen Fisher, a professor at Rutgers university, 'this dopamine acts like drug addiction, which is all very fine when all is going well but can be devastating, when it is going poorly. A broken heart, thus, acts like craving or severe withdrawal reaction. No wonder people kill for love and die for love.'

Dimming passion in a marriage coupled with a drug-addiction-like urge for it paves the way for infidelity.

A landmark study by the Gutmacher Institute sought to identify risk factors for infidelity. Scientists found that cheating was associated with some specific risk factors like:

- Being male
- Having a high number of sex partners before marriage
- Thinking about sex several times a day
- Living together without marriage
- Being in a long relationship with another woman before marriage

INCOME VIS-À-VIS CHEATING

Men on both extremes of the income scale tend to cheat more. Those who make less money than their wives feel threatened by the traditional notion that men should be the breadwinners. They feel incompetent and this leads to low self-esteem. Seventy per cent compensate with the conquest of another woman.

If the wife is dependent on the husband financially, he is again more likely to cheat.

Women, on the other hand, tend to cheat more if they earn more or if they are the sole breadwinners. And they cheat less if they are dependent on the husband financially.

In both situations, marriages in which the wife earns more are doomed to deteriorate.

Call centre jobs have also fuelled this raging fire of infidelity. Young adults, emulating American accents with American pseudonyms, tend also to emulate what they perceive as American culture in their private lives. A survey conducted among India's leading call centres shows that 38 per cent of respondents are fine with premarital sex, whereas more than 25 per cent admitted to having had casual sex (*India Today*, June 2008). Seema Mehta, a call centre veteran, believes that these numbers have more than doubled for the younger lot in last four years.

Scientists also found some factors that protect against infidelity:

- Having many friends in common
- Believing that extramarital sex is wrong led to a 50 per cent reduction in chances of infidelity
- Sharing social networks with the spouse decreased the odds of infidelity by 30 per cent
- A generally happy family life, with children, reduces chances of infidelity
- Both partners being satisfied with their personal relationships
- Both partners with similar religious ideas or if they follow the same religious sect
- The more educated the couple, the less the chance of their straying

- Women are like fruit . . .
  Every woman has her own unique taste and colour.
- The problem is men . . .
  They love fruit salad.

Are males more prone to infidelity?

With changing times, is male infidelity just a myth? As matrimonial lawyer, Mrunalini Deshmukh, points out, 'The ratio of men and women indulging in infidelity is 50:50 today. Ten years ago it would have been 70 per cent men in such relationships...'

Ekta Kapoor, creative director of Balaji Telefilms and the original creator of the saas-bahu serials, puts forth this argument: 'Women today are sexually liberated, free-spirited and are willing to acknowledge their libido. . . It's all about strident self-gratification.'

On the other hand, studies by John Lyndon, a psychologist at McGill University, Montreal, have shown just the reverse. Lyndon studied how people in a committed relationship react in the face of temptation. In one study, he asked married women to rate the attractiveness of some men. When he later told them that these men were interested in meeting them, the committed women gave lower scores to those men they had found attractive. It was as if they now rated these men lower as they were likely to threaten their relationship.

> Dr Louann Brizendine explored the male mind to confirm what women have long suspected—the hormone testosterone makes men sex-obsessed, makes them hide their emotions and cheat. Testosterone produces what Dr Brizendine calls 'man trance'—a glazed-eye stare at women's breasts. (from *Male Brain—A Breakthrough Understanding of How Men and Dogs Think*)
>
> In another survey done in the UK, half the male respondents confessed that they look at a woman's assets even before they look at her face.

The McGill University research has revealed a gender difference in our commitment response. In a study of 300 heterosexual spouses, it was found that after a bout of flirting with actors/actresses, the men focused more on the mistakes of their spouses, suggesting that flirting had clipped away on their commitment. Women, on the other hand, became more forgiving of their spouses' mistakes, suggesting that their flirting had elicited a protective response to their commitment. It was as if, 'women had the contingency plan—where the attractive alternative sets off the alarm bell.' Women implicitly code that 'flirting' is a threat, men don't.

Is it your fault or is it genetic?

First, the consolation. Studies have proved that some people are genetically more prone to cheating on their spouses than others and males are genetically more predisposed to cheating than

HUNTING THE HUNTER

Men go out to find partners to have sex with, while a woman's focus is on accepting or rejecting suitors. Interestingly, men's choice of partners is largely governed by biology. Men check for clarity of skin, hip-to-waist ratio and symmetrical faces, all the features that point to fertility in females.

Women, on the other hand, generally look for men who will make good providers, that is, wealthy men.

females. Hasse Walum, a biologist at the Karolinska Institute, studied 552 sets of twins to learn about genes related to the body's regulation of the bonding hormone, vasopressin. The study found that the men who had a variation in the gene were less likely to be married and if they married, were much more likely to have serious marital commitment problems. This trait is called the 'fidelity gene' and most men who carried two copies of the gene variant experienced serious relationship crises.

So it is no fault of yours that God has designed us to cheat. Right? Not quite, because studies have proved that this tendency can be overcome by the right kind of conditioning. Genetics does not absolve you of all your sins. All they show is that we need to work on our marriages and our commitment more than others do.

There are parameters in a marriage other than love and loyalty that decide the level of commitment that each spouse feels towards the relationship. Psychologist and relationship researcher at Stony Brook University, Dr Aron, tried to measure the qualities that add up to commitment.

His studies have shown that your commitment grows proportionally to certain factors:

- How much does a partner enhance your life?
- How much 'self-expansion' does the partner contribute to, that is, how much does she broaden your horizon or expand your capabilities?
- How much of a better person has knowing your partner made you?
- How many challenging and exciting things do you do together as a couple? How much time do you spend doing them?
- As a corollary to the above, how many things do you celebrate together? that is, how many occasions do you have or do you invent to be together and enjoy yourselves?
- Lastly, the ratio of small, positive interactions for every negative one is important. The negative interactions can be sneering, eye rolling, cutting the other person short and withdrawal.

HIRE HELP

Supermodel Cindy Crawford has advised cheating husbands to hire housekeepers because this would give their over-worked wives more time to spend with their husbands, groom themselves, and keep up a healthy sex life. As she puts it, 'If you can afford a prostitute, you can afford a housekeeper.'

Positive interactions can be:

- Touching fondly.
- Smiling recurrently, just on seeing the other's face.
- Paying a compliment.
- Pre-empting the other's need and providing what she requires.
- Accepting the spouse's idiosyncrasies.
- Laughing and enjoying the other's jokes and wit.
- Getting comforted or feeling secure by the mere presence of the other.

A healthy ratio, like 5:1, suggests a lasting bond and commitment. When the ratio of positive: negative interactions drops or, worse, reverses, the risk of infidelity, or even divorce, rises proportionally.

What is the solution? Let us see.

IN A NUTSHELL

Marriage counsellor M. Gary Neuman surveyed 200 husbands and found that 48 per cent of men rated emotional dissatisfaction as the primary reason they cheated, and only 8 per cent of men said that sexual dissatisfaction was the main cause of their infidelity. Only 12 per cent of cheating men said the mistresses were more physically attractive than the wives. Thus, a husband living in a harmonious relationship was least likely to cheat.

PART III

THE SOLUTION

A Word from the Author

'What did you (or do you) expect from marriage? Be very specific and answer truthfully.

- Was it happiness/bliss? Look within, for nothing external can ever do that.
- If you got married to fight loneliness you will soon be overwhelmed with company and crave solitude.
- If you got married because you loved her figure, what will happen when that figure is lost, say after your first child is born (remember the thick hair analogy)?
- If you got married because time was running out you, will realize that it runs out even faster now.
- If you got married because you wanted money, be ready to pay for the rest of your life. You might have all the money in the world but won't be spending a penny of your own will.
- If you got married to please your parents, you will end up displeasing them very badly.
- If you got married because it was a compulsion from society, you will end up being very unsociable.

- If you got married because you felt incomplete, you will be made a complete fool of.
- If you got married to have sex, your passion will decline with every passing day.
- If you got married because you 'fell in love', this love, lust or infatuation will soon be clear and tested.

Marriages with the most positive outlook are the ones which are entered into with a level head.

If you are getting married for any of the reasons mentioned above, you are going to be saddled with unforseen problems. Let us try to find their solutions—an arduous task but so compelling that your whole life's happiness depends upon your success in finding and implementing these solutions in your life.

14

The Choices We Make—the Need to Choose Wisely and Resist Our Inherent Attraction to Wickedness

Husband after eating a hearty dinner: 'I'm really sorry for my obnoxious comment about you being heartless. Forgive me.'

'Apology accepted, dear. I am a very reasonable person. Now drink this quickly.'

Husband: 'What is this?'

Wife: 'The antidote to the contents of your dinner.'

Pammi came a bit late. She had that naughty expression on her face which made everyone anxious. 'You know who I met today?' she asked, fluttering her eyelashes.

A chorus of voices asked, 'Who, who?' Pammi could have bet there was a male voice in that chorus.

'My ex-flame! Actually, I was his ex-flame. He was more of a time pass for me.'

Now, this was of universal interest.

'He is a doctor. He was a resident in the hospital where I was admitted for my fracture. The guy used to check my blood pressure every four hours and would come rushing every time I squealed, which I did often. His hands shook with excitement every time he touched my leg. Wouldn't it give you immense power to know that the most sought-after guy in the place is wrapped around your little finger?'

The listeners nodded, Savvy a bit more vigorously than the rest.

'It also taught me a very important thing. Guys just can't resist assisting a damsel in distress. That is how I actually ensnared my hubby.'

All ears were virtually outstretched. 'He had come to the marriage function of my cousin. We tormented the friends of the groom so much that they labelled us "wild vixens", unfit for even befriending.' Pammi giggled.

'I had become besotted with this smart young man, who seemed well off. So I decided to use Jassi's foolproof trick. During the running around to search for the hidden shoes of the groom, this man accidentally pushed me lightly. I promptly fell down and feigned a sprain. As I hobbled around acting as if I was in pain, he apologized profusely and was on my duty for the rest of the night, fetching food for me and helping me around, even helping me wear my shoes and what not. After he had apologized for maybe the tenth time, I expansively pardoned him and said in a coy voice, "It was not your fault, dear. You are the kindest and most caring person I have ever come across."

'With that shot, he fell head over heels and, forgetting all my earlier wickedness and bitchiness, cooed, "How decent of you to pardon me, you are very large-hearted, I've never met a person like you," and what not. From then it was all downhill.'

'You said you used Jassi Didi's trick. Does she too feign a sprain to catch a boyfriend?' Savvy was almost taking notes.

'Jassi is in another league and why not? She is not looking for a hubby for keeps, she is actually just looking for a good time. She does use the sprain method but then she goes a step further. When the man offers her his shoulder, she whets his appetite with a few brushes of her boobs. Then she enacts a wardrobe failure, making him inadvertently ogle at her thigh or bosom and the prey is hooked. Once, when the innocent guy was not taking the bait, she took him home and literally dropped her towel while coming out of bath. She always gets what she wants. In fact, every female can get what she wants if she is hell-bent on acquiring it because these stupid men have a blind spot when it comes to assessing a girl's character.'

~

Joginder swore under his breath, ostensibly at the wretched young beggarwoman who was pestering him to get alms. 'Bloody wretched woman, why don't you work for your livelihood?' He swore again at the woman but in his mind; he was venting his angst at these so-called high-society ladies who hoodwinked men to get their pound of flesh. Also these bloody stupid men . . . what kind of women they choose!

~

Shravan was transported back to the restaurant where he had got hooked. He was already mesmerized by Maya's mannerisms. Every action of hers or her family's was praised no end and in his mind always ended up further belittling his own family and himself in comparison. He was on cloud nine and considered himself very lucky to have a girl like Maya as his friend.

That day, when Maya agreed to meet him, he was overjoyed. But she came pretty late and appeared sullen. On repeated questioning, she revealed that her father was pressurizing her to get married to an army officer and for that he was introducing her to a new young man every week. 'I hate the artificial, pompous life of army people. And it is so infuriating meeting people and rejecting them or getting rejected by them. Today, when I told the army officer that I am not really interested in him, he felt slighted and said, "It seems you don't have the warmth to be able to like or love anyone." I literally ran from there.'

A tear had formed at the corner of her eye. Shravan had the strong urge to wipe the tear but he was hesitant as he wasn't sure if he was ready to move their occasional friendship to the next level. On seeing him hesitate, Maya's tears welled up further.

Still, Shravan was unsure how to respond and gave her his handkerchief and offered a few words of encouragement.

Then Maya asked, 'Am I really that cold and unlikeable?'

This melted all Shravan's reservations and resolve. He quickly moved to the other side of the table and patted her beautifully manicured hand. 'You are a very warm and lovely person. Any man will give all that he has to be with you.' Maya had now put her head on his shoulder and was sobbing uncontrollably. The feel of her bosom made Shravan's head dizzy. All his resolve not to get married before thirty, not to get involved with opposite sex lest it distract him from his duties towards his family, to go in for higher education before getting involved, all vapourized at her touch. That day he committed to things that he thought only very naïve people did. He was hooked.

He had been very happy with his life but now another question was knocking at his door. Was Maya using a ploy like one used by Pammi? Or was she employing something like Jassi's entrapment technique?

The answer to both questions was not a resounding 'No!'

Daiv was lost in thought about his own ex-wife. She was very different from these three women. He thought, 'These women are really an assorted lot.' He scribbled, 'Categories of women . . .'

~

Do you remember the times when you had to sit down and choose your career path or a new house or a vehicle? Did you go to finalize the deal in an alcoholic stupor? You're probably saying, 'What do you think I am—crazy?'

Quite right! Only someone really crazy would do a thing like that. And yet, you choose your life partner in a stupor. No, no, not the alcoholic one, but a hormonal one. Yes! You are dead drunk on testosterone, the male sex hormone raging full blast in all unmarried males. In that stupor, you tend to seek an excellent mate for sexual desires and disregard qualities you know would be excellent in a wife for someone of your temperament.

Most young men whom I asked the question, 'Why do you like this girl?' replied with something like, 'She is cute, 'She

Charles Darwin proved more than 150 years ago that an animal's choice of partner is not a random process but rather, a well worked-out 'genetic strategy' ingrained in our DNA, influencing evolutionary patterns. Female animals tend to choose male partners who are the strongest and fittest available, and males will look for the youngest, best-looking and healthiest females (Evolutionary Fit) that would help pass on his genetic material to the next generation.

Somewhat similarly, subconscious selection works in humans also, more obviously in males, maybe because women have learnt to camouflage their sexual preferences better. Thus, men are naturally attracted to a waist–hip ratio of around 70, large breasts with cleavage, and rounded protruding buttocks.

is beautiful', 'She is hot' or 'She is sexy'. One or two said, 'She is very innocent.' The somewhat more intelligent ones said, 'She is smart.' So it was good looks, good looks, good looks, said with different tongues.

This is not your fault. Your genes incite you to choose a partner for sex and procreation. (See preceding box.)

The problem is with changing social norms and requirements—women have ceased to be just the sexually fulfilling and child-bearing partners of yore. Not only are they taking up the role of an intellectual partner but they are also contributing as a provider for the family.

Alas! Men forget this while selecting a partner and give into their primal instincts. So if you marry for sexual gratification alone, God help you.This selection becomes the beginning of strife, because after you take a woman as your wife, you will want to keep her for yourself and ask her to cover the sultry exposed curves that once made you fall madly in love (or was it lust?), and she may not appreciate or even submit to this.

When you are looking for a life partner, a wife with whom to spend your life, you should think and look for the qualities that you associate with a good wife. Better still, look for the qualities that are compatible with your nature, not what you associate with a socialite, who makes the whole college drool when walking next to you in mini-shorts.

Your own nature, the kind of life you wish to lead, and even your idiosyncrasies should be examined. Small things, like a love for fast driving, listening to old film songs or even using deodorant, when resisted by your partner, who may have phobias where you have fancies, can cause turmoil in married life. You need to identify your 'triggers'—your passions, your goals and your moral leanings. A materialistic wife might scoff at her husband's penchant for social work in his native village. A girl bought up in a puritanical moralistic environment may not be able to tolerate the dishonesty and lack of integrity of a business family.

So before taking a plunge, consider a few important aspects that should be compatible:

- Core values and beliefs
- Intelligence and education levels
- Emotional needs and behaviour
- Ambitions and dreams for the future
- Status and style of living
- Importance of and need for money
- Ability to arouse and provide respect

~

Opposites attract but . . .

When it comes to choosing a life partner:

- Why do quiet guys choose chatter-boxes?
- Bookworms prefer activity-prone sports enthusiasts
- Livewire casanovas opt for shy girls
- Happy-go-lucky people fall for the meticulous types

A psychiatrist at L.H. Hirdandani Hospital, Mumbai, Dr Harish Shetty, says, 'We look for an alter ego who will complete us—that is, one looks for what one is not.' A Mumbai-based psychiatrist, Dr Nirmala Rao, comments, 'Relationships are about getting our own needs met, often at an unconscious level. We look for someone complementary, not identical.' You may also be looking for qualities that you may yourself lack.

People find differences exciting. We also tend to dislike some of our own qualities. For example, if we have been overweight most of our lives, we marvel at slim people; the disorganized man may be intrigued by the immaculate planner who has everything in place.

The problem is that when couples are thrown together for a prolonged period of time, the novelty and excitement of the differences tend to wear off. When you realize that your wife has nothing in common with you—no common hobbies, no common interests, no common tastes—you may start resenting the differences: 'Why does she eat so much?' 'What is this fixation with keeping socks properly folded?' 'Why doesn't she read?' 'Why does she shop all the time?' Personality differences are a very common cause for conflict in marriages. In a marriage where the husband loves home food and the wife always wants to eat out, trouble will brew.

The solution: First assess how many of these differences you are ready to overlook for the sake of a long-term relationship. Then sit down and talk about your differences with an open mind and how you two intend to cope with them. This would avoid conflict after marriage.

~

> Love at first sight is fine, if you are careful to look twice (or even better, thrice) before you take the plunge.

Love at first sight is a misnomer. Or is it?

MEN FALL IN LOVE AFTER JUST ONE DATE

The *Daily Telegraph* reported a study by a team led by researcher Elizabeth Noble, which found that men fall in love more easily than women. Most males reckon they know whether or not it is the 'real thing' after a single date, whereas females wait until at least the sixth date to make up their minds. Accordingly, males were more likely to say 'I love you' first.

What you believe to be love at first sight is really physical desire, your biological instincts to procreate acting overtime, which fuel your anxiety to see those beautiful assets and feel that heavenly skin and to indulge in . . . you know what.

These biological factors and sex hormones are so overwhelming that they make you take leave of all your senses, rationality and higher brain function for the primal instinct of sexual gratification. Your 'right brain', that is, the emotional side of your brain feels a cocaine-like rush when you look at that someone you consider special. At the same time, your rational, 'left brain' assesses the female from the single parameter of how good she is for giving sexual pleasure and as a producer of your children.

What you have at first sight is sexual infatuation. Love is a

WOMEN AFFECTING MEN

- **Men can't think straight when women are around** (*TOI*): A study in London revealed that men suffer a mental decline—lapses of memory or mindlessness—when good-looking women are around them. However, the same does not hold true for women. Researchers attribute the findings to 'evolutionary pressures'.
- **Beautiful women make men reckless:** Researchers conducting a field survey with young male skateboarders found that they were more at risk when they were being observed by attractive women. While there were more spectacular successes, there were also more crash landings.

higher brain function which develops after your carnal desire has been met and your forebrain (sex centre) satiated.

So stop fooling yourself and know what is what. The biggest mistake you can make is confusing lust with infatuation or worse, with love.

I am not against premarital sex, though I do caution against it—but I'm dead against making and, worse, keeping promises made under the heavy influence of your sex hormones. As my friend Dr Tuli remarked, 'Getting a promise when you are at the peak of your lustful passion is like giving a promise of peace with a gun to your head.'

~

THE CHEMICAL ASPECTS OF DESIRE

The chemicals called pheromones, which are produced by the body, also determine who we choose as a partner. These hormones send a strong chemical signal, communicating reproductive ability. Most animals, especially dogs and cats, are able to consciously smell out these hormones, which indicate whether the female is ready for mating. In humans, the perception is more subconscious and though we can sniff and be influenced by these chemical triggers, we are not able to realize consciously what we are drawn to.

Women can smell male intentions, especially sexual ones. Dr Denise Chen, assistant professor of psychology at Rice University, used fMRI (functional MRI) to study female brain changes in response to the sexual sweat of males (*Journal of Neurosciences*, January 2009). The researchers used sweat pads kept in males' armpits while they were watching pornographic films or sweating from exercising and gave these pads to nineteen women to smell. They recorded the women's right orbito-frontal cortex, the brain area that helps in perceiving emotions. The findings clearly indicated that the women were able to gauge subconsciously the males' sexual intentions fairly accurately. Imagine how gullible that makes you: You thought you were the hunter but your prey knew what you wanted all through and went ahead with the game. That makes you the prey.

~

Categories of women

Self-effacing to aggressively dominant

1. Doormat—I'm not OK, you're OK
   - Gives power to others, regarding even her own life
   - Accepts everything in the name of fate
   - Doesn't comment on anything
   - Tries to get sympathy with sob-stories
   - Scant respect for self
   - Does things to please others
   - Does what she believes others want her to do

   Example: Semi-literate wives

2. Aggressive—you're not OK
   - The quick decision-maker, even for others and even when unsolicited
   - Reckless
   - Often abusive
   - Believes others are inferior to her

   Example: Womens' rights activists

3. Indirect aggressive—you're not OK but I won't let you know that I think so
   - Uses manipulation rather than direct challenge
   - Uses deceit
   - Controls and dominates by making decisions for everybody

   Example: Products of joint families or girls with many sisters

4. Sensibly assertive—I'm OK, you're OK
   - Has strong personal qualities but shares power and decision-making
   - The balanced woman

   Example: Educated women who follow the middle path between domination and subjugation

PREFERRED PARTNERS OVER THE YEARS

Changing trends regarding what men prefer
(Source: Ranjana Kumari, Centre for Social Research, Delhi)

1960s: Pretty, virgin, accomplished in household chores, from right caste and family

1970s: Convent-educated, smart, fair, innocent girl

1980s: Tall, fair, slim, well-qualified but homely girl

1990s: Earning, well-educated, attractive; can manage the home

2000s: Compatible, professionally qualified, working girl who is intelligent. Caste, horoscope and even looks are not important

(About 47 per cent men now want their wives to continue working after marriage and are not averse to taking on some domestic duties themselves. Professionals preferred girls from co-ed schools, whereas men from conservative business families preferred those from 'girls only' schools)

> Wife to a friend: 'My hubby got me a mood ring. When I am in a good mood, it turns green and when I am in a bad mood, it leaves a red mark on his forehead.'

A popular saying goes: Heaven is an American salary, a British butler, a German car and an Indian wife. Hell is an Indian salary, a German butler, a British car, and an American wife.

You can modify this for today to: Heaven is an aggressive job (and salary), a docile maid, a sensible (sensibly assertive) wife. Hell is an aggressive wife, a docile salary and an indirectly aggressive (instigating) maid. Maybe a combination of a doormat-wife /indirectly aggressive wife will be par for the course for the majority of males, who know they don't deserve heaven but don't want to be saddled with hell.

Toxic wife

A new category needs to be added to the four above—the toxic wife. She is the wife who is out to rip off her husband in every way. She quits her job after marriage, supposedly to take care of home and kids, but instead hires an army of domestic staff and spends extravagantly without bothering about her husband's financial condition. In the UK, it was reported that many such wives divorced their spouses when they lost their jobs/finances (*TOI*).

When Archie, the ever-romantic hero, decided to tie the knot, he first proposed to his heart-throb, Veronica. Most readers however voted that Betty would be better wife-material. Archie eventually proposed to Betty.

It is as if the world could see what Archie couldn't. Veronica was a great date, but Betty was definitely the right choice as a wife.

The toxic-women syndrome refers to women who marry rich guys and take him to the cleaners. It is almost a lucrative career option for many today. Tara Winter Wilson, who coined the term, writes in the *Telegraph*, London, that toxic wives are not exceptions and that this 'syndrome' is becoming more prevalent by the day. Toxic wives believe that the most lucrative career is to get married, have a child and then get divorced, with a hefty alimony and millions of dollars worth of assets. Such women lurk in high-society bars, looking for potential prey.

IN A NUTSHELL

Take your time—do not rush into marriage just because most of your friends have tied the knot. In any case marriage is a gamble. Do not make it even a bigger one by rolling the dice in a hurry. Choose your mate rationally, not under the influence of sex hormones. The sauciness that seems alluring from afar might become a nightmare when you are saddled with it day in and day out. Think of long-term compatibility, not short-term pleasure. Do not marry on the basis of how good she looks on your arm or how envious your friends will be of you.

Easier said than done. We add to our woes by . . .

15

Praise but Don't Appease

> Question: Why are men losing this battle?
>
> Answer: Because in this war between the sexes there is too much collusion with the enemy.

Pammi looked a bit fatigued. She slumped into the chair and said, 'I've decided to raise my nightly rates.'

'What rates?' asked a flabbergasted Savvy.

'Some time back, we devised a system in which my husband shells out a fixed amount to have sex with me. After yesterday's explosive night, I've decided I deserve more.'

Sally raised an enquiring eyebrow.

Pammi said with a sly smile, 'I rewarded my husband with the most torrid sex that he has ever had or even dreamt of.' She gave a naughty giggle. 'If you think I am looking fatigued, you should have seen my hubby dear in the morning. He looked as if he'd been hit by a truck.'

'So the libber cat became a libber tigress yesterday,' winked Sally. 'What made you so generous that you rewarded your enemy?' goaded Sally. She was hinting at Pammi's accusation of infidelity against her husband.

'Two things: first, we finally decided who our inner circle of friends will be. These are the people we will be spending our vacation weekend with. The good point is that out of seven invites, six are my friends and the last one is his boss. After a big tug-of-war, he finally eliminated most of his idiotic bum-chums. Then when we got together, he praised my choice of friends lavishly in front of them.'

SOCIAL PERSONA

You marry the entire social persona of your spouse, including her family, friends and acquaintances. In *Tipping Point*, Malcolm Gladwell shows that at one time, humans tend to have the 'emotional energy' to justify ten to fifteen close relations. Any more leads to an overload of social capacity. That means, after excluding immediate family members, you can have only six to seven friends in your inner circle. After marriage, another set of six to seven friends and an equal number of close family members are added. This generally leads to an overload and, as a result, you have to trim some of your former close relations.

Pammi was upbeat. 'It took me two months to wear him down to agree to adopt my friends and give up most of his own, including that idiotic best friend of his, who insisted on yelling out 'bharjai!' every time he spotted me. We had many fights over him. Ultimately, hubby not only parted ways with him but also praised me. He deserved to be rewarded.'

Sally smiled, 'Something similar happened in our home too. Though he would never go as far as giving up his friends, he did something great and got rewarded with something similar.' She giggled shyly. 'We had invited some of our family friends and I didn't like the concept of serving them alcohol, when we don't drink at home at all. Not only did he defend my decision not to serve alcohol but even snubbed my sister-in-law, who was voicing her dissent, and said, "This is her party in her house, so she gets to decide. She is intelligent enough to know what is good for our family." This is the first time ever that he has snubbed his sister.'

'So what did you reward him with?'

'Well! I was initially reluctant to get a pedicure and waxing, though my husband had requested it many times, for… for… more pleasure during . . .' She winced at this uncharacteristic revelation. 'The lavish praise and support made me relent and I decided to go in for a complete wax.'

'Complete?' quizzed Savvy.

'I mean . . . Brazilian wax.' Sally looked down, embarrassed. 'Hubby was ecstatic that night. He showered so much praise on my beauty that I think I will make trips to the beauty parlour a part of my life.'

Savvy said, 'My husband never praises anything I do and I can't refuse him sex either. I get my waxing and pedicure done for Rehaan, who copiously praises my efforts. He touches my legs and says such flattering things that it makes my heart melt. I will definitely try this . . . what you say… Brazilian wax . . . if I get a chance to be with Rehaan alone.'

~

Shravan was seeing a pattern emerging with every visit to this restaurant. Every episode outlined by these ladies brought back a memory of his interaction with Maya. Unfortunately, the incidents that reminded him of Maya were always Pammi's, though he wished they were Sally's.

Today, he remembered another sentence uttered by Maya. 'Shravan darling, your friends are all so ghaati and how do you even tolerate that surd Gurmukh? He doesn't speak one sentence without swearing or slapping your back. Never bring him to our get-togethers at least.' Since then, he began ducking all calls from his best friend.

He is the only one who always gives me true and sincere advice and never hesitates to call a spade a spade. Such people are rare. I should call on him today itself, he now thought.

~

Joginder, on the other hand, was thinking, 'I don't even remember the last time I praised Roshni. And that is when

I know that she not only loves being praised by me but is ready to do anything for it. My praise might bring back her zeal to dress and deck up better. I'll try it today.'

~

Daiv, too, rued the fact that he had never soothed his wife with praise, as he wrote:

PRAISE—THE ULTIMATE SOOTHER

You all know the power of praise in the beginning of a relationship; otherwise how could you have written all those poems/ letters/ emails and SMSes, eulogizing some existent, some non-existent virtues of the lady? Right up to the moment you take your marriage vows, praise remains the dominant theme of your talk. 'Oh, you are so beautiful!', 'You look so elegant in this dress', 'You are so considerate', and so on flows out and usually this praise is also reciprocated in equal measure.

Despite that, one of the first things that you have amnesia about are the virtues which made you fall in love with the lady in the first place. Even worse, you forget that her virtues have to be communicated to her in proper language. Believing that

> Praise and smiles are like boomerangs—throw them and they always come back.

a grunt at the end of a great meal is praise enough is the biggest communication blunder that starts the downward trend of the relationship after marriage.

Praise, somehow, over time gets replaced by proclamations regarding her shortcomings that suddenly start coming to your notice. Familiarity breeding contempt?

Why do you stop praising? What do you gain by praising?

You stop praising because of three reasons. First, you believe that praising is a frivolous thing, fit for amateur bachelors but unbecoming of the now-married master of the house. Why should you praise someone who belongs to you? You wear the mantle of an old man, in whose eyes romance is bad for the self-image.

Second, you get the idea that praise will go to her head and make her haughty and she will start considering herself superior to you.

Third, and most important, you start thinking about your social image. What will my friends and family, especially parents, think of me? 'A henpecked husband'?

Add to this the fact that in the rigmarole of setting up your house, taking care of your career and managing the children, you just forget the power of praise.

So let us see what praise does for a relationship.

First, praise is a manifestation of mutual respect and admiration and is thus reciprocated. In itself, this is a huge reason to set the ball rolling. Second, praise raises the stock of

WHAT MAKES HER HAPPY?

A study of 2,000 females by the 'Dental Care Plus Implants Centres' came up with these nuggets on compliments:

- Women love being asked, 'Have you lost weight?'
- They love being told, 'Don't tell me—You don't look a day over (what-you-think-her-age-is minus ten years).'
- All moms like to hear 'What a cute baby (or intelligent child)!'
- Compliment what the lady may be a bit insecure about. For an obviously beautiful lady, praise her wit or how well-read she is—not her beauty; she already knows about that.
- Compliment her family or family members but never someone who might be considered a competitor, e.g. her close friend or her younger sister, especially if she is better-looking than her.

self-esteem of the wife. She starts feeling positive about herself. This feel-good factor is bound to make her lighthearted and happy, making her the kind of person you want to be around. It also makes her strive for improvement in herself and her surroundings, because praise is addictive and the praised person craves for more. The most important thing that praise does is that it conveys your faith in your wife. It tells her that you appreciate her or her efforts; you care for her feelings and you want her to be happy. In short, it tells her you love her.

This is the material of which the marital bonds are made up of. You can see how very small gestures get you huge dividends. But be careful that the praise is honest, that is, what you say or the virtue you are appreciating should actually be present in her and it should be praiseworthy. Your wife may not be able to spot phoney praise instantly, but once she gets a hint of it your relationship will be adversely affected. All your future comments will be discounted and everything you say will be doubted. I am not saying you should not call a spade a spade. I am just saying, dwell on the actual positives that she possesses. Instead of praising the culinary attempts of a poor cook, praise her well-organized kitchen. And instead of raving about the dress sense of a casual dresser, compliment her cool demeanour. Truth will reflect positively in your relationship.

Don't be stingy while praising. Throw away all that MCP trash from your mind about praise going to her head or that she will become haughty or think you are below her level—blah-blah-blah. Because praise is a feel-good gesture, it lifts the self-esteem of the receiver. The receiver of praise is not only more likely to return the gesture but also will think ten times before hurting one who has raised the level of her self-belief.

Chain reaction of praise and appreciation

You start by appreciating one aspect of your spouse and you will find that she reveals a hitherto unseen positive sentiment which is worth praising. This ever-escalating chain reaction can make your marriage an evergreen romance.

If still not convinced, start by mixing praise with jest, so that the comments can pass off for lighthearted conversation. How? One way is Catch-22 praise.

~

Catch-22 praise

Catch-22 praise involves tongue-in-cheek praise in which the partner is bound to respond with praise because the comments are indirectly complimenting the one who is praising.

For instance, your saying, 'You have good taste . . . for you chose me.' How can she refute it? Only by saying, 'No, you have good taste.'

Another example: 'My relatives are better than yours.' She disagrees. 'Okay. I was talking about my mother-in-law or brother-in-law vis-à-vis yours.'

There is a Punjabi proverb, 'Changyan nu change hi milte hain', meaning 'Good people attract good people (in marriage).

This kind of witticism sets in motion a lighthearted praise competition, instead of fault-finding bouts, especially during the early months of marriage. Used subtly and sensibly, it can provide special moments and diffuse some tense situations.

~

Appeasement versus praise

There can be a thin line dividing the two. It is imperative to distinguish between them because the consequence of each is diametrically opposite to the other. Praise lifts the self-esteem of the praised, making her reciprocate the sentiment and aim to come up to your expectations in the future. Appeasement, on the other hand, generates the feeling of vanquishing the opponent. The appeased person is likely to try to get the other to bend over a little more the next time and then some more . . . in a never-ending process.

Sally's husband praised her, raising her self-esteem, and she reciprocated by doing what he liked. Pammi's husband, on the other hand, simply gave in and agreed to abandon all his friends to appease her. His praising her choice of friends after that smacks of unfairness and sycophancy. He inadvertently set in motion an ever-increasing avalanche of appeasement that is bound to take a heavy toll on his social life. He has inadvertently raised the bar of his wife's unfair demands. The natural corollary to this might be that he is asked to sever relations with his relatives or even his parents.

It is imperative that you steer clear of appeasement at all costs, especially in the early phase of your marriage. Though I know that in this phase it is easier said than done.

~

A word about appeasement—mum is the best word

Men have to be careful of what they commit to in the throes of passion, especially during courtship. You can be made to admit anything, including the murder of the US President. Unfortunately, unlike in legal courts, these confessions made under the effect of a drug (testosterone is a drug, for sure) are admissible in the court of emotions—your wife will hold you to it when you have a disagreement after the wedding. Be careful not to commit too much to impress her because you will find it difficult to wriggle out of it after marriage.

IN A NUTSHELL

Praise her positive traits and actions but avoid appeasing. Appeasement doesn't endear you to her because your abject surrender is not seen as a caring gesture that begets respect. It is seen as a weakness and you are perceived as a wimp.

Are you a wimp? Let's find out.

16

Don't be a Wimp—or a Dictator

Question: Why is a man like the weather?

Answer: Nothing can change either of them.

'Why can't my husband be like my Dalmatian, Timid, back at my parents' home?' asked Pammi.

'What is a Dalmatian? asked Savvy.

'A dog,' enlightened Sally.

'Not just any dog. Timid or Timy, as we fondly call him, belongs to a wonderful breed. He is good company and looks aggressive but is really docile and that is why we named him Timid. Occasionally, when irritated, he does bare his teeth but confront him and he will never bite. He sits when I tell him to sit, eats what I give him to eat and bites whom I tell him to bite. That is how husbands should be—smart as company but obedient. The occasional bark will do but he should bite only when instructed to bite.'

Savvy laughed at Pammi's comparison.

'My hubby is just the reverse,' Pammi continued. 'He doesn't do my bidding but becomes a wimp in front of others. He is such a sissy; at times he starts crying. I feel embarrassed at his being so unmanly.'

Sally countered by saying, 'Didn't you say that he has grown a spine?'

A young man goes to ask his girlfriend's father for her hand in marriage.

Father: Where do you intend staying after marriage?

Young man: God will provide.

Father: What about the finances required to arrange for a house after marriage?

Young man: God will provide.

Father: And household expenses?

Young man: God will provide.

The girl's mother asked the father what he thought of the young man.

The father replied, 'What is more important is that he thinks I'm God.'

Such a spouse is unlikely to gain respect from his wife or in-laws.

'Spine for the wrong things—emotional things and for listening to his parents and admonishing me. He doesn't have the spine to stand up against his boss or even his mom. Then, he tries to soften me with tears to agree with his mom.'

Savvy nodded. 'This is true for my husband also. With me he is a dictator but lacks the spine to confront any other issue or person. Just because of this attitude of his, I'm being pushed towards Rehaan.'

Sally also pitched in. 'My husband is a perfectionist and it is difficult to adhere to his expectations at times but I have learnt to adapt to his perfectionism. Once you understand his viewpoint, it is easy to understand and even appreciate his system.'

~

Shravan was suddenly reminded of two sentences spoken within a couple of days by Maya. 'I just don't understand—why can't you be forthright and stand up to your parents once and for all? This is your life and you should live it the way you deem fit.'

And then, 'Don't you ever talk to my dad like that. The least you can do is to show respect and try to agree with him. You must realize the effort with which my parents have brought me up.'

Shravan was rueing that he hadn't responded with, 'So did my parents. In fact they had to cut down on their rations so I could study. Then how can I turn my back on them?' Somehow, the injustice of it all had never occurred to him till today.

'It is too late now to correct that,' he thought.

~

Daiv started writing . . .

THE FINE BALANCE OF PERSONALITY

What clicks for a husband is subjective. More often than not, there is a big gap between the extremes of absolute domination and total subjugation, which has to be found and adhered to for the sake of a happy marriage.

Let us take the trait of aggressiveness in males. The commonest grouse of women, especially of some generations earlier, is that men are too insensitive to really care about them. An equal number of females, strangely, have the grouse that their husbands are too meek to take a stand on anything.

The sensitive husband is as much despised as the insensitive one. Can a person possibly be delicately sensitive to your needs but a snorting bull for the rest of the world? In real life, when a man is faced with a particular situation, he can display either of the qualities—softness (and sensitivity) or aggression (and roughness), unless he is a split personality. Not many wives would like to live with a schizophrenic, but their expectations are somewhat akin to Draupadi's (see box), when they wish for a perfect husband endowed with mutually contradictory qualities. Even worse, they want the husband to be docile in front of them and dynamic for the rest of the world.

Draupadi prayed hard and God asked her to state her wish. She said she wanted a husband who had:

- Handsomeness
- Great strength
- Exceptional martial qualities
- Great wisdom and learning
- Sensitivity and an artistic nature

God found it impossible to create a single man with all the five traits. So, he destined that Draupadi be married to five different husbands by the decree of Kunti, mother of the five Pandavas.

The middle-of-the-road balanced personality, neither too sensitive, nor too insensitive might be the best bet for the wife but then whatever trait is there in the husband would have to be the same for everyone.

~

DON'T BE A WIMP—OR A DICTATOR

Don't cow down to irrational demands but don't be scared or ashamed of showing your love for your wife either. Don't take a cue from your dad; he married your mom not your wife.

Be a man, not a sissy

'This concept of a genderless society . . . has turned men into tragic "nappy-changing sissies" and women into frumps who neglect their husband's (sexual) needs'—Anna Anka, Miss Sweden (*TOI*, 21 September 2009). Anna felt that dads should work and provide for families—'Men are men and women are women'. It was felt the Scandinavian push for gender equality had gone too far, with the recent emergence of males wishing to breastfeed their babies—(*TOI*).

Most men are neither wimps nor dictators. They are reasonable people who care for their friends and families and don't like to be looked down upon. The problem is that you

THE PRESSURE OF BECOMING A SUPERMAN

The ever-increasing prevalence of nuclear families is putting new strain on the male partner. He has now to get in touch with the feminine aspect of his personality to be able to contribute to household chores as an equal partner. This requires men to be more sensitive and multi-tasking. It also requires that they become emotionally tougher and able to manage stress at home, after having done just that in office. As psychologist D. Vasanthar R. Patri comments, 'Men are biologically not made to handle pressure well.' Dr Sanjay Chugh says, 'He has to begin by creating a Self-concept: a fine balance between his "masculine" and "feminine" sides.' The male is poorly adaptable by nature and this dual role stresses him hugely.

BATTERED HUSBANDS, CHANGING PARADIGMS:

In a role reversal of sorts, men are getting punched, kicked, beaten with brooms or scalded with hot water or coffee. Many are so traumatized that they go into depression and even contemplate suicide, says Swaroop Sarkar, co-founder of the 'Battered Men Helpline'.

The problem is compounded by social norms that make men too ashamed to reveal this, even to their near and dear ones. Most men in such situations do not hit back or complain to authorities because they are scared that the law will side with the wife and worsen their condition.

Women's newfound financial power and an increasing consumption of alcohol is resulting in their increasingly aggressive behaviour and resultant violence against men.

Not surprisingly, of all the suicides, married men account for 65.35 per cent, while married women account for 34.65 per cent. (Data from All-India Men's Welfare Association, Hyderabad)

come to believe, or are made to believe by your advisors, that to succeed in marriage you have to change this way or behave that way, otherwise you won't be appreciated or loved or respected or you will be dominated, and so on, and you tend to put on a mask of a wimp or a dictator.

If in the most intimate and sacrosanct of all relationships, you can't be yourself, then when will you be yourself? How can a life lived with masks on be blissful? Be yourself, that is, be the person your wife married. Better still, be yourself before she marries you. If you've projected a different image, please correct that impression at the earliest before your marriage becomes a farce.

~

The Wimp Test

Who is a WIMP?

The parameters vary from place to place. In Afghanistan, anybody who allows his wife to show her face to another male is considered a wimp. Even one who allows the feet of his wife to be touched by a stranger, for example, while taking her shoe size, is considered a weak male. In the West, a man who afraid of a showdown and glosses over his wife's one-night stand is considered a wimp.

Most cultures regard a wimp as unmanly. This raises the question: Who is considered manly? The answer generally boils down to someone lacking in courage and power. A typical wimp has these features:

- He is afraid to confront injustice, whether to someone else or even to himself
- He is scared of taking responsibility
- He sidetracks or postpones contentious issues

- He avoids a display of emotions, especially of love and compassion
- He is more concerned about peoples' opinion rather than what is right, and acts accordingly
- He avoids giving his opinion for fear that it might be wrong
- He usually covers up his true feelings with displays of undue aggression or complete withdrawal
- He feels powerless without the approval of others.

~

The art of chivalry

Chivalry is as widely admired as wimpiness is despised. Even so-called 'women libbers' admit that they would rather deal with a chivalrous person than a wimp.

The word chivalry is derived from the French word *chevalier*, a man on a horse or a knight. In the Middle Ages, knights displayed an attitude of courtesy, honour, generosity and humility apart from their riding and martial skills to prove that they are worthy of noble ladies.

In today's context, chivalrous conduct would entail the following:

- Pulling out a chair or opening a door for an accompanying lady
- Minding your language; refraining from obscenities or abuses
- Being polite, even when proving your point in an argument

- Offering to pay the bill, unless you have decided to go dutch beforehand, in which case, concede to share the bill.

Don't go overboard with the chivalry though, because if your actions smack of chauvinism, the results can be disastrous. You need not display as much chivalry towards an aggressive business rival or your senior and avoid chivalry if she has strong women's lib leanings. The idea is to be considerate and polite, without giving the lady the impression that you consider her incapable.

~

Powerful is sexy

It seems the power of office gets added to the persona of men. Their success reflects on their overall personality and they become more desirable to women.

Obvious examples will have to come from the celebrities. Carla Bruni, for example, despite saying that she didn't find short men attractive, married the French president at the time, Nicolas Sarkozy. Monica Lewinsky and Paula Jones couldn't resist the woman-magnet, Bill Clinton. Women are attracted to men in power because they connect a man's identity with his position. This also holds true in our day-to-day lives, with women giving more attention, love and adulation to men who have control over their families or companies or even neighbourhood. Thus, you would always be more appealing if you are assertive and powerful rather than a wimp.

~

IN A NUTSHELL

So, dear friend, refuse to be taken for granted or, worse, trampled upon by your spouse because of your infatuation for her. Be clear about attitudes that you will just not accept in your relationship. This is especially important in the early phase of your marriage.

17

Conflict Resolution in the Early Phase

Question: How do you know your honeymoon phase is over?

Answer: Your husband stops smiling while scraping burnt toast.

Pammi appeared and waved a casual 'hi'. Then she sat down quietly. The silence was most unusual for the usually effervescent woman.

'What happened? Why are you so quiet?' asked Sally.

'Nothing!' replied Pammi in a very hoarse voice. 'I have a sore throat.' She swallowed hard and grimaced. 'All because of that stupid hubby of mine.' She coughed.

'Did he wring your neck?' asked Savvy. She had seen something similar in last episode of a saas-bahu serial.

Pammi shook her head as if the very thought was an affront to her dominance. 'No, he dare not! I tried to resolve the conflict about his extramarital affair by providing what he wants at home.' The other two looked at her with question marks writ large on their faces. Pammi rubbed her throat and took a big swig of coffee to soothe the pain. 'I obliged him by doing what he has always been asking for...' She enjoyed speaking in riddles to create suspense and get undivided attention. 'Uhm . . . oral sex,' she whispered.

'What did she do?' Savvy was utterly perplexed.

Sally sighed and bent forward to decipher for Savvy what Pammi was saying. Savvy's face grew crimson as she bit her tongue to avoid her customary giggling. Oral sex seems so modern, she thought.

Pammi shook her head at Savvy's childish gesture. 'I agreed for fear that if I don't provide what he wants, the other woman will. I could think of no other way to resolve this problem. How was I to know that I would land up with—' She wheezed. 'Don't you ever do it?' she asked Savvy, whose tongue was still between her teeth.

'I might have but my husband doesn't allow me to even touch his you-know-what. But I have found the solution to my sexual dissatisfaction. You know what—I slept with Rehaan and it was so great. He lets me do everything. Maybe I'll try this also.' She giggled with the anticipation. Then turning serious, she said, 'However, another problem has arisen from the solution. That wretched landlord of mine got a whiff of it and now whenever he finds me alone, he smiles very suggestively. I'll have to do something for him next week so that he doesn't squeal on me.'

'Sex is the biggest conflict in the early phase of marriage, isn't it? Savvy asked Sally.

Sally looked up and her sombre expression indicated that her conflict was not quite as titillating. 'I have no problems with the matter under consideration. I'll tell you what my conflict has been—my outspoken mother-in-law. Of late, she has been unwell, which has made her pretty irritable. Her bossiness combined with irritability makes for a deadly combination which can test anybody's patience and mine was running out fast. I work from home, and there is just no respite from her demands and comments. She's always been domineering but used to contribute in full measure to the household and with chores. Now she lies in bed and gets on my nerves.'

Both the ladies listened, for this was the first time that Sally was speaking against her MIL. 'Fortunately, my husband was able to realize what I was going through, without my having to say it. He acted very maturely. He knew that his mother wouldn't change overnight and that I was near breaking point. So, to compensate, he started letting me control things and even allowed me to decide in spheres so far earmarked as his fiefdom. For the first time, he literally handed over our financial decisions regarding our main purchases and vacation expenses, exclusively to me. He even recorded the live sports telecast that he is so enthusiastic about, instead of recording my cookery programme so that I could watch in my free-time slot. These small things pleased me immensely. Then he roped in my father-in-law and explained to him the source of my strain. My father-in-law is a thorough gentleman. He volunteered to take on all his wife's calls during the day so that I could work peacefully. He even insisted that I have a nap for an hour in the afternoon. This has helped me tide over the situation. In time, my mother-in-law's health improved. So, you see the issue that could have torn our marital bond asunder got resolved with a bit of mature handling.'

~

Joginder thought, 'Now that is what I call a true master of the house. Not like my father, who takes a conflict and turns it into an inferno. Can I become as mature as Sally's husband?'

~

Shravan, however, was still thinking about the sex escapades of the other two ladies. Maya had for the first time offered to go with him for a weekend to Agra and the way she had suggested it, he was certain that sexual intimacy was on the cards. Up to now he had been exhilarated at the thought, but now he was not so sure. 'Is she sizing up my sexual prowess to see if I can satisfy her?' he thought. 'Or worse, will she make me do any of these unnatural acts like oral sex?' He shuddered.

~

Musical phases of life:

LOVE: When all songs seem to describe exactly how you feel.

LUST: When it is just the same mushy crap.

MARRIAGE: When you never listen to music but face the music for your actions.

Daiv was frantically taking notes. He knew conflict resolution was of utmost importance early in marriage. He wrote:

Marriage progresses through certain set phases. Each phase can be categorized by the predominant thought process of that period:

Phases	**Predominant thought**
1. Premarital phase	Parents say, 'You are God incarnate.'
2. Honeymoon phase	Everything about you is perfect.
3. Rejection (fault-finding) phase	Everything about you is flawed.
4. Blame-game phase	You have wronged me.
5. Acceptance phase	Whatever you do is OK.
6. Transformation phase	I like being with you—let's evolve together.

The first three phases together comprise the early phase, lasting from two to six years, depending upon understanding, tolerance and maturity. Occasionally, couples who tide over the early phase uneventfully, tend to get stuck in phase 2 or 3 and are never able to reach a mutually satisfying relationship. The young age of the couple and their high expectations make it very difficult to negotiate this phase without hiccups. Learning to deal with reality and conflicts is an integral part of evolving in a relationship.

According to marriage counsellor Dr Nirmal Khurana, 'Ninety per cent of newlyweds who face problems after marriage do so within three to five years of getting married, irrespective of whether they had an arranged or love marriage.' Eighty per cent of all married couples admitted that they found the initial couple of years of marriage the toughest. They suddenly changed from all-romance-no-fight couples during dating and honeymoon to all-fights-no-romance couples within months of marriage.

A recent study in the *Connubial Crucible, Journal of Personality and Social Psychology* found that the way couples deal with problems in the initial years of marriage paves the way for their future.

Warning signs of trouble in the early phase

Life in the early phase of marriage changes so rapidly that we ignore our increasing disenchantment with each other till it becomes irreconcilable. It is beneficial to detect the early signs of conflict. Some basic signs are:

- Frequent and hurtful fighting
- Avoiding each other
- Small issues turning into fierce arguments
- Finding faults in everything that the spouse does
- Blaming each other for problems
- No meaningful conversation with the spouse, though the partners converse with everyone else
- Issues are generally left unresolved and partners give up trying to resolve them

- Both partners feel stressed out and irritable when in each other's company
- The partners find it very difficult to have good times or fun together
- Both partners are fearful about arguments
- Partners lose respect for each other
- Partners publicly humiliate each other, a very serious sign, and indicative of an imminent breakdown.

The origin of early conflict

From the early warning signs, you would have understood that conflicts originate when the partners lose respect and admiration for each other. This down-gradation does not occur in a straight line but rather in a sine curve, in which the relationship goes up the curve as the bar is raised and then starts sliding down when the bar is abruptly lowered.

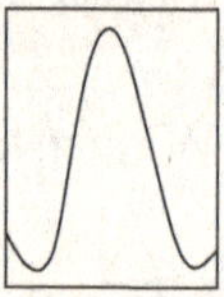

Raising the bar

To begin with, there is a sudden spate of respect and high regard that in-laws shower on grooms. One who was called by a nickname—Billu, Neetu, Monu, Jeetu or, worse, abusive distortions of his name or attributes—Kalu, Cheekhu, Chhottu, or Lambu—suddenly finds himself addressed respectfully, with 'ji' suffixing his name, as Vinodji, Sunilji or Vishalji. If he is a professional, he may be addressed by his exalted designation—Doctor Sahib, Vakil Sahib, or Engineer Sahib. All this makes the so-far unaccustomed groom go weak in his knees and he over-commits, as if to repay all this undeserved respect, thus raising the bar of expectations of the newlywed wife.

Something similar happens with the wife—during the courtship and honeymoon she is made to feel like a queen who has virtues fit for a goddess.

The honeymoon is over

Now the marriage begins. This is the phase of conflict, when the real situation is out in the open. The husband feels burdened with the effort required to make the transition from a carefree, even flamboyant bachelor to the responsible head of a family. The wife, on the other hand, feels as if she has fallen with a thud from cloud nine as she is loaded with responsibilities befitting a dutiful wife and daughter-in-law. She has additionally been saddled with sky-high expectations, courtesy you.

Thus begins the acid test of 'the rejection phase' in which it dawns on you that your spouse is not perfect. Everything about him/her may seem flawed, and your partner may have the same view of you. Marriages that come out of this phase unscathed are likely to be sustained in the long term. If the fault-finding is not resolved early and amicably, it leads to the 'blame-game phase', in which each partner, usually the wife, feels she has been wronged.

Lowering of the bar

In the final stage, both sides, with parents in tow, tend to lower their regard for the other party. Abusing, rebuking, name-calling and character assassination may be involved. The loss of mutual respect makes the situation untenable.

Escalation of conflict by faulty resolution

When faced with conflict, each partner tries to resolve the conflict in his or her own way, and this is what, inadvertently, escalates the conflict.

Attempt to change the spouse

After the honeymoon phase, the young spouses start focusing on each other's incompatibilities, something they hadn't paid much heed to during their courtship. These become stumbling blocks in the relationship as the couple envision that they have to bear them all their lives. The spouse, generally the woman, attempts to change the partner—his habits, likes and dislikes to match her own.

What the couple doesn't realize is that it is impossible to change the basic nature of a person without breaking his or her spirit. Can spending one's life with a broken-down person bring happiness?

Shooting off your mouth without thinking of consequences

Here, one of the partners attempts to resolve the conflict by becoming an aggressive speaker in the belief that this verbal outrage will make the partner cow down. It might prove successful, but in most cases either the verbal volley is returned shot by shot or the partner withdraws into a shell. In both cases, conflict increases.

Making conflict public

This may be resorted to in the belief that the partner will cave in to avoid social ridicule. This is a strategy often adopted by women but some men are also not above it. The problem is that if both partners play to the gallery, the conflict goes into overdrive.

Bringing the parents and relatives into the conflict

In the blame-game phase, the couple is very likely to bring in the parents and relatives. The parents first try to advise the other partner and if he or she does not listen, they tend to become accusatory and join the mêlée. This is the worst way to solve any conflict, as this scars the fibre of your marital bond irreparably.

How does the groom chosen by the parents as the best possible match for their daughter, one considered nothing short of perfect in every sense, suddenly become useless? Likewise with the bride. How does the ideally suited, carefully chosen, perfect wife, become Chandi, the incarnation of evil? What

> 'When you continually place your parents' opinions and views before your spouse's, you are planting seeds of destruction, and you will eat the fruit of divorce'—Dr Myles Munroe

do the saat pheras do to convert a devi or devta into a Chandi or laloo?

> 'Ego causes most of man's problems in dealing with one another'—John Bendix, US-based spiritual writer

Ego tussle—rein in your ego

Our minds create the ego to be able to cope with the fear of the future and regrets from the past. When you are threatened with conflict in marriage, your ego comes to the fore to defend you. Problems arise, however, when our ego gets inflated and starts perceiving even normal gestures as threats to our being.

The stupid, inflated male ego can mar a good marriage even with the best of partners. From inception, males are bombarded with many subtle and not-so-subtle hints about the superiority of the XY chromosome, which is bound to enter impressionable heads of young boys as his MCP ego.

With today's changing paradigms, where an alteration or even role reversal is imminent for sustenance and career enhancement, this ego is a huge stumbling block. No wonder the commonest grouse of the females who have opted out of a marriage is that 'it was his ego that prevented them from having a meaningful relationship'.

So, dear to-be husbands, before you enter a new-age metropolitan marriage with a working wife, please take a day off to rinse your soul free of most of this troublesome ego. If you find this difficult, I strongly suggest you opt for a conventional, single-earner-type set-up and find a partner to whom this appeals as well. Otherwise, you will end up spoiling not one but two lives.

Cutting off communication

This is another stupid reaction to a conflict that spouses enter into, believing that resorting to the silent treatment will force their partner's hand to succumb to her demands. Though indulged in more by women, new-age men practise it to force their spouses to come to them for settlement. In its exaggerated form, it results in one partner's pulling back into a shell. This measure inevitably fails because it blocks the main path of conflict resolution.

Developing mistrust

This is a serious development and occurs when conflict resolution has failed miserably. To save oneself from getting hurt again, the partner develops this defence mechanism, convinced of never trusting the partner's suggestions to resolve a conflict.

Advice to newlywed husbands

To begin with, forget about the ongoing conflict and its resolution. Instead, try to change your attitude to resolve the conflict:

- Don't focus on incongruities between you and your partner. Focus instead on the positives. Compromise and make some concessions for your partner's choices, even though they are in contrast to yours. If you remain as self-centred as you were as a single person, it will spell the ruin of your marital happiness because 'me, me, me' leaves no room for a 'we'.

- Develop a thick skin.

Dear husbands, don't be shocked when you find that your wife is not all sugar and honey. As my uncle in the army exclaimed in his hidden diary that we, his nephews, stole from his bag, 'I was shocked to find that my beautiful, delicate wife farts almost after every meal.'

Be witty

Good humour saves many skirmishes. As the story goes about one Mr Webster: Mrs Webster once caught him redhanded kissing the maid. She said, 'Mr Webster, I am surprised.' Mr Webster, coming up for air, said, 'Actually, I am surprised, my dear. You are merely astonished.'

Keep your wits around you—only they help one crawl out of the holes that we invariably dig with our own hands.

Be mature

Maturity in relationships, especially when coming from the husband's side, is a major slayer of conflict. The biggest sign of maturity is the ability to control your behaviour and your expressions in front of your spouse, especially when subjected to an unpalatable response. Showing your true feelings will only worsen an already heated situation. Deal with that frustrating situation later, after tempers have cooled down.

Let the wife dominate

Give in to her trifles and allow her to be happy and feel dominant because that raises her self-esteem and makes her happy from the core, but never make the mistake of letting her think that she is superior to you. Intelligence lies in accepting that when the frogs start croaking in rains, it is better for the koel to keep quiet but don't let the frog think that they sing better than koel, a mistake most husbands make in the early phase.

Don't bite but definitely hiss—advice for the snake and husband

Once there was a deadly snake whose bite caused many deaths. A renowned saint met the snake and asked it to stop biting people. The snake agreed. Soon word spread that the snake never bites. As a result, people stopped being afraid of it and children starting throwing stones at it. A few months later, the saint came to the village again and he met the injured snake. On being told of the atrocities the snake was being subjected to, the saint said, 'You are really naïve. I said don't bite, but I never told you to stop hissing. Be gentle but don't forget to hiss and raise your hood if somebody steps on you.' The same advice applies to husbands—don't fight but don't lie prostrate to be stepped upon.

Two hours of divorce a day

This saves your marriage. Look at the progression of your relationship:
Unknown individuals→meet for two hours a week→meet for two hours a day→living together on a twenty-four-hour reality show is too sudden a transition for both→friction is bound to develop.

My wife ceases to be my wife between 9 a.m. to 11 a.m., when the maid brigade comes in—no requests are entertained and even suggestions or reminders bounce off unheard. She even puts it in so many words by saying, 'Wife department closed for two hours.' In the beginning, it felt odd, but with time I have learnt to use these moments of separation for writing in complete solitude. Similarly, when I go to my clinic, I make it a point not to call her, despite her being just on the next floor, until something extremly urgent comes up. My wife uses those hours for her favourite dance programme or financial channels,

KAHLIL GIBRAN ON MARRIAGE:

- You were born together and together you shall be for ever more
- But let there be spaces in your togetherness
- Stand together, yet not too near for the pillars of the temple stand apart
- The oak tree and the cypress grow not in each other's shadow

in which I have no interest. We have both thus carved out our own personal spaces and times. If this is done by newlyweds, it would do wonders for their relationships.

Midas touch: small tips, big rewards

Tips to help you negotiate the early phase of marriage better:

- Tone down your expectations to match reality
- Accept that you are different people
- Base your perceptions about your spouse on hard facts, not imagination
- Understand your spouse's perceptions and expectations
- Focus on solving the problem rather than indulging in the blame game
- Don't rake up the past
- Emphasize points and ideas on which you two agree rather than those on which you disagree
- Learn to say 'sorry'
- Create and give personal space
- Be patient
- Think—am I right in asking my spouse to do this?
- Discuss—how can we be happy?
- Adjust
- Enjoy yourselves together
- Forgive . . . forgive . . . forgive and then forget

Touch and sexuality

Studies by social psychologist Susan Sprecher of Illinois State University show that sexuality can make people feel closer emotionally, especially women. The simplest touch can produce warm, positive feelings, and a back rub can work wonders.

It would be naïve to underestimate the power of sexuality in marriage. Let's see why.

IN A NUTSHELL

Immature attempts to resolve early marriage conflicts can boomerang, worsening the situation to no end. Maturity and patience are required to succeed, and a bit of wit is always welcome.

18

Sex versus Love

One friend to another: 'Our love life is like the Olympics.'

Other friend: 'Wow! How exciting.'

First friend: 'Well, not exactly. It takes place once every four years.'

'You will be surprised to know what Paulo Coelho writes in *The Winner Stands Alone*,' gushed Pammi. 'That all males, when they see a woman, do one thing—they mentally undress her.'

She waited for the effect. The male eavesdroppers nodded a silent assent. The young man mentally unzipped the front of Pammi's top.

The women listened with rapt attention. 'He writes that as long as you have great breasts, thighs, buttocks and belly, you can conquer the world.'

The other girls were lapping up every word of hers. Even the usually indifferent Sally was all ears as the conversation pertained to Coelho, her favourite author. Pammi eluded the fact that she had not read the book but was quoting Jassi, who had a knack of quoting out of context.

'As they say, charity begins at home. So, I've decided to conquer my husband with sex. Now, every time he refuses me anything, he finds that the tension of not getting what I desired has given me a headache for several days, or rather several nights. I dress up in the sexiest negligee and seductive make-up and feign a headache at the last moment, dousing his aroused libido.'

'I don't have that luxury,' Savvy said, 'as my husband doesn't believe in taking my consent to have sex. He sort of forces himself onto me without bothering to find out whether I'm in a mood or not. Then when he is done, he dismounts, without bothering about whether I am satisfied or not.'

'That is terrible—then you can't use sex as a weapon.'

'Well, I had not thought of it as a weapon till I met Jassi Didi! But I have devised my own way of extracting my pound of flesh. I had agreed to be quiet when he came to me at night, in exchange for the weekly movie and dinner. Now I am learning how to avoid it, when I'm tired because of . . . you know Rehaan, or that lecher landlord.'

'Landlord?' queried Sally.

'Yes, I had to give in to him, too, otherwise he would have spilled the beans to my husband. In any case, he gave me gold earrings the first time and showers me with gifts every time I . . .' Her giggle was free of guilt.

WOMEN'S MOANS IN BED MOSTLY FAKE

UK researchers polled women between the ages of 18 and 48 and found that over 25 per cent faked moans 90 per cent of the time. They did this to manipulate their male partners to either speed up lovemaking or finish then and there.

'So how do you avoid having sex with your husband?' asked Pammi.

'When I'm tired, I become very aggressive and demand that he come and fulfil… you know… by moaning passionately. This aggressive and demanding moaning just puts him off. I don't think it's only because of sound going to the next room, where his younger brothers sleep. I think he gets scared that he won't be able to satisfy me in my demanding mood. Maybe he has realized that he is not able to fulfil me. Whatever the reason, he quickly loses his erection and his desire. He really hates the feeling of being left high and dry. One thing is for sure, I get a huge sense of power by using this weapon and holding three males in my muthi.'

'Isn't sex a manifestation of love, especially for women?' interjected Sally.

Two cold stares shot down her suggestion.

She persisted. 'You talked about Paulo Coelho. In *Brida*, he writes about sex. He says, "It (sex) will always be a total experience, because it's the only experience that touches... all five senses. All our channels with the other person are wide open. At the moment of orgasm, the five senses vanish and you enter a world of magic, you can no longer see, hear, taste, touch or smell... It is exactly the same ecstasy as that attained by hermits after years of renunciation and discipline." That is my idea of sex.'

Pammi waved her fingers dismissively. 'Okay, even if we take that romantic view of sex, remember what he said about orgasms, that a man loses all his senses and becomes powerless. Women are not lost in the same way. That is why Jassi says that women are superior to men, especially in matters related to sex. I quote her: "The male perceives himself to be stronger as he has been provided with a lance to poke us with, but he forgets that he does not have a shield to protect him. Add to that the fact that post-coitus he becomes utterly defenceless, lying at the mercy of his superior enemy and God forbid if he has failed with his weapon to satisfy her, then she literally has him by his balls. The conniving female just has to say, 'Give me more. Give me more. Don't stop now,' even though she knows he has discharged and his self-esteem hits rockbottom. At this time if she magnanimously chooses to pardon his lapse, his gratitude is akin to a person who has his head on the chopping block and is let off. He is her slave for a week if not for the whole month."' Pammi smiled menacingly.

~

Shravan shook his head in dismay. Once again he was subconsciously making comparisons between Maya and Pammi, not with whom he wanted to—Sally. Their two-day sex escapade in Agra had turned out to be everything he hadn't wanted it to have been. He had ejaculated prematurely the first night; the second night the demands of Maya had extinguished his libido so that he had feigned a headache and avoided sex. She had magnanimously pardoned him and, yes, he felt hugely obliged to her for the pardon.

Was it all staged to subjugate him?

~

Daiv started a new chapter:

SEXUAL INCONGRUITY

Sex is not merely a physical act. Very few couples are perfectly matched in their sexual needs and this has far-reaching repercussions on marital relationships. It is very important to pay attention to your partner's physical needs.

> Worry occurs when you first realize that you can't do it twice.
>
> Panic occurs when you realize for the second time that you can't do it once.

'Sex-starved marriages are causing a divorce epidemic'—Delhi High Court

A man put forward the case that not having sex with his wife amounted to mental cruelty. The Delhi High Court agreed that 'marriage without sex will lead to an insipid relationship'.

The problem is that more often than not, the Indian male is fixated with an age-old mindset and believes in clichés like, 'Man gives love to get sex and a women is willing to give sex just to get love'; or 'A woman needs a reason for sex, a man just needs a place.' This somehow presumes that sex is not as important for the female. It is ironic that this mindset prevails in the land of the *Kama Sutra* that refers to the act of sex as sambhog or equal and mutual pleasure to both partners by the sexual act. As well-known sexologist Dr Prakash Kothari puts it, 'Indian women are sexually unhappy because the Indian males use their partners as sleeping pills.'

This unhappiness is now coming out of the bedroom and the Indian woman has started demanding her right to sexual satisfaction. Dr Kothari validates this: 'When I started practice thirty-six years ago, a female patient would never complain about sexual dissatisfaction. Now, women are voicing their concern. I get about 150–200 complaints (from women) daily.' This is further documented by Chicago-based psychologist Dr Shaifali Sandhaya, who researched 400 urban middle- and upper-class Indian couples. She says, 'The Indian marriage

> NO SEX—Finances on their minds (*HT*, 8 May 2012)— A sex survey 2012 of 25,000 respondents threw up a nasty surprise. It said that a majority of those in the age group of 30–39 years were unhappy with their sex lives. The cause: worries regarding money, taking care of babies and other demands of modern life.
>
> Couples who were 50–59 years old, however, and even those 60–69 years old said they had a good sex life and were sexually more confident.

is burning and about 80 – 85 per cent divorces are initiated by women.' In fact, one-third of her female respondents said that they were unhappy with their sex lives.

One factor that always puts a strain on the marriage is a sexual mismatch. In such a marriage the partner with the bigger sexual appetite and desire becomes more sexually demanding and as a consequence becomes the dominant partner. If his or her needs are not fulfilled, that partner is perpetually dissatisfied and in turn makes the other's life stressful.

In the West, this problem is less significant because of the prevalence of premarital sexual indulgence and live-in relationships. In India, though premarital sex is no longer taboo, very few couples have prolonged the sexual relationships required to assess their individual needs. When they stay together over a prolonged period, they are shocked to find that their sexual appetites are so different with regard to frequency as well as intensity.

In young couples, however, this mismatch is less profound and easily resolvable. Those of you who have experienced this difficulty are in all likelihood misconstruing your sexual competence. Unfortunately, a large percentage of males enter the arena of marriage overloaded with misconceptions about their sexual prowess, based on either trashy sex magazines or ignorant peer groups. Add to this performance anxiety and bachelorhood abstinence from sex and you have a Catch-22 situation. The male worries about his performance and the more he worries, the more likely he is to fail. Stress is a well-known early discharger. Many men start believing that the pussycat they married may be beyond their sex zone.

Relax, and let the marriage grow on to you. You will find your bearings. Don't do anything drastic, except maybe have a

TYPES OF LOVE

TAMSIC love is selfish.

RAJSIC love is when you develop understanding, caring and respect for your partner. It involves give and take.

SATVIK love comprises give and give (and it will be reciprocated with give and give).

SPIRITUAL love is soul-to-soul.

Marriage is like a bank. It survives if you put in more than you take out.

word with a professional, who would assure you that occasional premature ejaculation in the early days is common.

If you let the guilt get to you, you will end up taking a subservient position in the relationship, which is not going to get corrected in a hurry. As Jassi puts it, 'He is so thankful for being let off the hook that he is literally ready to become a slave, if only out of gratitude for my not exposing his inadequacy to the world.'

Another concern: size of the penis

In a *Cosmopolitan Durex* sex survey (September 2008), 43 per cent women felt that when it came to sexual pleasure, the size of the penis was of no consequence; for the remaining it was of minimal consequence. The Indian Health Bureau (*Femina*, January 2009) gave these dimensions:

a. The G Spot, the source of the female orgasm, is located two inches up the front wall of the vagina.
b. The average length of the vagina is three inches.
c. The average erect penis is five inches, not one-and-half feet as shown in porn movies. Also, when looked at from above, it appears smaller than it actually is.
d. A smallish penis when aroused will enlarge much more (100 per cent or more) than a well-hung one (less than 75 per cent).

A four-inch erect penis then is all that is really necessary. The rest is essentially window dressing.

The well-known research of Masters and Johnson reveals

> Pay a fine for not having enough sex: A judge in France asked an ex-husband to pay a fine of 8,500 pounds for failing to have sex with his wife for twenty-one years. The judge said, 'A sexual relationship between husband and wife is the expression of affection.' He also added, 'By getting married, couples agree to share their lives and this clearly implies they will have sex with each other.'

that women prefer girth over length. As Dr Kothari puts it, 'Performance anxiety is more common than the common cold but it can be eliminated with a bit of common sense, which sadly is very uncommon.'

Apply common sense, and relax. If you have to learn something about sex, it is to learn to enjoy it, for that is more likely to be the deciding factor of good sex than anything else.

~

What gets you slapped?

We are in a process of finalizing a match for our Sunny. Though he has had absolutely no sexual experience, Sunny is all ready for the D-day, and has no doubts about his sexual prowess or his ability to satisfy his wife. He has not asked his peers for advice regarding the first encounter nor read any articles with titles like, 'Twenty-one ways to keep her sighing' or 'How to have your best sex ever' or 'How to keep your bitch happy'.

Sunny is my beloved Dalmatian. Unlike humans, dogs don't indulge in sex with their minds; they simply use their penises. Had I asked him if he needed any advice, he would have said, 'Why take advice? Sex is an absolutely natural act and I've been ready for it ever since I was six months old.'

Humans have the odd habit of over-analysing the simplest of things in order to make them better and in the process complicate them. If you can't complicate it yourself, you tend to take the help of studies and surveys to understand what ails you or your sex lives. Some of the more enterprising ones might even take tips from bombastic friends or even pornographic sites.

Why? Because you are convinced that something is amiss and that requires to be corrected for you to be able to enjoy great sex.

Sex is such a dynamic force that it leaves you totally defenceless at its peak. As Paulo Coelho writes in *Brida*, 'Sex has a life of its own. The moment you begin, you are no longer in control; it takes control of you.' Though there is a give and take of pleasure, the woman is somehow able to control the man by letting her emotions seduce him, leaving him without any defence mechanism to set in motion to remain in control. The male resents losing even this momentary control, which occurs during sexual orgasm.

In cases of extreme give and take, where the male perceives that he has received more than he has given, he becomes overtly obliged and the woman takes complete control. This is akin to a situation in which you bungled in office and were caught by your boss but he magnanimously did not report you and save you from getting sacked.

What happens? You become so indebted to him that you accept every bidding of his as the last word. Using this analogy in marriage, consider a guy who has some sexual inadequacy, say premature ejaculation, which might be because he was anxious or nervous. After a couple of tries, he gets performance anxiety and this further shortens his release time. The woman generally realizes what his problem is. If she is mature and wants to correct the problem, she can relax him and put his fears to rest and he could improve with time. In a case of a genuine sexual dysfunctional disorder, she can suggest that he go to a sexologist to resolve the problem.

More often than not, none of these scenarios happens. The partners usually both keep mum and she becomes the proverbial statue of sacrifice that has put up with his inadequacy (give) and in return he hands over the reins of his life to her (take).

He becomes the slave of her sacrifice and she, either through ignorance or through design, stands on the altar of her sexual desire and reels in everything else. Some women are crafty enough to keep crying wolf long after the man has started performing normally. A woman may continue to pose as the wife who remains unfulfilled by her husband and bask in the warmth of sympathy and gratitude.

Something similar occurs in cases of male infidelity that is pardoned by the female. Here the male actually ends up 'giving' to two parties and perceives that he is 'receiving' from them, poor fellow.

Statistics Research Organization C-Fore conducted a survey in four metros—Delhi, Mumbai, Bangalore and Chandigarh. Here are the findings:

1. Does marriage naturally ensure sex with your partner?
   34%: Yes 54%: No 12%: Can't say
2. Would you allow your partner to force himself/herself on you?
   23%: Yes 67%: No 10%: Can't say
3. Would you adopt, if you were unable to have a child of your own?
   20%: Yes 64%: No 16%: Can't say
4. Do you keep your romantic details—past or present—from your spouse?
   62%: Yes 25%: No 13%: Can't say
5. Would you end the relationship if your partner socializes overwhelmingly with members of the other sex?
   54%: Yes 20%: No 26%: Can't say
6. Is it all right for a person to be sexually involved with more than one person at the same time?
   17%: Yes 73%: No 10%: Can't say

THE ADDITIONAL SLAP—OTHER MALES' REACTIONS

When you go out in the world and your conduct with your wife is one of extreme appeasement, other men will consider you to be suffering from some inadequacy that makes you give in completely to the female. Some men try to dominate a man dominated by his wife and may even try to flirt with his wife in the belief that she is not getting fully satisfied by the husband.

Improving your love life

The saying goes: 'Love may make the world go around, but it is the romance that makes the ride worthwhile.' To bring romance into your marriage, it is you, the male counterpart, who has to change.

Why? According to statistics, the Indian male is burdened by nonsensical notions and ignorance-induced guilt about sex and romance. Need proof?

- A Durex survey found that less than 5 per cent of Indian boys are taught even rudimentary sex education in schools/ colleges.
- Three out of ten males in India learn about sex from movies or pornography.
- The Indian male on the average loses his virginity at 20 years and 8 months vis-à-vis less than 16 years in the West.
- Ninety per cent males do not consider foreplay and afterplay to be essential for good sex, or even as a part of sexual process. For 90 per cent of females, it was just the reverse.

> 'He who knows how to make himself loved by women, as well as to enhance their honour and create confidence in them, becomes an object of their love. But he who neglects a girl, thinking she is too bashful, is despised by her as a beast ignorant of the working of the female mind'—Vatsyayana, *Kamasutra*, Chapter II

Sixty-eight per cent of people in the *Outlook* 'Moods' sex survey felt that sexual satisfaction was the most important factor for a happy marriage. Another 29 per cent ranked sex as the most important thing in their lives, even more important than family support or their own house.

How can you improve your love life?

For this you have to understand your partner's perspective on love and sex. This is not easy, especially in India, where it has been ingrained in the psyche of Indian women that it is not proper, decent or civilized to talk about or demand sex. You, the male, then has to:

1. **Open your ears:** Women know what they want but refrain from voicing it openly. You have to keep your antennae primed to pick up the signals like moaning or her verbal encouragements ('yes! yes!') to know where she needs to be stimulated. This knowledge will also improve your performance.

Men seem to be changing—at last.

No more just wham-bam-thank-you-ma'am—A survey of 1000 middle-aged men in the US, Spain, Japan and Germany revealed that 'closeness' and 'intimacy' are the most valuable things in the sex lives of men.

Congrats!

2. Open your mouth: To know her perspective, learn to communicate during sex. Wham-bam-thank-you-ma'am-type sex is very frustrating and brings a disconnect for females. When you whisper sweet nothings into her ear, it opens her up and she is able to communicate what she likes and what she doesn't. This also keeps her mind from wavering to other anxieties, which are likely to distract her from sex. A *Cosmo Durex* sex survey (September 2008) reveals that during the sex act, a good percentage wonder about things like 'Was it good for him? (28 per cent), 'Do I look fat? (6.9 per cent) or 'Does he have any new moves?' (24.8 per cent). It would really help your cause to voice your amorous feelings and fantasies. She may not oblige with all of them but she would love to hear what you want to do to her in the shower.
3. Open your mind: Remove age-old perceptions and worn-out beliefs about what she'd want and learn about her current preferences, which are bound to develop as she explores the physical side of love.

Horny woman: A poll conducted by *More* magazine revealed that young women (especially in the West) are becoming more promiscuous. The 2000 respondents revealed that by the age of 21 they had had sex with an average of nine lovers, as compared to seven lovers for men. The women were also twice as likely to be unfaithful as compared to the men, with more than 50 per cent admitting to have cheated.

4. Open your purse strings: As Vatsyayana says, 'Shower her with gifts . . . you should try in every way to make her look upon you as one who would do everything that she wants done.' Chivalry works as foreplay for women.
5. Open your knowledge gates—read up: Good sex is not in people's genes. To become a great lover, you need to observe, learn and read up about sex from experts on the subject, not roadside sex clinics with half-baked quacks doling out advice and adding to the confusion.
6. Keep your eyes open a wee bit longer after an orgasm: Most women hate it when you turn away after sex. Spend a few minutes talking warmly or at least listening to her. Remember, before and after are equally important for her.
7. Open your attitude: Love is not the same as sex. She might not climax as obviously and as frequently as you do, but she still needs to be in tune with you to be able to love you, physically and otherwise. Nothing fine tunes a woman's coordination with you better than romance. Buying a card, flowers or chocolates for her, or taking her out on a romantic dinner will add a zing to your love life.

Before and after:
A survey of 5000 Japanese women reveals that 50 per cent of women want longer intimate interaction (like cuddling and hugging) after sex, whereas 44 per cent ranked foreplay as the most important aspect of getting intimate. In a nutshell, foreplay and afterplay are the ways to satisfy your woman.

Sex on our minds—Difference in perceptions:

- The average male thinks of sex once every one minute
- The average female thinks of sex once every one to two days

8. Open your bedroom to let in some fun: Monotony is the bane of sex after marriage, more so for the female. An *India Today*–AC Nielsen-ORG MARG sex survey (7 December 2009) states, 'Urban Indians are cautious tourists in the new world of sexual fantasy.' Women are now becoming more aware and demanding. To make sex invigorating, keep your mind open to creativity and variety. This can be in forms like strip rummy, bathing together, reading erotic literature like the *Kama Sutra* together. Even some fantasy-related roleplay, for example, playing a masseur or a doctor and exploring her body can be great, but don't get too kinky. Different positions during sex, new toys, different settings and, above all, getting her away from all the routine of the household work for a few days work like magic. I can say this from personal experience.

IN A NUTSHELL

Men have a tendency to hang their self-esteem by their penises. If she refuses to have sex with you, she is not rejecting you as an individual. She may just not be in the mood or she may be tired. Remember, it is not the amount or quality of sex that will make or break a marriage—it is your understanding of each other's needs and capabilities and your thoughtfulness that will determine your marital bliss.

So what do wives really want?

19

What Wives Really Want and Need—Seeing from Her Perspective

> A genie popped out of a bottle and granted a young man one wish.
>
> The lad, who was scared of flying, asked for a bridge to LA.
>
> Shocked, the genie said, 'Are you all right? Can you imagine the effort and materials required?'
>
> 'Okay, then just tell me—what do women really want?'
>
> The genie sighed, 'Okay—you want a two- or four-lane bridge?'

Pammi sat down with a sigh. 'I don't understand my husband. I cannot understand whether he is innocent or too smart to be caught in his adultery. I have been giving him the benefit of the doubt because my detective came up with nothing against him, but then he does something that sets my antennae at high alert.'

'What did he do?' Savvy was, as usual, wide-eyed with anticipation of some spicy gossip.

'Well, nothing conclusive, but he did some things which made me suspicious. But when I confronted him, he defended himself so staunchly that I became all the more suspicious. His mother must have overheard our heated exchange and the next morning she took up the defence of her son, which made me even more sure that there was definitely something wrong. The weirdest thing was that he had proof regarding his innocence. Can you imagine? Foolproof evidence that he was not in the city when she was there. Who keeps the bills of tea or cold drinks they've had at a restaurant? Not only that, he also had a bill to prove his ex-girlfriend was in another city on that day. When I saw all this evidence, my sixth sense told me that there had to be something amiss.'

Savvy was beside herself with excitement. This was a combination of the saas-bahu and *Crime Patrol* serials—thrill and sex together.

Sally, on the other hand, was shaking her head in dismay. 'I don't understand you, Pammi. If he has no evidence of his innocence, you perceive him as guilty. If he has evidence, you still perceive him as guilty. It is as if you've already judged him irrespective of what he does. People say that men don't understand women, but I don't get you either.'

'That's because you have not seen his body language. It reeks of guilt. The very fact that my husband doesn't understand me at all indicates that his attention is somewhere else. I am all frustrated from the monotony of sitting at home.'

Savvy pitched in for her. 'Pammi is right. Even my husband doesn't understand me at all. I also believe that it might be because of another woman. Even that landlord understands me better. He told me that he'll leave his house to me in his will as he has no other relatives. Maybe then Rehaan and I can have a future together here. The only problem is that though he keeps saying he is suffering from so many ailments, his performance in bed doesn't indicate that he is going to leave us any time soon—the wretch!'

She took a bite of her dosa and continued. 'Still, on days when Rehaan is not here, he at least provides some respite from my monotonous household chores.'

Sally's expression indicated that she was preoccupied with her own thoughts. When specifically asked by Pammi, she thought for a few moments and reluctantly decided to get it off her chest.

'Last fortnight has been very stressful, not only for me but for the whole family,' she started. Pausing to gather her thoughts, she continued. 'There has been a big complication in my husband's life. He's been accused of molesting a female colleague in the office.'

'You always said that he is a very decent person,' Pammi's said with I-told-you-so overtones. 'Jassi maintains that inside all decent males are equally . . .'

'No, no!' Sally cut Pammi short. 'I said he has been accused, not that he did anything like that; that lady is lying.'

'How do you know that she is lying?'

'I know my husband and I know the woman—she and my husband are competing for the same promotion. This is her way of pushing him out of the competition. And the kind of acts she has accused him of and shown as evidence are just too bizarre for my husband to even contemplate. He hates things like using his tongue sexually or even the slightest hint of bestiality. Just imagine what she accuses him of : squeezing her breast to cause welts, biting her ear, pinching her bottom so hard that there are bruises and biting her lips and that, too . . .' She sighed '. . . and that, too, on a day when it was impossible.'

'Why?'

'You see. . . my husband becomes totally refractory for at least two days after we have had a busy night. . . you know what I mean. How can he possibly eat, when his stomach is full to the brim? That day was definitely one such day.'

'You can never be sure with these men.' Pammi voiced her opinion but an angry stare told her that she was treading dangerous ground, so she kept quiet.

'I'm 100 per cent sure about my husband. I know he is an honest, upright and fair man. This is a trap and I'm sure he will come out of it unscathed.'

'However, this kind of a thing does cause suspicion and weaken the marital bond.' This was the most Pammi could muster against Sally's unflinching faith.

'Not our bond,' said Sally dismissively. 'It has actually got stronger because of this controversy. I believe marriages become stronger when they are put through challenges.'

Shravan sat bewildered. He was at an utter loss to understand these women. One was suspicious without an iota of proof and the other was disregarding concrete proof and standing by her husband. 'What do these women really think?' he thought. 'Is Maya like Sally or Pammi?'

A small voice answered, 'Sally!'

But the voice didn't seem too sure, maybe because Maya had been overtly critical of him and always praised her parents.

~

Joginder, too, was flummoxed by the women's behaviour, but he had the great consolation that his wife always supported him, irrespective of the issue. She is perfect, he thought. But would she support me, if I were charged with sexual molestation?

Something told him that she would. Though you can never be sure with women, he then thought cautiously.

~

Daiv smiled wryly. 'Had I understood women as well as I do today, I would still have been happily married.' He started writing:

'What makes a wife happy . . .'

~

PERFECT HUSBAND?

Not a single one of the 2700 women surveyed by the British company Remington, in December 2011, thought there was such a thing as the 'perfect man'. No wonder the number of single women in Britain has more than doubled over the past thirty years. On the one hand it shows that women now expect more, pushing American writer Lori Gottlieb to write *Marry Him—The Case for Settling for Mr Good Enough*. On the other hand, it also shows that maybe men are unable to understand what a modern woman really wants from them.

The biggest bane of marriage is one or both partners' insistence pursuing self-oriented agendas, as if they are refusing to be part of a whole. It is always about me-my-mine, rather than we-us-ours. This invariably leads to a power struggle and unhealthy competition. The only way around is to understand the perspective of your partner and by finding out what she wants.

After marriage, a joint space of 'we and ours' has to be created, carved out of each partner's personal space—a part of his 'me and mine' plus a part of her 'me and mine'. Whether you use 'give and take' as a tool to create this space or resort to 'snatch and chop' will determine the harmoniousness of your marriage.

A HAPPY WIFE→A HAPPIER HOME

When I said, 'A happy wife means a happy home,' Pramod cut me short.

'Who doesn't know this? What we don't know is how to keep the wife happy. I just can't figure why she is always unhappy. After all, I'm a good husband who takes care of all her needs and never prevents her from doing anything she wishes, despite being the sole earner. I also juggle my stressful private bank job with shopping for household goods and teaching my daughter. And who shows her frustration on a daily basis—my wife.'

'Which is the most loathsome task in your bank?' I asked him.

'Counting the notes and making wads of the day's collection in the afternoon. It is so bloody monotonous that nobody wants to do it two days in a row.'

'What will happen if you have to do this day in and out for years together?'

'I'll go bonkers.'

'Exactly! That is what your wife is going through. A lot of work but most of it is excruciatingly monotonous. Not a ray of excitement filters through the entire day to up her spirits. Add to this the fact that your wife has never really enjoyed cooking or home decorating and it is obvious that she is doing a task that she detests. Won't she be frustrated?'

~

The malady of spending the day carrying out non-exciting chores is so widely prevalent that I would hazard a statistic of 80 per cent in young non-working wives and up to 40 per cent in working ones. The younger the woman, the more profound are her frustrations. For those who have worked outside the home for an appreciable period of time, it may still

THE RIVER OF MARRIAGE

Marriage is akin to a river with distinct phases:

- Its 'conception' is the thaw of ice that the opposite sexes feel towards one another in the beginning
- In the 'premarital' phase, it begins its journey, with the pulsation and excitement of a mountain rivulet
- In the honeymoon phase, the sheer pace and turbulence takes it down a slope, overlooking the boulders in its path
- In the 'consolidation phase', just as the river reaches the plains, the journey becomes placid. But it is here that it is most likely to run through its embankment and cause floods, if the embankments are not strong enough or if more water than it can manage is poured into it
- Last, it enters the 'compromise phase', where like a river approaching a delta, the marriage becomes slow and steady. But, like the river, it runs the risk of becoming stagnant. It requires a channel to be able to complete its journey

be acceptable to settle down as a housewife but for a lady who has never seen the life of working outside, the tedium of her unglamorous work gets compounded by wishful thinking—perhaps of her coveting that glamorous job that her neighbour is doing as a receptionist.

This frustration typically sets in for the wife as the children start going off to school. Till then, there was an urgency and excitement about a new person in her life, a new home and later, of events like the honeymoon, pregnancy or the arrival of a newborn baby. When the novelty wears out, the wife stares in the face of the stark reality of the situation that this is now her fait accompli.

Let us take Pramod's wife's case:

- She joined university in 1998: excitement +++→
- Graduated in 2001: excitement +++→
- Got a receptionist's job in 2002: excitement +++→
- Courtship in 2002–03: excitement ++++→
- Marriage in 2003 end: excitement ++++→
- Honeymoon in 2004: excitement +++++→
- A newborn arrives in 2005: Cumbersome but exciting ++→
- Child grows up in 2006 + husband busy in office—very busy life + excitement +→
- Child goes to school in 2008 + husband very busy—Monotonous household chores—excitement 000→
- Child goes to school in 2009 + husband very busy→ excitement 000→
- Child goes to school in 2010 + husband very busy→ excitement 000→

- Child goes to school in 2011 + husband very busy→ excitement 000→
- →excitement 000→
- →excitement 000→
- →What year is it?

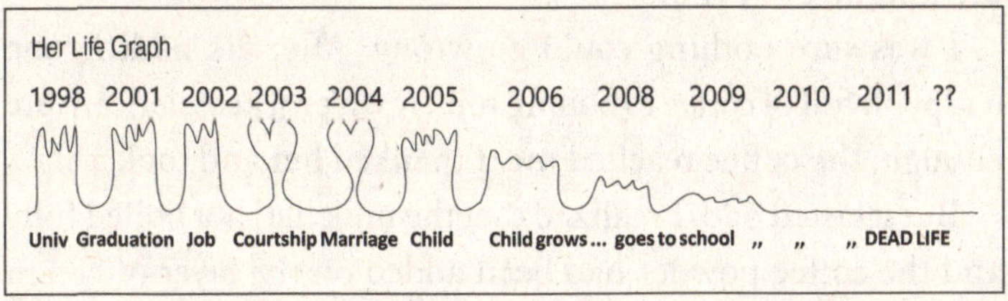

~

Priorities of the spouse—Coffee versus shade of lipstick

One day, I was surprised to find my uncle, an army officer, making his own tea in the morning, while his doting wife was already up and working in the kitchen with the cook. When I asked about why he was making his own tea, he told me, 'You know, Sunil, your aunty has never been able to make tea to my liking. Every time she makes it, I end up feeling irritated.' I was surprised, for not only was Aunty a good cook but because they had been married for forty-five years.

> The most terrifying thing a wife can say to a husband: 'Notice anything different?'

How is it possible that a person can't learn as simple a thing as making tea according to another's taste in such a long time? I realized it was possible when one day I told my wife of twenty years to give me my morning cup of coffee for which I'd mixed in the correct amount of milk and sugar and left in the microwave to boil.

I was sure nothing could go wrong. After all, adding one teaspoon full of coffee to boiling milk wasn't rocket science. Sure enough, the coffee reached me. I thanked her and took a sip.

But it tasted odd. I realized that the milk had not boiled fully and the coffee powder had been added on the layer of cream

DO YOU KNOW WHAT SHE WANTS?

A South Korean wedding agency conducted a survey regarding what women wanted or expected when the man proposed. They found three vital points:

1. The men presume that women simply wanted sweet words or love songs while most women preferred diamond rings.
2. The men believed taking the woman to his favourite neighbourhood joint would be ideal to propose, but the women felt this showed his stinginess and she would probably even feel insulted.
3. The men believed that she would love a public announcement of the proposal or a glitzy display on stage while the women felt that such displays were crass and not romantic at all.

and allowed to stay there. Because it wasn't immediately stirred, the coffee was now lumpy.

When I pointed this out to my wife, she said, 'Oh God, what difference does it make—warm or hot, less or more coffee. It is after all just coffee.' This, coming from a lady who a day before had tested twenty-five shades of mauve lipstick (all of which looked the same to me) was galling to me. I also realized how idiotic I must have seemed to her when I had said, 'This mauve or that mauve—what is the difference?'

All of us want beautiful relationships. Are we ready to invest the thought, time, effort and sincere emotions required to understand our partner?

Only this would decide how good a marriage partner one is.

~

Changing focus and perspective

The woman of yesterday was single-mindedly focused on trying to adjust to new circumstances or at least, making sure that the husband was content.

The man of yesterday was focused on providing for the family and being the head of the family or at least, giving the semblance of dominance.

Today the focus has changed.

The woman of today is now clear that in marriage she wants freedom, financial independence, no interference from relatives and not being tied to household chores.

Today's man, on the other hand, carries the baggage of the

Why women never have time for you—because they spend a huge part of their lives:

■ Dieting	10 years
■ Shopping	9 years
■ On the phone	4 years
■ Preening before going out	3 years
■ Wearing make-up	2 years
■ Styling hair	2.5 years
■ Planning the next meal	2 years
■ Using the washroom	1.5 years
■ Deciding what to wear	1 year
■ Removing unwanted hair	58 days

This is besides essentials like sleeping and eating.

Why you don't have time for her?

Shopping website Kelkoo conducted a study on 1000 men and found that on an average a British man spends in a lifetime:

- Eleven years in front of the TV
- 10,585 hours in the pub
- One month finding socks
- Four months learning to cook four meals

And maybe to assuage his guilt, he says 'sorry' 1.9 million times.

past that tells him that he should be dominant and the provider in the family while his rational side implores him to be more flexible to keep pace with changing mindsets. Just as women have taken over partial responsibility as providers, men too, should take on the responsibility of running the household. Sexual equality is not only looming large, it is being splashed onto his face and forced down his throat by the strident stance of his female partner.

This discord is making the metrosexual male insecure and tense. The changes are being thrust upon him by a changing system and he resents them. Hence the power struggle.

~

Life's motto: husband versus wife

A male who thinks he is smart says to his would-be wife:

- What I think, I don't say.
- What I say, I don't do.
- And what I do, nobody can fathom.
- So have faith in my rationality and, without criticism, go along with my well-laid-out plans.

Then after marriage the husband realizes that his wife was thinking something else:

- What I think, I am unable to say.
- What I say, I am unable to do.
- And what I'll do, even I don't know.

Neuro-psychiatrist Louann Brizedine in *The Female Brain* maps the brain circuitry and hormones of a female. She writes that being a woman is like having giant antennae that are beholden to the emotions of others. She shows how the female brain is different from the male brain:

- She has 11 per cent more neurons in her brain centres for language and hearing. Result: She uses on an average 20,000 words a days as compared to 7000 by a male.
- Her brain is 9 per cent smaller than the male's but the hippocampus, which is the hub for emotions, is larger than the male's.
- Sex-wise, the space devoted to the sex drive is two-and-a-half times smaller than the male's. Result: She will think about sex about once a day, compared to the male, who thinks about sex every 58 seconds.

- So accept me as such and do as I tell you to, rationality be damned.

~

What does a wife really want and need?

This is a million-dollar question that many sages, philosophers and even a few genies have failed to answer with any real conviction. Let us take the help of scientific data and research to answer this eternal question.

The broad guidelines were provided by economist Allen Parkman, PhD, of the University of New Mexico. He said that until recently, women were more likely to initiate divorce proceedings for reasons linked to severe faults of husbands, like cruelty or infidelity. But now, a lack of qualities like understanding, communication, empathy and affection are the more likely relation breakers. Based on data from 340 divorced adults, Parkman found that 59 per cent of ex-wives said that it was they who wanted to end their marriages, compared to 28 per cent cases, where the ex-husbands wanted out. When the husband switches the wife off and the TV on before the day is over, it leaves no doubt in the mind of the female where his priorities lie.

As sexologist Dr Mahinder C. Watsa, says, 'A successful marriage is based on 4 Ts: trust, time spent together, touch and talk. Any impediment in these can lead to conflict.'

Having stated the crux, let us see the specifics that make women happy:

1. According to a study compiled by wedding-planning website, www.confetti.co.uk and reported in the *Daily Telegraph*, the secret to a happy marriage has very simple elements:
   - Four hugs a day. Another study has pointed out that a woman's happy hormone, oxytocin, starts flowing in just twenty seconds of hugging
   - Seven evenings spent together every month
   - Two romantic walks in a month
   - At least one visit to a pub or theatre (without children)
   - Sex three times a week

WHAT WOMEN LIKE:

A study in *Behavioural Ecology* asked men and women to rate pictures of men from their countries. Women showed a preference for clean-shaven men. Bearded men were considered meaner, older and more aggressive by the women. As a consolation, bearded men were considered of higher social status and commanded more respect, especially from other males.

Take your pick.

- Two shared hobbies
- Three cuddles a day
- Saying 'I love you' at least once a day
- Two romantic meals a month

2. Great sex keeps women healthy and happy: Author Sonia Davison of Monash University found that 'women who were sexually dissatisfied had lower well-being and lower vitality,' as reported by the *Daily Telegraph*. They also found that when it came to sex, it is the quality that matters and sex is linked to good health and positive well-being.
3. A good night's sleep for the wife is a must for a blissful marriage: A study, presented at professional sleep societies at Minneapolis, found that sleep-deprived wives, especially those who had difficulty falling asleep, tended to be more cranky and irritable and their marital interactions were more negative the following day. Researchers studied sleep

patterns of thirty-five couples and found that while a male's deprivation barely impacted marital relationships, the wife's impacted the relationship rather acutely.

The way you sleep as a couple says something about you.Another study by Faraway Thomas, author of *The Secret Language of Sleep*, showed that how you sleep says a lot about your prevailing relationship. He noted that there were thirty-nine distinct sleeping postures depicting emotions ranging from complete intimacy and total reliability to complete estrangement and resentment. Naturally, how you sleep would point towards the future of your relationship.

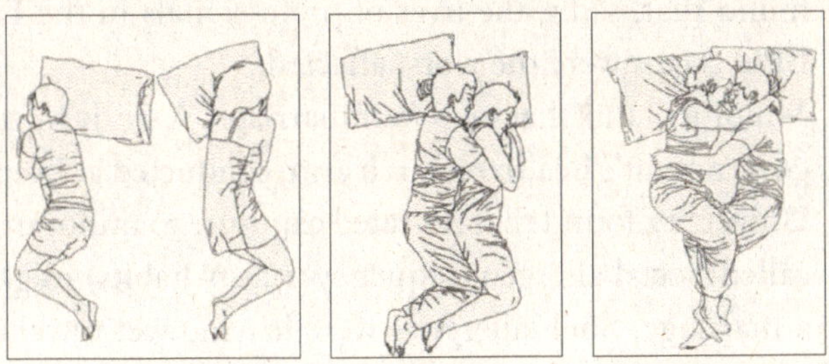

Cliffhanger　Classic spoons　Patient–doctor

4. A senior in her life: From my personal experience I can say that women look for father figures in their lives. This is especially true of women who were close to their dads. It is no wonder that many women address their husbands

as 'Papa' or 'Daddy' and some conservative ones as 'Pappu's father' (where Pappu is her kid). Research shows that women look for a senior who can take over some responsibility in their relationship. In cases where they consider the husbands to be immature or incapable of taking over responsibility, they grudgingly take over that role but then they don't respect or look up to their husbands. If such a husband insists on dominating the wife, there will be a power struggle.

5. Work–life balance: Long hours in the boardroom wreak havoc in the bedroom. The *Week* C-Voter survey on a person's profession's impact on personal life showed that over two-thirds of the 1071 respondents admitted that personal relations are ignored due to work pressure. It also found that, sadly, the lives of professionals in the IT and BPO sector were the worst affected.
6. Minor irritants that mar your marriage: A study by the US government's health research arm, conducted at Louisville University, found that repeated exposure to minor irritants called 'social allergen frequency' (nasty habits) might end a marriage. Such allergens were leaving wet towels lying around, leaving a new toilet roll on an empty one, using a fork as a back-scratcher, nose picking, burping, etc.

   Another survey by the British company Remington came up with top peeves for women:
   - Not getting along with her family
   - Using her toothbrush
   - Leaving the toilet dirty

- Hating her friends
- Not being good with children
- Being lazy
- Having a big bushy beard
- Leaving nail clippings around
- Driving like a boy racer
- Being grumpy
- Watching too much sports on TV

LAST—THE PROBLEM OF OVERFAMILIARITY

After you have learnt about what makes your wife happy, you still are left with one major wall to climb—overfamiliarity. There is a saying in Hindi—'Chandanpur ki Bheelni chandan det jarai', literally, the tribal woman of the sandalwood forests burns sandalwood in her hearth at home. Or familiarity breeds contempt. You forget to extend even the minimal courtesies, chivalry and protocol to your wife that you would normally

WOULD YOU MARRY YOUR SPOUSE AGAIN?

- Fifty-eight per cent of respondents in fifteen countries would again say, 'I do' to their spouses.
- In India, 68 per cent said they would, whereas in China 83 per cent would marry the same person again. Italy topped in dissatisfaction, with 42 per cent not wanting to remarry their present spouses.

RELATIONSHIP QUOTIENT (RQ):

RQ comprises an ability, capacity or skill to perceive, assess and manage one's relationships. It is closely linked to Emotional Quotient (EQ), which has five components:

- Self-awareness—knowing your emotions
- Managing your emotions
- Motivating yourselves
- Empathy—recognizing others' emotions
- Handling relationships

The biggest factor that undermines RQ is taking the partner for granted.

extend even to complete strangers who have no bearing on your life. With the passage of time, this turns into indifference and then into apathy, which is a major grouse of females.

If you know what she wants, go ahead and do it—you might be among the lucky few considered to be Mr Right by the wife and then you will be able to stand together as a unit against the world . . .

IN A NUTSHELL

Advice for the newlywed husband: Try to be that father figure by carrying the mantle of decision-making maturely on your own shoulders. If you succeed in this, and your wife accepts your position as the father figure, your marriage will be stable over the long run. This maturity should also ensure that you avoid the nasty habits she abhors.

20

Fight the World Together—Marry Early

Man: 'My wife's fighting is becoming ridiculous.'

Friend: 'Why do you say that?'

Man: 'The other day she looked at my calendar and said that I was having an affair with "May".'

Savvy entered wearing oversized black goggles. As she took off her glasses to get adjusted to the dim light inside, a large bruise became visible, along with a swollen eye.

Pammi raised an eyebrow, 'What happened?'

'This is the sign of my first open fight with my husband. He had come late and was reeking of cheap scent. So I confronted him and bluntly asked him if he had gone to a prostitute. He got infuriated, more so because his brothers were present there. He slapped me and his heavy wristwatch hit my eye.'

'Bloody brute!' Pammi almost shouted. 'How dare he? You should report this to the police and let him face the consequences.'

'It was my fault. I should not have accused him thus, without any proof and that, too, in front of his brothers. I just got carried away.'

Sally, though mum, was shaking her head with disapproval. She knew that the seed of this suspicion had been taken from Pammi's baseless suspicions. Pammi, however, nodded at Savvy's story. 'I, too, got carried away and had a big tiff with my hubby yesterday. Only the mark of confrontation is on his face, not mine.'

'You hit him?' Savvy's shocked voice masked an echo of jubilation.

'Well, almost, but then he wanted me to become a hypocrite, to say something and do something else.'

'What did he want?' enquired Sally in a soft tone.

'He wanted me to take part in the family ritual of bringing home the Granth Sahib and doing jagrata, that is sitting down and reciting the pages for the whole night. I refused point blank. I told him not to ask me to do something in which I have no faith. Yes, I am a Sikh, and I do go to the gurudwara, but I don't believe in mindlessly reciting pages that I don't even understand. He wanted me to sit down with the others and recite the verses just to make his parents happy. I told him that I wouldn't do anything just to please others. This led to a serious argument and a tiff. He said I was insensitive to others' sentiments. I said so be it and anybody who doesn't agree with me can go to hell for all I care.'

'So you hit him?' Savvy realized that the juicy part was still missing.

'I didn't really hit him. I threw a book at him in a fit of rage.'

'That caused the bruise?' This was not as exciting as Savvy had hoped for.

'Actually, he ducked the book but in the process banged his temple against the showcase, resulting in a big swelling on the right side of his forehead.'

Savvy's flustered 'Oh!' indicated her disappointment at the anti-climax. Despite herself, Sally couldn't stop herself from smiling at Savvy's disappointment.

Pammi then turned to Sally and asked, 'What happened in that case of molestation against your husband?'

Savvy's rapid nodding indicated her eagerness to know the lurid details.

'It is still going on . . . but as I told you, my husband is innocent. So . . .' her voice trailed off, indicating her fatigue over this issue.

'One thing I must say—under similar circumstances I would have made my hubby's life hell, with much less proof,' ventured Pammi. 'I don't understand how you are so sure that your husband is innocent in the face of such overwhelming evidence.'

'There are many things. Apart from the fact that such sexual bestiality is totally against his overall personality, you know what he did on that night? He came straight to me and told me that she had tried to seduce him and divulged everything, much before the accusations were levelled against him. At that time, he was contemplating complaining against her and the thought had never occurred to him that she would become the accuser. Moreover, if he was so savage, shouldn't there have been some marks of retaliation on his body or face? The lady is a long-distance runner. She could break his arm if she were accosted. Last and most important, a couple of maintenance staff saw my husband leave in a huff and also heard that lady call him back to his office. Now, why would a woman being molested call back her molester? It all just doesn't add up.'

'How did your husband take it?'

'There was a lot of turmoil to begin with. He was shattered. When both his senior manager and the CEO of the company sided with the lady without hearing his version, he decided to quit his job in disgust. He was even told by the manager to either quit his job or face legal charges. He was so shaken that he pleaded with everyone he met, including me, to believe him. I told him to snap out of it because I believed him totally. He should roar like the wronged one and take the battle to the court.' Sally was uncharacteristically loud, maybe because she was giving vent to anguish embedded deep in her chest.

'Then?' asked Savvy, as if seeing a reality show serial.

'He got the point and threw in the gauntlet to defend himself. The manager issued him a show cause notice and de facto suspended him. I took in more work so that he could fight unfettered by family and financial pressures.' Sally took a sip from her coffee that was getting cold.

'Then?' This time Pammi asked. Her furrowed forehead indicated how seriously she was following it. Something was stirring inside her, telling her about a new type of relationship between husband and wife, which was diametrically opposite to what Libber Cats had taught her. Can such a relationship exist for real? she thought.

'Then we went to the homes of all the witnesses to request each of them to give their statements. One of the maintenance staff told us about one of the manager's ex-secretaries, who was wrongly sacked by him. I went to her house alone and what she told me changed the whole scenario. She told me that this accusing lady had had a relation with this manager and she herself was sacked because she had caught them in a compromising position. Now the manager was getting promoted and the only way they could remain in touch, was if that lady superseded my husband and became second to the manager. Thus, on the manager's advice, she had staged this drama.'

'Oh my God!' exclaimed Pammi. Even as Savvy sat unblinking, trying to recollect which serial had a twist like this. 'What happened then?' asked Pammi.

'Armed with the evidence, we approached the CEO. There was a protracted and exhausting battle but ultimately, the big boss understood our point and we were vindicated. Just yesterday, a colleague called up and told us that the orders were being prepared to sack the manager, who in any case has not been coming to office ever since, and reinstate both my husband and that sacked ex-secretary of the manager.' A contented smile spread over Sally's weary face.

'Wow! What happened to that lady?'

'She has gone back to her hometown. The real good news for my husband is that he will be promoted as the senior manager, a two-step jump.'

Pammi and Savvy congratulated Sally. She smiled and added, 'For me, the real good thing is the new equation in which my husband envisions me as an equal and able partner. Even my mother-in-law's attitude has undergone a sea change. This is real happiness.'

~

'Sir, her coffee has gone cold. Should I heat it?' asked the waiter.

'No, no. Heating the coffee spoils it. Give her a fresh one, from my side.' This was the first time Joginder had gone against the business tenets taught by his dad of never giving anything complimentary.

He had also decided to go against another of his dad's tenets—'Never share your financial details and bank account with your wife.'

~

Shravan was still looking at Sally with awe, when another question raised its head to spoil the moment. 'Will Maya support me through thick and thin? She might, if . . .'

He had seen that Maya had very firm beliefs about everything. If she felt an issue was wrong, no amount of cajoling, arguing or wisdom would be able to change her stance.

Would she consider him innocent and support him wholeheartedly, like Sally had supported her hubby? The problem was that an unequivocal 'yes' was not forthcoming.

~

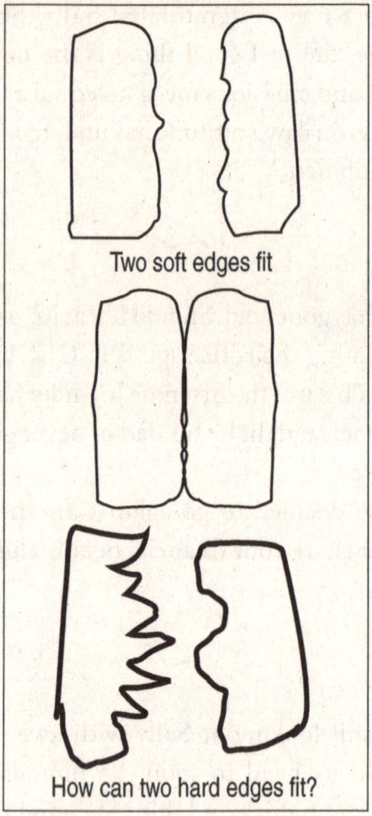

Daiv tried to write but realized that his vision was blurred because of a thin mist forming in his eyes, in appreciation of the lady's belief in her husband. He wiped his eyes and scribbled: 'Fighting the world together versus fighting with each other . . .'

~

MARRY EARLY—FIGHT THE WORLD TOGETHER

'This will go against the advice of the government, which espouses that people marry as late as possible so that they have fewer children. I believe that the whole concept of settling down before getting married is lopsided. This concept is taking hold in metros. Youngsters want to enjoy their freedom for longer periods and want to settle down financially before they tie the knot and parents agree to this as it suits them too.

'This has two fall-outs. First, marrying late means the partners already have firm ideas of what people want from life and how exactly they want to live. Hardened attitudes hurt—a square peg cannot be fitted in a circular hole. Second, as one becomes financially sound, there is less struggle for existence. You might ask how this affects marriage. The strongest bonds form when you fight together as a team, as in fighting to set up a business; fighting financial constraints when one partner's salary goes out to cover the mortgage of the house; fighting a legal battle; fighting a social stigma like intercaste marriage; or even fighting together for a social cause like alleviation of illiteracy or rural upliftment.

'These struggles make the bond between the couple super-strong in the post-honeymoon phase of life, when unbonding can take place after discovering negative traits which so far may have been hidden. From personal experience, I can tell you that when, after two years of my marriage, we got embroiled in struggles both within the family and on the business front, it then seemed like a mountain of trouble and resulted in a lot of strain at the time, but a positive outcome was the renewed bonds our strife created. Despite being from vastly different backgrounds and monetary statuses and having dramatically opposite tastes and mindsets, we gelled so well as a couple that people sometimes felt envious. My uncle said then, "You are blessed to be fighting the whole wide world . . . together. Nothing bonds a couple as this kind of struggle does."

'In fact, our frictions came to the fore much later, after some twenty-five years of marriage, when we hung our boots from the hectic business and thus stopped fighting the world together. Then, for the first time in our lives, we started fighting with each other and we separated.

'So, if God has been kind enough not to have given you turmoil of your own, it is not a bad idea to find a common cause to fight for—any cause, even a social cause in your spare time will do the trick of strengthening your bond.'

~

Working together

In today's world, the best examples of fighting the world together come from couples who are either working together in the same office or doing business as partners.

Advantages: Couples who work together stay together. Many professionals choose to work for the same employer.

Let us enumerate the things that make such a relationship work:

- More quality time spent together, such as commuting together

- Sharing more private moments, like eating lunch together
- Both partners understand the demands of the job better, and this reduces the possibility of misunderstanding. This holds especially true for professions such as those in the medical field or BPO executives, where heavy demands on the time of the employee can be misunderstood by a non-working spouse. It reduces the chances of infidelity creeping into their lives.

The flip side of working together is that on a long-term basis, these arrangements might show fissures that are invisible in the beginning. The commonest problems are:

- Both partners might start competing with each other. In cases where promotions are being gauged vis-à-vis their partner's performance, it can spell disaster.
- Too much proximity might lower the overall respect that the partner deserves, especially if either is senior. So be careful—your spouse should be treated with the same regard and courtesy that another colleague would be accorded.
- You might get too personal in the office. Don't spill your family quarrels into the boardroom and vice versa.
- You might take your office worries home.
- A small concern can be that if one partner has to take a decision regarding the career of the other, he/she might not be entirely objective. But that is a small undetectable blip.

If the couple keep the competition among themselves out of the workplace, the benefits outstrip the negatives.

Fight between partners

What happens when the couples are not fighting the world together? They simply tend to fight between themselves, especially during the post-honeymoon phase. This in itself is not that bad a thing if done properly.

But can't life be perfect without any fights? No!

- Spring doesn't last twelve months
- Sunshine doesn't last twenty-four hours
- An erection doesn't last two hours

Accordingly, your harmony can't last forever. Fighting is a way of manifesting your thoughts and understanding your partner's sentiments. Without fights, you would remain strangers all your life. The only care you have to take is not to make these fights pathological. There are certain don'ts:

- Don't drag hurtful issues of the past, to settle the score
- Don't be vindictive
- Don't deliberately attack your partner's sensitive spots
- Don't be mean. The memory of it is long and bitter
- Don't bring in a foreign hand. Your interactions have to be a mutual business, with no third-party mediation. This is so because, first, finding a truly impartial judge is very difficult. Second, exposing your inner feeling to another person, however close, always leads to ego hassles that make apologizing and reconciliation that much more difficult
- Don't leave issues unresolved

This last point is particularly important. The strength of a marriage does not lie in how many conflicts you have or how much you fight but in how well and how completely you resolve the issue that led to a fight. Leaving nothing smouldering under the heap is what you should look for.

~

Fight till the end—resolve issues fully

Fighting is the spice of life. Just don't add too many red chillies, which will burn up the relationship.

Why do couples fight? An online, 'Can't buy me love' survey revealed the top five causes of arguments and discord as:

1. Money: 31 per cent
2. Household chores: 28 per cent
3. Problematic in-laws: 25 per cent
4. Children-related: 22 per cent
5. Sex-related: 18 per cent

Spurred by the fact that every third Australian marriage ends in divorce, Richard Ronay, University of Queensland, Australia, researched why lovers fight. Putting conflicts and their causes under a scanner for couples who have been together for more than one year, the study focused on lovers' reactions like:

- Door slamming
- Fiery verbal exchanges
- Cold shouldering

FIGHTS REVEAL A COUPLE'S CHANCES OF STAYING TOGETHER

R. Keith Sanford, Baylor University, studied dozens of fighting couples and concluded that:

- Couples used positive or negative communication during arguments and this determined whether they would stay together or break up.
- There are two types of negative emotions—hard and soft.
- Hard emotions were associated with asserting power and always escalated fights towards a break up.
- Soft emotions were associated with expressing vulnerability and were beneficial for long-term relationships as they increased a couple's chances to resolve a conflict. The more the couple fought this way, the stronger their relationship emerged.

The conclusion was that an improper resolution of conflict always escalated the conflict to the next level.

WHY ISSUES ARE NOT RESOLVED FULLY

In rural or where people are illiterate settings today, as in the past, male dominance is absolute with the husband accepting no dissent from the wife. This unjust and demanding behaviour suppresses any conflict that the wife feels. Because of this suppression, issues fester and lead to stress in the relationship and an unhappy marriage.

In modern-day urban settings, the reverse is true, with even worse results. The husband tries to somehow postpone confrontation by giving in to the wife's unjust call. He gives in to her, whether it is a matter regarding their respective relatives, of who should be their friends, where to go on vacation, or even what level of cleanliness or organization is desirable in the house. The husband does this to avoid confrontation, to avoid settling issues in front of others, or maybe because he is simply fed up of constant arguments. He believes he has overcome the problem by avoiding the fight and the existing conflict would resolve automatically.

I have seen that the worst problems occur in marriages where one partner, usually the male, tries too hard to avoid confrontation. This abject surrender forges a feeling in the mind, usually of the woman, that she was right all along and was justified in starting the fight. What this temporary truce does is that it actually escalates the confrontation, if

In medicine, Q waves in an ECG indicate serious trouble, i.e. myocardial infarction or a heart attack

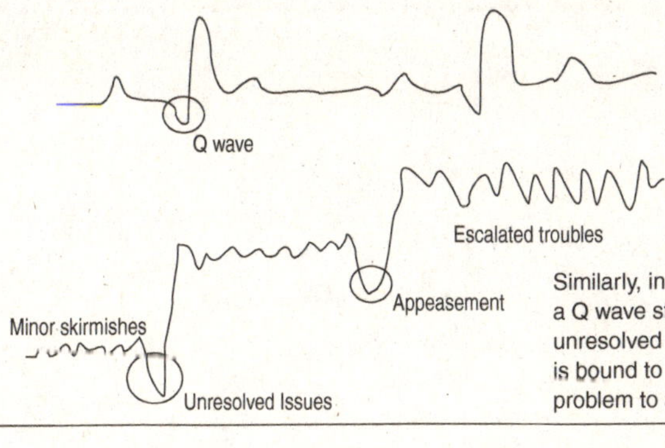

Similarly, in relationships, a Q wave stands for unresolved conflict, which is bound to escalate the problem to a new level

some time later, to a higher level. It should not be difficult to visualize where this postponing and subsequent escalation of confrontation will lead→breaking of the male or breaking of the marriage. That is why I call these unresolved issues, and appeasements to scuttle the issue, Q waves (Q waves in medicine denote heart attacks).

IN A NUTSHELL

Resolve the issues completely, irrespective of how prolonged the conflict or arguments are. If the confrontation is getting too heated, you may allow a cooling-off period, but sit down again at a mutually agreeable time to discuss, and fight if you have to, this very issue to its logical end.

When you fight, remember two things:

1. Keep communication channels open.
2. Be prepared to apologize if you are wrong.

21

Communication and Apology—a Mighty Weapon Whose Swoosh Can Amputate Your Own Nose, if You Are Not Careful

When she asks me, 'What do you think?'

I think I really should have been listening.

Pammi, Sally and Savvy walked into the restaurant almost simultaneously.

Despite a heavy rush of customers that day, Joginder had ensured that their cabin was vacant—a 'Reserved' sign hung over the curtain.

Pammi looked at Savvy's face and said, 'You have recovered quickly and your face has a new glow. It seems as if your husband is taking extra care to compensate for his slap. Did he apologize?'

Savvy took a deep breath, 'That husband of mine is beyond such niceties. He keeps snubbing me. It is always, don't do this, don't do that, don't behave this way, don't wear such clothes … blah, blah. We have no communication apart from these don'ts. He just doesn't listen to me at all. So now I've stopped listening to him. And after the slap incident, he has started behaving even more haughtily. Sher ban gaya ho jaise (as if he has become a lion). Let him be. I'm going to teach him a lesson soon,' she said, fluttering her eyelids conspiratorially.

'What do you plan doing?' Pammi enquired.

'It is more like an unplanned thing. I have missed my period. It is just three days overdue but I feel I might have conceived.'

'What? Really? Wow!'

'I'll know for sure in a couple of days. If it is true, then I'll turn that lion of mine into a jackal. My mother always says, "You can get release from this household grind only when you are pregnant. That is the only time when your husband is forced to follow your diktats." Now I'll tell him what to do and what not to do and he will bloody well listen to me. I'll also pass on all the strenuous work to the men in the house and they will dance to my tune.' Savvy snapped her fingers.

Pammi sat mesmerized. Her eyes twinkled with a devious plan which was taking shape in her mind. 'Yes! This could be the answer to all my problems,' she thought.

'Well, tell me, is it only mine or do all husbands not listen?' Savvy asked.

Seeing Pammi still lost in her trance, Sally answered, 'You know what—now that you mention it, my husband also doesn't really listen to me. If your husband keeps telling you what not to do, then my husband keeps telling me what to do. Actually, he is trying hard to help me in his own way. Ever since we won that battle together, he's going overboard with his concern. He says, take care of yourself, take some rest, take a cup of coffee, I'll make it for you, put a pillow behind your back, have a proper meal, and so on and so forth.'

'That is so good—what is wrong with that?' Savvy felt a twinge of envy.

'Nothing really, except I don't want any of this. I keep telling him that I want to do my things my way but he just won't listen. On weekends, when he is home, this problem really gets escalated because he barges in every fifteen minutes, offering to help. He is so sweet and well-meaning that I just don't know how to tell him, without offending him, that he is not just disturbing me but also getting on my nerves.'

Pammi by now had come out of her reverie. She joined in, 'I absolutely agree. Their attempts to help us are as tiresome as their indifference because they are just not in sync with our thoughts. Ever since our last tiff, my hubby has been out to appease me. He keeps jumping up to do everything even before I ask for it. When I tell him that this is not what I wanted, he says, "Sorry! Sorry!" This is becoming so annoying—I dread telling him anything, in case he starts apologizing.'

'You have turned your lion into a mouse!' laughed Savvy.

'Right! Dar gaya becahara.' Pammi sniggered. 'But it hasn't improved his listening capacity. Our communication is still like that between two people coming from different lands and trying to fathom what the other is saying. It is very true that the commonest cause of fights is this lack of communication between partners.'

~

The word 'bechara' stung Shravan like a scorpion. The more he wished that there was nothing common between Maya and Pammi, the more common traits popped up to torment him—like the word 'bechara', that Maya frequently used for him when she wanted to show her sympathy for him. In the beginning, 'hai, bechara' in Maya's anglicized accent had seemed so cute. Now, he was getting the feeling that it was another put-down remark. 'I'll tell her not to call me "bechara". I also have to remember not to say "sorry" for everything.'

~

Daiv started jotting down:

COMMUNICATION—WHAT IS THE PROBLEM?

Men and women have different problems regarding communication.

Men generally abhor talking about their problems even to their near and dear ones, including their wives, because they believe that not being in control will be perceived as a weakness, and thus lower their standing in others' eyes. They tend to bottle up their emotions, resulting in a stressful existence for themselves.

Women, on the other hand, generally communicate quite freely about their problems and tend to take the advice given rather seriously. When a woman finds that her husband is not communicating enough, she turns to others who are available. As a result she often exposes herself to detrimental advice from people who might have ulterior motives or are plain jealous of her.

Incorrect communications

In this age of a communication-gadgets' glut, the one thing missing is communication. Before marriage, there are all-day phone calls and all-night chatting with would-be beaus. During the honeymoon, communication takes the form of 24x7 live chats, in which your past and future lives are shared. Then comes married life, and communication is reduced to the occasional phone call from office, then to the occasional SMS with a cut-pasted 'P.S. I love you' suffixed to appease the spouse for your coming late. In the late evening, or maybe night, when you actually meet face-to-face, most of your energy has deserted you and the only conversation left is informing each other of the big things, generally the emergencies of the day: 'I got shouted at by the boss', 'She stole my presentation', 'I have to go to Mumbai tomorrow morning', 'Your mother-in-law was saying you never call her'. Then a quick meal and maybe a 'quickie' once every fortnight, or when she is in the mood, followed by musical communication via snores.

They say the foundation of a relationship is communication because communication is sharing and sharing is caring. From that account, the scene described above is the biggest snub. What it would do to a relationship is anybody's guess.

Separation through the unsaid word

Husband and wife constitute the most intimate social nexus. In such a close relationship, partners share most of their thoughts, ideally their thoughts and views about everything, right from career prospects to the choice of toothpaste. Still, there are things that are unsaid between the partners, usually regarding personal biases and past history.

When the present-day unsaid words increase, so does the gap in the relationship. In marriages where the 'unsaid' part becomes more than the 'said' part, the chasm becomes increasingly irrevocable. The marriage becomes progressively dysfunctional and if this communication failure persists, it results in the dissolution of the marriage. In more conservative families, the marriage may not get dissolved because of the social pressure to stay married or a concern for children, but it becomes an unhappy, unfulfilling relationship.

To make a marriage work, both partners need to take care that the present 'unsaid' part is minimal and doesn't pile up.

Couples more likely to TEXT 'I love you' than say it: A survey by mobile phone company, Good Mobile Phones, of 2137 people in the UK found that 61 per cent of people texted 'I love you' as compared with 22 per cent who said this face-to-face. Women, on an average, texted this message once a day as compared to thrice a day by men.

This can happen only if both partners find a regular time, preferably on a daily basis, to get things off their chests. Then, on a weekend or so, they can get the pending 'unsaid' also through.

INSUFFICIENT SKILL IN THE SUBTLE ART OF CONVINCING

The subtle art of convincing, hitherto a hallmark of female communication, is quite lacking in today's generation, especially in literate, working females. Even the passionate arguments of women activists, who ardently and vociferously emphasize their point, are gone. A haughty take-it-or-leave-it stance has taken its place, in which women do not need to justify or even explain their position. They will just go away in a huff if you don't do exactly as told or commanded.

This is as irrational as the former stance of the MCP and leaves men with two options:

1. Behave in the haughty manner of the wife→marital chaos
2. Take over the task of subtle convincing to drive home his point, one for which he is neither made by nature nor groomed for by his parents. Worse, when he tries to softly coax, the wife thinks the hubby is a wimp and dislikes the new face that is so different from the dashing confident manly mien of the young male she liked—another Catch-22 situation.

GENESIS OF A FIGHT

Not listening

The commonest grouse of a wife is: 'My husband just doesn't listen to me.' This complaint is a recent phenomenon. No,

> The wife is seriously complaining, 'You don't listen to anything I say, so I'm leaving you forever.'
>
> The husband is watching TV. He replies, 'Whatever you cook, honey.'

no, not the problem of men not listening. No. Men since time immemorial have been bad listeners. They are geared to focus all their senses on the project on which they are working. Then, when they rest after the project, they tend to shut off all their senses and become refractory to listening.

A man in this switched-off mode, in front of a TV, watching a cricket game, is like a hibernating bear who registers very little. He has been that way since the days of hunter-gatherers. What has changed recently is that women have started voicing their complaints. Why? Because earlier, wives had the company of other wives and relatives. With the breakdown of joint families, and more and more women working with men, the burden of listening now rests on the shoulders of the husband. This is an area in which the shoulders are rather weak.

The solution is simple but not in your hands. Women need to keep communication short and dish it out with a meal or when you are working on something—not when you are hibernating in front of the TV or reading a magazine. It is when the husband is doing something routine that his senses are focused and he is likely to register what the wife is saying properly.

SPARE HIM/HER

Don't expect your partner to be the sole provider for all your emotional, gossipy and spiritual communication needs. He/she (especially he) is bound to fall short of such lofty expectations and this could be the start of your frustrations. Go find a friend instead.

Listening but not understanding what she wants:

Step1: As you are made aware of a problem, the male tendency to find a solution or become the protective guardian takes over. This leads to→Discussion.

Step 2: To help her, you try to convince her of your point of view. The Discussion then leads to→Disagreement.

Step 3: Your efforts backfire as in your zeal to find a solution you brush her point of view under the carpet. Disagreement then leads to→Fight.

Dismissive remarks like 'Don't worry, it is nothing', 'Don't bother and stop thinking about it', 'It is not that important', 'Do as I say and the problem will be solved', 'I would have done . . .', 'Relax, I'll take care of it', though well-meaning, invariably end up aggravating the situation.

Step 4: This infuriates the wife as she feels her problem is being misunderstood. At that point, you pour ghee on that fire by saying something like 'I got it, I got it', 'I understand', 'Say no more' 'It is simple enough, don't repeat it'. The fight then leads to→her Frustration.

Step 5: Then when she has become absolutely enraged, you add the proverbial last straw by saying 'Relax! You are getting mad over nothing', 'That is not what I said/meant', 'This is very irrational', 'You don't get it at all'. This definitely converts her frustration into→Withdrawal and Depression, as she gives up all hope of ever improving the communication. This leads to→a perpetually strained relationship.

~

Communication problems and their impact

Based on the video recordings of thousands of conversations between couples and their long-term outcome, social scientists have outlined a few communication patterns that are detrimental for the marriage:

1. Avoiding communication to avoid conflict. Couples often believe that the peaceful path of no confrontation can solve all their problems. As one study that followed married couples over a three-year period showed, this approach works to begin with. Couples who argued the least had the highest levels of marital happiness. By the end of the three-year period, however, most of them had serious differences and were headed towards divorce. On the other hand, couples who argued had resolved most of their differences, resulting in a big increase of marital satisfaction with the passage of time.
2. Showing contempt in communication is a sure sign of serious trouble in marriage. While discussing marriage indices,

American psychologist Dr John Footman commented that the regular use of contempt in communication was the most telling predictor of divorce.

3. If your communication indicates that you are disappointed about how your life has turned out after marriage, and that you are repenting having married, it is a serious predictor of divorce.

~

A) **The art of listening to a woman** is simple. Yes! This is an irrational statement and you might think that I am a moron even to suggest this. If you ask a woman, she will refute what I am about to suggest, and may also feel offended but try it.

- First, listen to your wife and let her talk till she is spent. Don't have any expectation, don't provide any solution. Sixty per cent of the problem solved.
- To solve the remaining 30 per cent, just repeat verbatim what she just said four times, with no input from your side. One hundred per cent problem solved.
- Yes, I know rationally this adds to 90 per cent but we need to put aside rationality while taking about the female thought process. I think that women don't want to solve 100 per cent of any problem. Otherwise, how will the issue be raked up in the next argument?
- Have patience and understand her need to converse, making adequate concessions for irrationality. Male conversation is mostly rational—about one focused

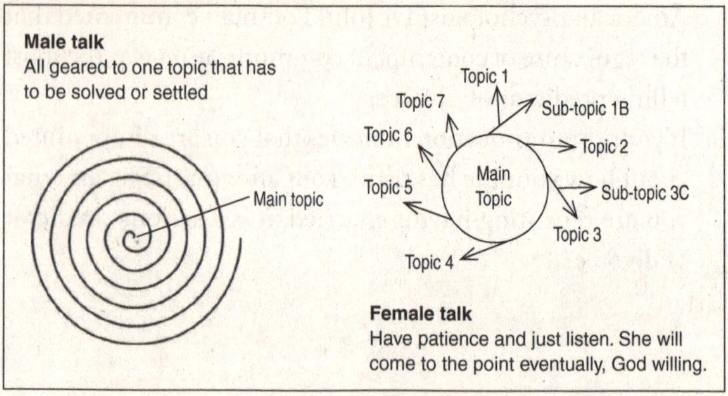

topic which has to be resolved before another issue is addressed. Female conversation is more scattered. It goes off on tangents and may or may not return to the main topic.

- You need great patience to be able to decode what is really intended to be discussed.

Note: A woman can avoid a fight even more easily. Just tell the repetitions to a female friend and tell your man just once (ONCE ONLY) what needs to be done. He will do it at all costs, especially if you throw in some appreciation at the end.

B) **Avoid saying this to a woman—hold your tongue**

- *Telling her what to do/what not to do:* This is exactly what she wants to know but you can't tell her until she herself asks. Sounds bizarre to the logical brain but that's the way it is. Keep your counsel to yourself and just listen without offering advice, till you're specifically asked for

THE SOLUTION IS THE PROBLEM

This is what I have told my wife a hundred times:
You are worked up→You tell me the problem→I tell you the solution→You don't follow the solution→Problem not solved→You are worked up further→You tell me the whole thing again→I tell you, follow my solution or the problem will get aggravated→You don't follow the solution→The problem gets aggravated→You are worked up madly and wonder why the problem has aggravated→I tell you, 'I told you so'→I ask you, 'Why didn't you follow my instructions at all?'→You say 'How does it matter? Heaven is not going to fall'→Now I'm worked up→And you wonder why I am worked up for such a trivial thing. WOW!

Rationality—RIP!

a solution. Even after specifically asking for the solution, it is possible that she never wanted a solution—she just wanted to hear something positive about her blunder.

- *Telling her 'I told you so'* after she commits a blunder, especially after she has gone against your advice. Males have the compulsive need to be proven right. When you are proven right you like to stand on the carcass of the dead issue—Tarzan-like—and howl at the top of your voice, 'I told you so.' Unfortunately, hitting with this remark at that point of time is like hitting a very enraged tigress with a pebble. Few live to tell the tale.

C) **The art of apologizing:** This is an important and mature act, especially if you believe that you were wrong or that you, too, were wrong but NEVER overdo it. Be specific about what you are apologizing for and don't let it become a tool to simply get the discussion off your head. Otherwise, the apology will lose its effect and your wife will assume that you are always wrong and she is always right.

D) **Be lighthearted in dealing with her**—use your wit
Use her dialogues—Say what you expect her to say in a lighter vein before she can and see her squirm uncomfortably in her chair, speechless, as she has nothing left to say. Unlike in her favourite serial, she can't go to the director and complain, 'He has stolen all my dialogues.'

For example, after clumsily spilling tea over her favourite tablecloth, say 'Sorry!' and then using her tone and words say, 'I am a totally clumsy guy, who has five thumbs and can't even do what any five-year-old can.' Now what can she add?

Accept a surrogate sorry

When egos are flared, don't expect a verbal apology even if your wife is completely wrong and knows it. Chances are that the apology will arrive in the form of exceptional food at night or the sheer negligee that you had been insisting on her wearing. Be wise—accept it and tell her in jest, 'Your surrogate apology is accepted.' This is important.

The conventional system of straightforward male talk and

the subtle convincing of the wife was the best combination possible because it meant that everyone knew their respective strengths and weaknesses. It is not just in communication that the golden conventional systems can help your marriage.

IN A NUTSHELL

Men tend not to listen to their wives easily. What men can do is to designate some time for communicating with their wives. And remember, you don't lose any stature by apologizing if you are wrong.

22

Golden Oldies—Concepts That Have Come a Full Circle

> My wife is blessed. She thinks, 'freedom of the press' means 'no ironing clothes'.

'How demeaning!' Pammi thundered so vehemently that the wooden partition around their cubicle reverberated in resonance. 'Now, women are being systematically reduced to second-class citizens.' She produced a copy of the day's newspaper with the headline 'Keeping hubby happy is big business!' The article talked about finishing schools charging 20,000 to 50,000 rupees for courses that teach skills to win over their husbands' hearts—cooking, party-planning, dress sense and applying make-up. 'The article is trying to put in the subconscious minds of women that our very existence is for the benefit of men.'

'What is the harm in learning basic home-management skills?' asked Sally. 'In fact, as a Home Science graduate, I feel that such a course does a world of good to ladies, whose main job is to manage the home. It makes tasks like managing home, rearing kids and hygienic cooking more systematic.'

'That may be your opinion but I believe in Jassi's dictum that she teaches the Libber Cats.'

The men held their breaths, for this was the missing link. 'Jassi believes that women-oriented courses, like Home Science, are a blot on human equality. Why should only women train for these chores? Why should women bear the onus of all the household work? Instead, they should take up jobs and be financially independent. Only then would they be able to kick the collective butt of these bloody men. Jassi, in fact, wants to start one truly female-centric course: a course on "Husband hoodwinking and in-laws management" where girls would be taught tricks to handle their in-laws and spellbind their husbands so they would obey at the snap of their fingers. They would also be taught the finer points of law pertaining to marriage and how to manipulate it to their own advantage. Imagine the impact of such a course, rather than courses that turn women into maids.'

Sally shook her head in dismay. Such extremist views always agitated her. 'That idea of hoodwinking the husband may hold promise for a minuscule percentage of women. For the majority, who have a traditional arranged marriage, household chores are a part of their job descriptions, even if they are working.'

'That is why Jassi is dead against arranged marriages and joint families. They shackle women to the hearth and take away all their freedom. They have no recourse to a better way of life because the whole system is against them. Jassi says, "Why should the woman compromise? If the in-laws and the husband don't agree with her, she should just kick the marriage goodbye and get out."'

'Will all that strife make her happy? What would happen to the institution of marriage if every woman starts following this advice?'

Pammi shrugged her shoulders as she had no answers to these questions but some men were getting answers, as was obvious from the vigorous nodding of their heads.

~

Shravan's mind was formulating a plan that could answer most of his questions. He was going to ask Maya if she would be prepared to live with his parents in case he decided to set up a business in his hometown.

Her answer would decide the future of their relationship.

~

The writer's hands were furiously at work, for in Jassi's rulings, he had at last found the answer to the question 'What can make a marriage happy?' He now realized that contrary to his belief, 'Romance' was not the answer—that the answer would lie in the 'golden oldies' systems from our past was something that his progressive mind could never have guessed had he not heard these injunctions today.

~

I have come a full circle. I am forced to deduce that despite their respective drawbacks, our time-tested concepts have much relevance today. Let us see what the studies indicate:

TYPES OF MARRIAGES AND THEIR RESPECTIVE CHANCES OF SUCCESS

A thirty-year prospective study on different types of marriages, by E. Mavis Hetherington, emeritus professor in the Department of Psychology at the University of Virginia in his book, *For Better (Or Worse): The Science of a Good Marriage,* categorized marriage into five distinct categories:

1. The traditional marriage, in which there is the male breadwinner and a female homemaker, was the most stable, that is, it has the lowest divorce rates. In the Indian context, traditional also means arranged by the respective families.
2. Cohesive-individuated marriage, in which the partners though living their individual, independent lives are bonded together by their need to return to an oasis of affection and companionship, which rejuvenates them. Such a marriage has the second-lowest divorce rates.

   The next three types all have a high risk of divorce.
3. In pursuer-distancer marriages, one partner is eager to confront the issues and discuss problems (pursuer) and the other partner tends to withdraw to avoid confrontation (distancer). In 80 per cent of marriages, the pursuer was found to be the woman. Men resist discussion by engaging in other activities like reading the newspaper or watching a game on TV. If nagged, men tend to just stay out of house.

In the end even the wife gets fed up and withdraws into herself.

4. Disengaged marriages unite two self-sufficient and independent individuals who don't need each other to fulfil their lives on a daily basis. Many such individuals fear intimacy and keep living as if they are single. Such cases are generally found in marriages of overage, well-placed professionals, whose careers/ businesses mean much more to them than the family.
5. The operatic marriage is characterized by dramatic highs and lows as these couples are emotionally volatile. There are severe fights, which are resolved by torrid sex. Though these couples are the most sexually satisfied of all types, still they have very high break-up rates.

FAST FACTS—LESSONS ON LOVE

1. About half of people's first marriages fail in the US, as do two-thirds of second marriages and three-quarters of third marriages. They fail in large part because people enter relationships with poor skills for maintaining them and highly unrealistic expectations.
2. A study of arranged marriages, in which love has grown over time, hints that commitment, communication, accommodation and vulnerability are the key components of a successful relationship. Other research indicates that sharing adventures, secrets, personal space and jokes can also build intimacy and love.

Let's see how the traditional marriage fares vis-à-vis the love marriage.

~

Arranged marriage versus love marriage

Robert Epstein, Harvard behavioural scientist and author of *How Science Can Help You Fall in Love* and *How People Learn to Love and You Can Too*' is a keen believer in the arranged marriage. At 54.8 per cent, the US has the second-highest divorce rate in the world (second only to Sweden) whereas India has one of the lowest at 1.1 per cent. He attributes this mainly to the system of arranged marriage. He says, 'love marriages flounder because most confuse lust for love. Moreover, love makes you blind to important characteristics in your partner. Typical example—the woman is dying to have babies and the man is dead against it. Eventually, one or both partners will be miserable because of it. In contrast, arranged marriages put everything good, bad and ugly on the table from the word go. These marriages do not start with love but with the right circumstances, that is, the right background, religion, caste, education and other factors. Sensible, isn't it?'

So, the right circumstances let love blossom with time. As Epstein put it, 'Studies have shown that love starts at a scale of 3–4 (on a scale of 10) in arranged marriages but grows to match the love score of love marriages in five years and is twice as much in another five years, whereas in love marriages the trajectory of love is always downwards.

GEN-NEXT is increasingly saying 'no' to premarital sex: After decades of increasing promiscuity, there has been a reversal of sorts with a majority in India saying 'no' to premarital sex. In a survey conducted by the *TOI*, in Mumbai and Bangalore, 65 per cent of the respondents between 16 and 22 said 'no' to premarital sex. Also, 90 per cent said they would not be willing to marry a non-virgin. This trend is catching on in the US too. In a survey, almost 57.4 per cent were virgins.

No wonder arranged marriages are on the rise.

~

THE BUFFER OF A JOINT FAMILY

Economic slowdown affects lives in unique ways. In the West, it is resulting in a gender-role reversal in the form of the husband taking up household duties and wife providing the proverbial bread and butter because she holds a job and he doesn't. It is also causing a revival of the joint family system. Even though financial constraints and the cost of living may be more compelling reasons than traditional family bonding, one thing is for sure: after entering into a joint family system, most young couples realize the benefits of this system, once considered obsolete.

The biggest plus is security, not only of the house but also of the children. In fact, most couples in places like Mumbai or Delhi, where two incomes are mandatory for sustenance, can

JOINT FAMILIES ARE BACK IN MUMBAI
(*TOI* headline, 24 March 2012)

- The population of households with joint families has gone up by 56 per cent in the suburbs and 37 per cent in the city
- 13.7 per cent of suburban and 14.5 per cent of the city households constitute joint families, up from 8.8% in 2001

only think of having children if they have some sort of support system at home, as is provided by the joint family.

A motive for entering into or continuing to live in a joint family is the benefit of buffering, especially for a newlywed couple. In the immediate post-honeymoon period, there is a discovery of the many hitherto hidden negative aspects of the spouse. This is certain to cause teething troubles, which if allowed to go unbridled can cause damage to the still delicate bond of the new partnership. The freedom of the couple staying alone as a unit family that can make love blossom can also make differences multiply as quickly and has resulted in many marriages floundering even before the partners really come to know each other.

This is where the buffering effect of joint family is invaluable. The presence of seniors make the fights and differences less tantrum-prone and the partners are less likely to shout profanities that they will regret later.

~

A SINGLE-EARNER FAMILY

In cases where financial constraints are not a problem, that is, the earning of the male member is enough to sustain the kind of lifestyle the couple wants to have, going in for a system of a wife dedicated to the family household makes sense. The only caveat is that both partners have to ensure that the wife gets adequate recognition for the job and that she has some form of mental stimulation to ward off the monotony that will set in with just household chores. I believe that wherever possible, home-office or freelance consultation from home is the ideal way to keep women gainfully employed as well as psychologically stimulated.

INDEPENDENT WOMAN—A MYTH?

Research has questioned the assumption that women dislike being dependent on men. According to Catherine Hakim of the London School of Economics, 'Women's aspirations to marry up, if they can, to a man who is better educated and higher earning, persist in a lot of European countries also'. In her fifty-two-page report, in 1949, 20 per cent of women in Britain married husbands with significantly higher levels of education and income. By the 1990s this figure had gone up to 38 per cent. Similar patterns are seen in the US and Australia. Hakim also says that women don't want to admit that they want to be housewives, as it is politically incorrect.

A German study found that among working women, the happiest were those whose husbands earned more than two-third of the household income. The high- earning woman was more stressed and resentful because she had to work full-time in the office and then also do the bulk of the housework. On the other hand, an unequal financial earning allows for a clearer division of roles and there is less day-to-day stress because the lady realizes that her main task is household work and not becoming the bread-earner.

The study also found that the happiest marriages were based on a mutually giving relationship, where each partner puts himself out for the other without a quid pro quo arrangement, as in, I did this chore on Saturday, so you do this on Sunday.

MALE HORMONE LOWERS EMPATHY

Scientists in London have found that testosterone, the male sex hormone, lowers the ability to empathize and contributes to the aggression that men display.

When a group of women were given small doses of testosterone, they,. too, showed lower empathy. The research also showed that women working in stressful and competitive environs have higher levels of testosterone and lowered empathy for their families. This might be the reason for the increasing frustrations and abrasive behaviour that some women in a demanding job display.

Psychiatrist Dr Jitendra Nagpal says, 'The incidence of depression is increasing among women, especially those who are in high-pressure jobs and don't have support systems at home.'

Answering these questions is Megan Basham's *Beside Every Successful Man*, which emphasizes that couples need to make the mental shift of considering their marriage a joint enterprise in which the individuals are equal partners but with different responsibilities. The woman has to think in terms of managing the home and supporting her husband, and his career being as important and essential as working outside to contribute to the household income. The man's responsibility is to be the provider and to acknowledge that his wife's job at home is as important as, if not more than, his job of earning. Basham

MEN HATE HOUSEHOLD CHORES

Researchers from the University of South Florida found that men doing jobs traditionally associated with women become more aggressive, because they feel their masculinity is being threatened (A *Daily Mail* report).

After doing traditionally feminine tasks, such as dishwashing or cleaning, men consciously behave in a more macho way to claim their self-esteem. Jennifer Boson, who carried out the study, concluded that men are extremely concerned about how they appear in other people's eyes. They suffer psychologically when their manhood feels violated.

believes that in this lies the bliss of a happy life, because otherwise, in her endeavour to have it all, the woman gets no time for herself.

One more nugget in this already controversial issue: I have stated that a single-income family arrangement can work only where the husband's income is sufficient to provide desired level of comforts. However, I believe that even in cases where the husband's income is frugal and not really enough to provide for all the luxuries of life, this system of a single earner can still work well if the wife wants it to. If the wife accepts what he earns and assuages his feeling of inferiority by showing contentment, they will be happy, despite the lack of amenities. If on the other hand, she compares him to his peers, he starts running around like a whipped horse, causing stress.

IN A NUTSHELL

Youth of today are realizing that systems like arranged marriages and joint families that were once being shunned can be fine-tuned to provide solutions to today's hectic cosmopolitan lives.

Another age-old practice that was almost an art form for women is making a comeback. Their newly learnt brashness is being replaced with pretence . . .

23

Pretence—the Magic Marriage-saver

Only two things are necessary to keep one's wife happy.

- Let her think she is having her own way
- Let her have it

Pammi entered the restaurant and moved very slowly, with a wobbly gait, to the cabin, where Sally and Savvy waited for her.

'What happened?' asked Savvy.

'What?' asked Pammi, innocently.

'You're walking strangely, not with your normal breezy style. Why do you have all this greasy make-up on and this oily hair-do? You normally abhor these things.' Sally was forthright.

'Isn't this the way expectant mothers behave and dress?'Pammi smiled mischievously.

'What! You, too, are pregnant? That is great,' chuckled Savvy.

'That is the least important thing that happened this fortnight.' She set up the preamble so well that Savvy clutched the edge of her seat so as not to miss any part of the riveting live-show. Her wide eyes begged Pammi to go on.

'Two weeks ago, another flashpoint arose. Mother-in-law said, "As your PhD is still some five months away, why don't you join my NGO and contribute?" Though I had no interest in that unpaid work, I thought it is better than to be saddled with the household work. But within two days, I realized that this was not my cup of tea. All that dust and heat and smell in those women's homes was terrible. I didn't know what to do. I asked my mom and she devised a plan. Accordingly, I started saying things like, "This is hypocrisy—everybody takes dowry and tells others not to"; "They fight so-called injustice outside and look how they treat their own DILs"; and "Even after marriage, people keep covertly asking for favours and gifts." This soon reached my mother-in-law. I had thought she would quietly remove me from the NGO to avoid embarrassment and it will be the end of the story, but she proved to be made up of sterner stuff. She ignored the reports and didn't react.

'Frustrated, I made a blunder. I blurted out these ver same things to an investigative journalist who writes stories about victims whom this NGO helps. She wrote down what I said but instead of printing it, she took it to my mother-in-law.'

'Oh my God!' exclaimed Savvy.

To add to the suspense, Pammi started nibbling on her sandwich and sipping her coffee.

Savvy could hold out no more. 'Leave the coffee. Tell me what happened next.'

'The next day was a Sunday. I was woken up by shrill voices coming from the dining room. I tiptoed out and heard my mother-in-law complaining to my hubby. As I heard my husband come up the stairs calling my name in a terse tone, I remembered your mother's comment, 'Only pregnancy can save you from the household grind.' So, I rushed to the bathroom and put my fingers in my throat to induce vomiting. After much retching, I came out feigning dizziness. My hubby by then had temporarily forgotten why he had come upstairs. When he enquired, I told him that I had missed my periods and, voila, everything was forgiven. Slate washed clean.'

'Have you actually missed your period?' asked Savvy innocently.

'No, you dumbo! I was just pretending and this gait and make-up are part of this one-act play.'

'What happens when they come to know the truth?' Sally was concerned.

'We'll see. My immediate problem is solved—no kitchen, no NGO, nothing. In fact another problem had cropped up. My husband wanted to confirm the pregnancy by visiting a doctor.'

'Then?' Savvy was still wide-eyed.

'My mom solved that problem too. Her rummy partner in the club is a retired doctor. She took her into confidence and she will help us pull off the sham. She has asked me to get a few routine tests done, just to keep up the pretence, and she will add a typed pregnancy report to the lab reports. Problem solved for a few months.'

She snapped her fingers mischievously.

~

Shravan blinked as if trying to ascertain whether he was dreaming. This was too close to be a mere coincidence and once again it was Pammi mouthing Maya's dialogues, not Sally. His mind drifted to last Sunday.

Gathering resolve, Shravan had decided to pose the question to Maya. The moment they sat down at the restaurant, Shravan gathered his guts and asked the question.

'Maya, I was thinking about leaving this job and starting a business in my hometown. We also have a piece of land there, you know. What do you think?'

Without batting an eyelid, Maya shot back, 'Oof oh! Shravan, you ask the wrong thing at the wrong time. I am so tense and you ask these purely hypothetical questions.'

Shravan wanted to shout that his question was not hypothetical but had to ask, 'Why are you tense?'

'I've missed my period, damn it.'

'How? We used protection, didn't we?'

'It's never foolproof and you know it.'

Shravan felt so perturbed and guilty that everything else was just forgotten.

Now, he sat thinking, Maya had effectively answered my question without answering it. Somehow he now knew that she had not missed her period.

It was just a perfect pretence.

~

Daiv wrote:

The word 'pretence' has severe negative connotations. Pathological pretence, as Pammi showed in the forms of vague pains and aches to shirk work or, worse, falsely accusing in-laws to cause grief, have brought a bad name to women. In fact, ancient literature has labelled such female behaviour as 'triya charitra', a term which essentially means 'pretentious devious behaviour'. That such behaviour puts a wedge in the husband–wife relationship is obvious.

The questions that need to be answered are:

1. Should we remove all pretences from marriage and speak out the plain truth and
2. Is pretence all bad?

The truth in communication

This is tricky. Most couples agree in principle that the relationship should be truthful but they all also agree that there are certain things that are better unsaid or at least not dwelled upon. Are there? I don't think so.

Aside from unsavoury details, most feelings and thoughts require to be shared, whether they pertain to spending too much time on getting dressed, or his habit of reading the

> Research by Aron and Sprecher indicates that people tend to bond better when they share secrets with one another.

newspaper all Sunday. Any festering sentiment will only induce more resentment in the marriage.

In the same way, when we circumvent touchy issues like sex, money or staying with the in-laws or if we try to deal with these in double-speak, hinting obliquely rather than broaching the subject, the relationship gets corroded.

What about the touchy subjects like your mother-in-law's interference in your marriage or your spouse's unacceptable habits, such as not maintaining proper hygiene?

These, too, need to be discussed openly, lest they fester under cover. Discussing these things in the heat of the moment can only create a rift. That is why I strongly recommend a personal discussion time, in which the couple should sit alone and discuss everything openly, without any reservations or repercussions.

~

Is pretence all bad?

No. Like all drugs, it is poisonous in heavy doses but it has some virtue when it comes to managing a marriage.

Early in marriage, drastic changes come into your life; more so for your wife. With time you realize that these are simply a different set of circumstances, which seem odd to you in the beginning, just because you are not used to them. If you baulk at them at the very onset, it can be very damaging for your relationship. This is especially true for the woman as she has shifted her home and is dealing with a new world. Here, a bit of pretence can be a marriage-saver.

Let me explain:

1. Intrapersonal pretence, that is, pretence between the spouses: During courtship, you both are at your best, with your best clothes, best hair-dos, best manners, best habits—a beautiful pretence. The same pretence goes on in the honeymoon period. Then, immediately after the honeymoon, as you settle down, you start believing that this pretence is no longer required. You come down straight to the bare basics, especially at home—basic clothes, basic mannerisms and, worse, absolutely basic communication. You can understand how disillusioned your partner will feel when her prince has suddenly morphed from an Armani-suit-wearing man to one in Rupa underwear. Even worse, his Gucci fragrance has been replaced by the stink of unwashed socks worn for three days straight.

   This is where pretence saves you from hurling that four-letter word that can make a huge dent in your marriage. Pretence teaches you to smile politely and gives you time to understand that just like there was a Rupa underwear beneath the Armani suit, there is a gentle caring soul hidden behind that uncouth exterior.
2. Interpersonal pretence—we versus the world: In most cases, all that a marriage needs is time, the very thing that this generation doesn't have. This is where the role of a senior person as a buffer becomes important because in that person's presence you have to keep up the pretence of decent behaviour, which gives you time to accept and appreciate the spouse's point of view.

~

Advice

1. Avoid damaging pathological pretence that would hurt your spouse or in-laws. For example, the wife pretending that the inlaws are demanding dowry, when they are actually not; or the wife pretending that the husband is impotent.
2. Observe the pretence of formalities, niceties and etiquette even after the honeymoon period at home. Don't give up all pretence and become too informal until you have come really close, something which usually takes years. You have to give your partner at least the same consideration as you would to any other respected acquaintance. Be generous with your 'you are welcome', 'thank you' and, of course, the most important marriage-saver, 'sorry'. You do this even to that unknown waiter and to that cab-driver, whom you are paying, then how come your spouse is not worthy of that treatment? And please maintain that dignity even when you two are alone. This is not a public relations exercise, it is a relationship-builder.
3. Chivalry and chivalrous behaviour: Showing common courtesies, like opening the door or pulling out the chair, might seem pretentious but would always endear you to her. These don't demean you, despite what your MCP friends might say. These are hallmarks of a true gentleman.
4. Some formality: Dressing up well, not just when going out but when you are with your spouse at home is very important. After all, your life is going to be heaven or hell depending on what your spouse thinks about you, not

relatives in far-flung places or people in restaurant for whom you dress well.

5. Protect her—Irrespective of how modern and liberalized she gets, this is one thing she always cherishes. This does not mean just physical protection, like a bodyguard, but emotional protection, especially when it comes to relations. Defending her choice or stand or action goes a long way in establishing a positive image of you in her mind. It is the highest form of praise.
6. Last, a small gesture that can smoothen a lot of rough edges of early marriage is the use of 'aap' and 'ji'. As my grandma said, try retorting to someone who has addressed you as 'aap' and suffixed a 'ji' to your name and you will find your tone softening by many notches. That is why you should use these two for the most important person in your life, your spouse. These two words bind you in a bond of decency. Try it.

Remember to do this, even when you two are alone in exclusive time.

IN A NUTSHELL

Soft pretences, like chivalry or formal etiquette, are marriage-savers, while devious pretences can harm your marriage. Remember your wife may like 'ji' being suffixed to her name as much as you do.

24

Time Out and Personal Space

Pammi entered the restaurant, visibly upset. She threw her bag on the table and murmured, 'These taxi drivers are bloody blood-suckers.'

'You didn't bring your car?' Savvy was worried about how she would reach the metro station.

'That is not my car and, in any case, I can travel even without a car. It's no big deal.' Then she turned to the waiter, 'What is wrong with you? Can't you bring a glass of water when a customer comes in?'

Sally could see serious strain in her tone but decided not to rake up anything just yet.

Over the next half an hour, Pammi's foul mood was apparent. She found fault with everything and snapped at everybody. 'The coffee is horrible', 'The spoon is not clean', 'The dosa is soggy', 'Why is the music so loud?'

Sally noticed the dark mood and decided to wait before saying anything. Savvy, however, was anxious to know the reason for Pammi's anger. She cleared her throat and was about to ask, when Pammi's mobile phone rang.

Pammi listened to the call with a brooding stance, just responding with 'hmm', 'Okay!' or 'yes'. Then visibly upset, she snapped back, 'No, no, no. Don't do that.' Then, realizing that this was not the right approach, she softened her tone and said, 'Please understand… Keep talking to the journalists. Shower them with some more gifts but we will be able to hold the press conference only after the results. Okay?' She tossed the phone on the table.

Savvy was concerned. 'Press conference? What is the matter? Is it about…'

'Shut up. Mind your own business.' Pammi shouted at Savvy. Then annoyed with herself, she shook her head and placed her head down on her arms, cutting off all communication.

There was a pall of tension in the room.

Shocked, Savvy tried to mutter, 'But I … I was only…' Seeing her distraught condition, Sally gestured to her to relax and wait without saying anything.

After what seemed like an hour, Pammi lifted her head and in an apologetic tone said, 'Sorry, yaar! This infidelity thing of my husband is really making me mad. He is just not giving me time to sit down alone and talk straight. It's driving me crazy. Sorry again. In fact, I have to go to the doctor. I think I should be leaving.' She hastily said bye and left without finishing her coffee.

'What's happened to Pammi?' asked Savvy. 'Why doesn't her husband clear the air about it all?'

Sally thought for a moment. 'You know what . . . I believe

the problem is twofold. First of all, Pammi has the habit of resolving all her issues in the heat of the moment. She keeps pushing the argument till something gives. Trying to resolve issues in the heat of the moment very frequently makes us take decisions that we regret later. Second, she and her husband don't spend time alone, and so they can't resolve the issue of her suspicions. Inside the house it's just not possible, because you can't vent your feelings for fear of being overheard. Our lives have become so busy that even though we stay together, we remain aloof from each other and discontent keeps simmering.'

'I can relate to that very well,' Savvy nodded. 'I believe our marital problems started and got aggravated just because my husband never had time to sit and ask me what I want. Even when he is at home and is free, he is busy doing some inconsequential task rather than spending some time with me. His ego gets bruised by the very thought that he might be labelled a "joru ka gulaam". He even avoids sitting within five feet of me when any of his brothers are home, which is most of the time. It's no wonder I open up my heart to others who listen to me and are more responsive to my requirements.'

'I agree with you totally on this point,' nodded Sally. 'In fact, we too, had this problem in the beginning of our marriage. We would always be together, so much so that it got on our nerves. We just didn't have any independent time, alone. Both of us were hostellers in college and this constant togetherness felt stifling. Then when we started moving apart, we moved to the other extreme. Things got so bad that we started feeling like strangers staying in the same room. Then, one day, we sat down and formulated a few things that we were to observe. Now, we've kept specific days in a week which are meant for two of us together, nobody else. We also have another set of specific times in which each of us can pursue whatever we want.'

'How I wish we could come up with some such thing. That would definitely improve our relationship. Also, Pammi would not have gone to such elaborate measures to get back at her husband. Can't we suggest this system to her?'

'We can, Savvy, but these systems work only after the couple themselves feel the need for them, otherwise they feel like these are forced regulations and are dissed. Imagine if I tell your husband to follow this system—how would he react?'

'Oh my God! He'd go wild thinking that I told you about our troubles. As such, he resents my coming here. You know what, if we are sitting together and drinking tea in the mornings and one of his brothers wakes up and comes into the room, he jumps away as if stung by a scorpion. Once I asked him, "Why are you jumping? We are married." He replied, "That is why it doesn't look nice. What will they think about us?" He can't even accept that somebody should see us smiling at each other. Conservative male's false ego.'

'Exactly! In these relationships, the most important thing is that the couple should spend time together alone. Because the process of heart-to-heart talk is definitely hindered by the presence of the onlookers. The male ego won't allow him to appear subservient to the woman and the woman can't really bond without a one-to-one interaction.'

~

Daiv started writing:

Listening to Sally, I was reminded of an incident of our twenty-fifth marriage anniversary. We had planned to celebrate it at Jim Corbett Park and had invited all our cousins and their spouses for three days to relive our childhood. To bring back the nostalgia and be able to remove the tag of seniority (all of us were above forty-five), we decided to be not just on first-name terms but on the pet-name terms of our childhood—Kuku, Pappu, Neetu, Pinky.

As luck would have it, a fraudulent manager at the resort absconded with our advance money and we spent a few hours trying to sort out the mess. In the heat of the moment, and the ensuing frustration, my wife and I exchanged some heated, accusatory words. After the situation got settled, we both breathed a sigh of relief and realized that we were spending our pre-anniversary day accusing each other.

To compensate, we sat down on the ledge overlooking the beautiful jungle stream, holding hands, sipping from a glass of juice together. I was surprised at the comments that were thrown our way: 'Kya baat hai, akele akele baithe ho'; 'mana rahe ho?'; 'bada romance ho raha hai'; 'aur koi nahi mili ki apni patni ko hi pata raha hai?'; 'sharam karo—itne barre bache hain tumhare, tum ishq jhar rahe ho'.

The more I heard, the more amazed I became—I was a bit sad too. I couldn't help pondering on the state of affairs where even such broadminded, well-placed professionals found it odd that a couple should spend some romance time, enjoying each other's company. I had believed that this kind of bonding is a definite marriage-saver.

To probe the matter, I decided to meet a few eminent HR experts handling large MNCs. What they told me further established my fears. Harish Joshi, from the HR firm, the Protectors, said, 'The reason executives don't want to take a break is their galloping ambitions. They become so insecure that someone will take their place that their leaves pile up and then get lapsed but they still don't avail them. In some firms, we had to make a policy of giving them forced leave.' Another HR executive, Priyanka Rohtagi, says, 'Vacations? Many don't even claim their weekend-offs. A newlywed employee chose a presentation over her honeymoon because she didn't want her boss to take all the credit for her hard work.'

Talking of the fall-out of such leisure-deprived lives, Dr Jitender Nagpal says, 'Some of the side-effects of workaholics are: edginess, abusive and reckless behaviour; smoking and drinking heavily; getting involved in irresponsible hit-and-run relationships.'

The lack of spending leisure time with the family is taking a heavy toll not only on the marriage but also on the person's psyche.

~

Personal space—the final frontier

The requirement of personal space is becoming one of the biggest incongruities in modern-metro marriages, especially between two working partners. The commitment-phobia that is shaking the very foundations of the institution of marriage is largely born out of fear of losing that precious personal space. 'In metros today, more couples mismatch with regard to their space, rather than anything else,' says Neeru Kanwar Chaudhary, a Delhi-based psychotherapist and member of the Indian Association of Family Therapy. 'The problem comes up when distancing becomes a convenient method to avoid confronting an issue.'

The requirement of space can be at many levels:

- An away space, where a holiday together is the most desired element
- Time without kids or even without a spouse
- Financial space is the need for independent bank accounts and independence in spending, without any restrictions from the spouse
- Working space is especially demanded, when one partner is working from home
- Creative space is an issue, where some form of art or creativity is involved. It is specially demanded when both partners are working together.

Finally, how much interpersonal distance is enough?

This is a tricky question but an essential one. Extreme nearness, in which partners share absolutely everything, seems endearing from afar, but over time becomes stifling. Partners start taking each other for granted, making the relationship stressful.

> A man's silence can make a woman feel alone if she wants to talk . . . A woman's talk can make a man feel abandoned if he doesn't want to talk.

On the other hand, there are couples who carve out such huge spaces for themselves that over time they start moving away from each other and become virtual strangers, even while staying under the same roof. Something similar happens in different-city marriages and marriages in which one or both partners has a job that entails touring. Then what is the ideal near-far balance? Near enough to feel together and far enough to retain the mystique. When a man after years of marriage can still look at his wife with appreciation and the wife, despite being the mother of his two children, can still be bashful and caring, that means that they have worked out the distance formula to perfection. This is only possible when the couple not only gives each other space to be on their own, but also carves out a together 'us' time and space, frequently, to nurture the relationship. As Sally and her husband have done.

> A couple feels less lonely when they are thousands of miles apart than when they lie on the same bed after a fight.

Mobile phones

Mobile phones impinge hugely on your interpersonal space. In 2011–12, out of 9800 cases registered with the marriage grievances cell, 80 per cent said that the cause of dispute was the mobile phone. In some cases, the disruption caused is because of prolonged talking with their family members. In others, the cause is the continuous disruption in married life by phone calls from the office. In many cases, the mobile phone also becomes the provider of evidence of infidelity.

~

Time out

Time is the one thing that this present generation of young people is deprived of.

But, however stressed out for time you might be, you always find time to quarrel. Why? Because you feel that the issues should not be left unresolved and pent-up steam should be let out instantly. As the saying goes, never sleep on a fight, that is, settle the issue then and there. So you have a quick tiff, even in that dash to get ready for office or during the car journey to or from a late-night party.

Is that wise?

No doubt, resolving conflicts and their ensuing issues completely is important, but not doing it in the heat of the moment is vital, because at that time you are actually only reacting and you tend to spew a chain of truths and half-truths, most of which you regret later. The deep hurt of these barbs will incite many more conflicts in future. These unkind, even if true, words, said in an accusatory tone, can weigh on you for years.

It is wiser to just stay quiet for the moment and give each other time to calmly and maturely assess the situation. Arguments and disagreements should be postponed to a later time, when you can sit down alone, during an 'exclusive time', and coolly iron out your differences.

If there could be a prenuptial bond according to which there could be no quarrels, arguments or angry outbursts in the first two years of marriage, most marriages would be successful. If we could just write down the points of differences and decide to solve these two years down the road, we would all have a great marriage.

Because writing down differences, without resolving them instantly, is akin to an analytical catharsis, a roundabout way to open your eyes to the facts of life without reacting spontaneously, and a 'time-out'. After two years when you pick up the list to settle the scores, you will be able to see your childish approach to issues in a new marriage and relationship.

I have kept diaries of my quarrels with my wife, just as I have kept diaries of our romantic banter. On our silver anniversary, we decided to look at them, as we occasionally do. We found these quarrel diaries to be much more hilarious and fun than the romantic ones. Sample these nuggets:

- She then: 'I hate his diplomatic approach. Instead of directly pointing out my mistake, he hints it to me obliquely.'

- Today, she thanks God for this tendency of mine.

- Me then: 'What the hell, I can't even raise my voice when I'm angry, just because my mother detests our quarrelling.'
  - Today, I know this is what sustained our marriage for so long.

- She then: 'He has an annoying habit of compulsively changing into fresh clothes and brushing his teeth last thing before sleeping, even if we reach home at 2 a.m. Worse, he insists that I do that too.'
  - Today, we both thank God for this because one of the commonest grouses our middle-aged friends have about their spouses is bad breath or body odour. So it saved not just rotten gums but also a potentially rotting relationship.

- Me then: 'She is maniacal about cleanliness and insists on cleaning and placing things in their place, even after coming home from a late-night Saturday movie.
  - Today, I am thankful for all that organization for I can find all my things with my eyes closed.

So, dear friends, whenever it seems that the temperature is rising in your arguments, take a 'time-out'. Schedule a fixed time to settle the issue, ideally at the end of your exclusive time.

Exclusive time

This is the time that you spend alone with your spouse, without a cell phone and inputs like TV. Ideally, it should be done outside the house—in a park, restaurant or any peaceful place. If, however, you have to sort out some emotional or disputed issues, you should use your house for this, but first make sure nobody else is home. Also, make special arrangements, akin to an official meeting, like ordering food from outside to be eaten after your meeting or flower arrangements on the table where you plan to sit. That reminds me: this type of a meeting should never be on the bed; use a table or sofa instead. The bed corrodes the seriousness of the event and makes you too cosy to complete the conversation. Furthermore, the bed must never be the scene of a battleground.

If you have never had exclusive time-out with your spouse, that's tragic. You can't imagine what you are missing. Your own happiness and contentment are some of the most critical ingredients of a happy marriage. This exclusive time is the best way to touch the core of her heart and find some joint space where you are happy.

At these exclusive times, sit down and pour your heart out. Let your emotions show because your partner needs to know: How big was that issue for you and why? What hurt or disappointed you? How did you feel at that time? What do you need from your partner?

At the same time, you too, need to learn about her feelings. Express clearly what you need. There is no shame in telling your partner what you really feel.

IN A NUTSHELL

Planning an exclusive time with your wife is the safety valve that prevents marriages from blowing up from pent-up pressure. Remember: the mobile phone is becoming the proverbial last straw on already strained marriages.

Don't be too selfless during these exclusive times. Don't think, 'If I don't say it, she will understand my noble motives and do justice herself.' That never happens because. . .

25

Don't Expect Justice—It Just Doesn't Exist

> Hear no evil, speak no evil, think no evil and you'll never be invited to my wife's parties.

Sally hardly recognized Savvy in her trendy goggles, scarf and high heels. Though she was still wearing a salwar-kameez, it was the body-hugging designer variety, unlike her flea-market-bought readymades.

'Despite being pregnant, you look very smart,' said Sally.

Savvy gave an enigmatic smile and rotated her keyring around her index finger, like Kamolika, her favourite TV vamp. 'As Jassi Didi says, these are the spoils of femininity. Rehaan bought me this dress and sandals and the goggles; the scarf and the gold earrings are courtesy the old lecher. They both believe it is their child that I am carrying, as does that stupid husband of mine.'

Sally had a strong urge to tell her to stop this nonsense or she would spoil her life but she stopped herself. All her attempts in the past had been brushed aside with indifference. Despite that, she spoke up.

'Really, Savvy, you should be very careful about saying all this in public. You are playing with fire, if you have told these two that they are the father of your child. I think you should...'

Savvy cut her short, 'Drop the sermon, dear...' 'Dear' was a new import into Savvy's vocabulary—from which serial, Sally didn't know. 'I've figured out everything. Last week, Rehaan's family suggested a match for him. I saw the photo. The girl was indeed beautiful. So I told Rehaan to refuse to see the girl. He was stalling—'How can I...'; 'At least I'll have to go and see her'; 'Mother will be angry'; blah, blah. I told him, nothing doing or I'd spill the beans about his being the father of my baby. He promptly told his mother that he didn't want to get married right now. Then he bought all these goodies for me. You know what he told me?' Savvy rolled her eyes suggestively. 'That he is getting a job in Dubai soon and that he hasn't told anybody about it except me. He told me that soon he would take me away to Dubai. He showed me the photos of Dubai. See.' Savvy was on cloud nine as she showed Sally the brochures and pictures. 'This is a dream city. I have already fallen in love with it.'

Sally was aghast at Sally's naïveté. 'Are you sure, he will...' She was cut short by the Pammi's entry.

Savvy quickly gathered all the brochures. She wanted to show it all to Pammi and take her guidance but one look at Pammi's face and she knew that today wasn't the day for that.

Pammi sat down and lit a cigarette. She asked the waiter for an extra- strong black coffee. As she took off her dark goggles, her eyes were bloodshot. There were dark circles under her eyes that indicated that she had either been weeping or missing out on sleep or most likely both.

At long last, Sally cleared her throat and asked, 'What is the matter, Pammi? You don't seem well.'

'It is that bastard husband of mine. He is sleeping with other women. Now I have proof of his debauchery. The worst part is that I can do nothing about it.'

'Why? You can always confront him and…' Sally was intercepted mid-sentence by Pammi.

'No. The proof is not of the type that I can openly expose.'

'Are you sure?' To Sally it seemed that Pammi was again making a mountain of the molehill.

'Yes. I am convinced and that is enough for me.' Sally kept quiet after that snub.

Now, Savvy asked softly, 'So, if you can't confront him, then what will you do?'

'I have retaliated by doing the next best thing. I have hit them all, the whole family, where it hurts most. Through my uncle, who is a senior journalist, I contacted a couple of page-three correspondents and told them they are all torturing me for dowry, especially my mother-in-law and my husband. I know my husband's weakness is his mother and her weakness is her status as a social worker. Defaming her is what would hurt the most. Mother and son won't be able to show their faces in the society where they roamed with heads held high as its custodians. I even called up all the hubby's friends and colleagues and told them about his infidelity. I also told all of them that he was impotent and was unable to satisfy me. Imagine what the papers would say about the head of an NGO who collects funds to fight for dowry victims and then demands dowry from her own daughter-in-law. I will finish this family and…'

'Just a moment, Pammi,' interjected Sally in a very firm tone. 'You have gone far enough with your accusations. Now just listen to me for five minutes. I am going to tell you a story of the wolf and the lamb.'

Savvy was all ears, for she loved stories. Also, she was petrified by Pammi's foul mood. Pammi, too, realized that she had said more than enough for the day. She nodded her head, encouraging Sally to go on.

'Once, a young lamb was drinking water from a river. A wolf spotted it from above the hill and came down to confront the lamb.

"I was drinking this water and you have dirtied it by putting your mouth into it."

"But, sir," protested the frightened lamb with a quivering voice, "I was downstream, how can I dirty the water upstream, where you were drinking it?"

"Maybe, but last year same time, I saw you drinking water upstream, and dirtying my water," boomed the wolf.

"But sir, I am barely eight months old." "How could I have dirtied your water one year ago?" protested the lamb.

"Hmm . . . if not you, then your dad must have done this," Saying that, the wolf jumped on the lamb and and killed it.'

Sally looked straight into the eyes of Pammi, 'Something similar is happening today. First, we try to find fault with our spouses, using a tainted lens. If, despite the taint, we don't find anything fishy, we say your forefathers did these brutalities to woman, so we will make you pay for them. You're doing the same—you accuse him of infidelity and then spread rumours of his being impotent. It can be only one of the two, right? You so desperately want to be the wronged one that you imagine shadows of non-existent evils hiding behind curtains. Worse, you are ready to set your own house on fire to be rid of these shadows. Be careful, you may repent when you realize there was really nothing behind the curtains.'

Sally waited for a response; when none came, she continued. 'I believe that you alone are not to be blamed. Your husband is also responsible because accepting injustice is as bad as perpetrating injustice. Both corrode the bond of marriage equally. But one thing I know for sure: the major blame rests on your shoulders because you are the perpetrator of this gross injustice.'

Pammi couldn't take this tirade any longer. 'Injustice? You think I've inflicted injustice? You don't know what injustice is. I've just finished their name and fame, but he has literally finished me. I didn't want to tell you this but the fact is that I have tested positive for HIV. I got the confirmation two days ago that that bastard husband has given it to me because he too is HIV positive. Now tell me who is unjust?'

Shock waves ran through the room, paralysing everyone.

There was nothing left to say or hear or even think, just a complete vacuum.

~

Justice does not exist

Nature is unjust. The tormenter oppresses and the oppressed suffers. The only way nature has taught the 'meek' to strike back is by procreating in ever-large numbers. Species at the bottom of the food chain produce offspring in large numbers to be devoured by those who are at higher rungs of the food chain. According to a rule of the mighty, the dominant devour the weak.

This law applies to humans as well, although its manifestation varies. When the battle was of the brawn, the physically weaker woman was inflicted with the unjust behaviour of males. Even today, the practice goes on in illiterate or bigoted societies.

In places where the battle has less to do with brawn and is more psychological and social, however, females are fighting for dominance. Where they are successful, whether because of social pressures or the male's weakness or even the law of the land, she does not desist from perpetuating her own form of injustice. From what I've seen, where the female is unjust, the injustice is ruthless and aggressive, just like when a new despot has recently acquired power.

What should you do if you are up against such injustice? I believe the middle path is the right path here. Accordingly, the first thing you do is just be yourself, because without this moral footing, you will not be able to take the second step sure-footedly. Keep the rules of the game fair and equal for all. If you are not a virgin, don't expect your wife to be one. If you acted greedily and asked for the sky in your dowry, don't expect her not to claim all your earth, that is, all your land and property, in alimony.

Second, don't accept injustice at any cost, even if the cost is social ridicule or mental agony or even a fight with the spouse, because, high as these costs are, they are nothing compared to the cost of giving in to injustice. Nothing fuels injustice as one's bowing to it unconditionally. Injustice gets escalated when one partner succumbs to the injustice.

While standing up to injustice does not remove the problem, the fact is that whenever there is gross injustice in a relationship, it spells hardship for all involved. It might seem that by succumbing to injustice, you have bought peace, but this is very transient. In the long run, it will make the marriage itself untenable.

~

You can avoid facing female injustice if you don the mantle of the senior partner in the relationship. This is not easy and may not always be possible, especially in cases where your wife is mature and smart. In such cases, she is bound to assume the seniority in relationship, but these women are generally intelligent enough to keep the male happy by apparently allowing him to dominate.

IN A NUTSHELL

When you don't accept injustice, it usually loses steam and peters off. But when injustice crosses a limit, it must be fought till the end. If despite all your efforts the injustice persists, it is better that you prepare for the ultimate solution to injustice—a parting of ways.

26

Legal Issues and Divorce

PRICELESS BARBIE

A man walks into a store to buy a Barbie doll for his daughter.

'How much is that Barbie in the window?' he asks the shop assistant.

She responds, 'Which Barbie? We have

- Barbie Goes to the Gym for $19.95
- Barbie Goes to the Ball for $19.95
- Barbie Goes Shopping for $19.95
- Barbie Goes to the Beach for $19.95
- Barbie Goes Nightclubbing for $19.95
- And Divorced Barbie for $395.00'

The man asks, 'Why is Divorced Barbie so much more expensive than all the others?'

'That's obvious,' the assistant says, 'Divorced Barbie comes with Ken's house, Ken's car, Ken's boat, Ken's furniture, Ken's . . .'

Savvy reached Rendezvous very late and was surprised to find that even Pammi hadn't come as yet. Only Sally was sitting there, sipping her second cup of coffee.

'Sorry. That husband of mine came home early and wanted tea and pakodas. That took so long that I got late. There should be a law to give independence to women also. Why should we remain shackled to the hearth for life?'

Sally couldn't help smiling at the change in Savvy's tone as she parroted Jassi's words.

'Some day, I'm going to make that husband of mine pay for all these atrocities. I only wish I could haul him to the police station and make him pay for all his marriage crimes, like Pammi is doing. Moreover, unlike Pammi's husband, he had actually taken dowry also. That is a crime, isn't it?'

'Yes, it is but had he not taken dowry, would you have staked a claim to your parents' ancestral property?'

'No, never. In villages asking for property from brothers is considered the meanest thing to do; not even the lowest castes do that.'

'Exactly! That was the original purpose of dowry. The girl was given streedhan, which was considered her right, by her parents at the time of marriage. Greed and materialism vitiated this system. Forget about that rosy picture you have of police stations and courts; these are hellish places, whose experience I don't even wish for an enemy, leave alone a friend. It is commonly said that both parties are losers in litigation, only the lawyer wins. I really wish that, despite her genuine grouse, Pammi somehow settles the issue without dragging it to the courts. It will be good for both——' Her sentence was interrupted by the shrill ringing of her mobile.

It was Pammi. Sally promptly picked up the phone, saying, 'Hello, Pammi. Where are you?'

After a pause, Sally responded gravely with, 'Oh, no. What now?' She listened to Pammi for a few minutes, then after ending the call, she slumped in her chair.

Anxiously, Savvy blurted, 'What happened? What did Pammi say?'

'It is not good news. Pammi has rashes on her body and that is why she hasn't come. She's also told her lawyer to prepare her case for divorce. She said she would meet us next fortnight.'

'Why does she have rashes?'

'I don't know but it might be that HIV is now manifesting itself.'

'These rashes mean her disease is increasing. Do you think we should meet her? I mean, are we at any risk or something?'

Sally shook her head and got up. Somehow, the whole thing seemed meaningless. She felt utterly helpless about doing anything for her friend. She also didn't know which news saddened her more—HIV or divorce.

~

Marital litigation—Daiv looked at his research papers:

FROM PROTECTORS OF THE TORTURED WIFE TO SAVIOUR OF THE WRONGED HUSBAND

The law has taken many turns in the path of changing marital equations. But justice still eludes most cases for there is no single key that can fit the myriad locks of human nature.

- Following a spate of dowry-related deaths, the stringent anti- dowry section 498A was inserted in the Indian Penal Code in 1983
- 'Accept what wife says'—Supreme Court. The Supreme Court bench advised a divorce litigant thus: 'If your wife gives a suggestion, accept it, irrespective of the fact whether it is sensible or not. Otherwise you will face trouble. Hum sab bugat bhogi hain.' (We are all sufferers.)
- 'Living in' is no offence'—Supreme Court
- Misuse of dowry law—4.2 lakh people, including 1 lakh women, were arrested between the years 2005–07, with less than 5 per cent conviction rate. The government has asked for legislation to review the stringent provision of this law.
- No divorce on grounds of 'irretrievable breakdown' of marriage, according to the Hindi Marriage Act (HMA), 1955. Divorce only on the grounds of adultery, cruelty, desertion, and impotence.
- Amend dowry law to stop misuse—Supreme Court said, 'Very large number of cases/complaints filed under anti-dowry law (section 498A of IPC) are either false or exaggerated.

- 'Irretrievable breakdown' of marriage is enough ground to grant divorce—Law Commission.
- 'Live-in relationships can be equivalent to marriage if they are continued for a long time'—Supreme Court, 18 August 2010 by a two-judge bench headed by Justices P. Sathasivam and B.S. Chauhan
- 'Such is the level of blatant exaggeration of cruel behaviour of the husband and his family that to find out the truth is a herculean task in majority of complaints'—Justice Dalveer Bhandari and Justice K.S. Radhakrishnan, Supreme Court, 17 August 2010. 'The Supreme Court has plainly told the government to take a relook at the anti-dowry law—Section 498A of the IPC—saying it has been misused by women to lodge false or exaggerated complaints against husbands and their relatives accusing them of cruel behaviour.' (*TOI*)

~

False litigation—SIFF (Save Indian Family Foundation) is a group which fights for the rights of men falsely implicated in dowry cases. 'The problem', says Rakesh K. Kalra, who represents many SIFF members, 'is that it is a non-bailable offence.' So a person can be imprisoned just on the basis of a single complaint, even before the trial and proof of wrongdoing.

~

TECHIE KILLS WIFE, HANGS SELF

In his suicide note, Amit said, 'I loved her a lot, even though she had an affair with her colleague . . . there was also discussion about divorce. I feared that she might file a harassment case against me, though I had not accepted anything from her. So, I killed her . . .'

Divorce

The Libber Cats recently celebrated the fastest divorce or rather separation of one of their members. That cat-libber left her husband on the wedding day itself because her husband couldn't satisfy her physically. The 'doli' was sent off at 4 a.m. and she called her father at 7 a.m. to take her back from the hotel, where she was to have spent her wedding night.

In a similar incident, one of my patients, a beauty-parlour attendant, told me that she had gone back to her parents the day after her wedding because her husband had failed to consummate the marriage. The husband had admitted that he suffered from premature ejaculation before marriage and that he had even visited a so-called sex clinic in Daryaganj to boost his sexual prowess. Knowing the kind of nonsense these clinics fill the clients' minds with, I persuaded her to go back to her husband and give him time. A month later, the girl told me that not only was the husband functioning normally but he was also hugely indebted to her for saving him from being labelled as impotent.

In the Indian context, where the boys have absolutely no day-to-day interaction with girls, it is natural to get overexcited by the mere touch of a naked female body and ejaculate even before penetration. How is a groom, who has gone through backbreaking festivities and rituals for two to three days and who has spent a couple of sleepless nights, to be expected to perform physical love, possibly for the first time in his life?

~

The situation today

According to an ANI report on a study on marriage and divorce, published in the *Times of India,* 50 per cent of the future first marriages would end in divorce. The data also showed that the percentage of population living together without marriage increased from 3 per cent in 1982 to 11 per cent in 2010–11.

What is fuelling this escalation in divorce rates?

Compatibility criteria—Neil Clark Warren, founder of eHarmony, conducted over 500 'divorce autopsies', interviewing the former spouses and their parents. He found that the rifts in the relationship had begun far earlier than expected. He says, 'Seventy per cent of relationships were already in pretty deep trouble when the couple first married, because their characteristics didn't match.' He believes that to find a soulmate, there are some twenty-nine criteria that should match, including curiosity, intellect, appearance, anger management, self-perception, honesty, spirituality and moral values. The most important criteria, however was emotional health, which encompassed interpersonal care, affection and sharing.

RISE IN DIVORCE RATES

Data from various courts and marriage cells show a huge increase in divorce rates, not just in metros but also in smaller, more conservative cities:

- Ludhiana's marriage dispute cell's complaint rate increased seven times in the last seven years.
- The number of divorces doubled from 237 in 2006 to 433 in 2007.
- In Lucknow's family court almost 300 cases are filed every month.
- Even in the conservative Muslim qazi court in Bhopal, 76 per cent claims are made by women—up from 20 per cent, seven years ago.

Causes of divorce

- **Intolerance:** The fulcrum of tolerance, the tipping point at which a decision, argument or even a relationship tilts towards breaking point, has shifted drastically to the left on the time-scale. Decisions lead to differences, which lead to arguments leading to a break-up without any discernible warning. Mutual respect and admiration is lacking to begin with, and it never gets a chance to develop.
- **Attitude**: According to marriage counsellor Rita Kapoor, 'Attitude and image problems top the list of reasons, followed by unrealistic expectations.' Divorce lawyer Ansuya Dutt elaborates, 'The attitude of the young towards

EVEN A MOLEHILL CAN DO US APART

In today's intolerant times, it doesn't take important issues to cause a divorce. Something as trivial as the wrong fragrance of an after-shave lotion suffices. The reasons:

- The husband insists that she dress in a clingy dress
- The wife serves tuna-casserole, his least favourite dish
- The wife tampers with the TV antenna
- The husband communicates only with Post-its
- The husband insists that his pet tarantula be kept in a glass case next to his bed
- The husband has body odour
- The husband changes channels too fast
- The husband demands sex daily

marriage is shockingly casual and frivolous.' The attitude of the modern Indian women is one of rigidity. Most are not prepared to invest in the relationship nor are they ready to wait patiently, unlike women in earlier generations. They want immediate gratification and will not settle for anything less than their dream image.

- **Facebook:** According to a recent survey in UK, (*TOI* 3 June 2012) Facebook was blamed for nearly one-third of all divorces. People spend too much time on FB, chatting or playing games, causing a strain in a marriage. FB has also made affairs or flirtations easy to indulge in without the need for any sort of commitment.
- **Mobile phone:** Digital footprints by way of SMSes are easy to spot and also leave undeletable evidence that can bring a

marriage to an early end, especially in the case of proving the adultery of a spouse.

- **The in-laws:** Marriage counsellor Dr Khurana says, 'Ninety-five per cent of people who divorce within the initial years cite the in-laws as the main reason, specifically, the mother-in-law.' This problem is more in love marriages than arranged marriages, maybe because the family doesn't feel the responsibility of choosing the spouse. Outside unsolicited advice, especially from the girl's parents, also makes it difficult for the new bride to adjust to the new family.

Experts believe the onus of solving this tangle lies on the husband, who should ensure that his wife gets her proper place and respect in the family. He also has to make his family's traditions and habits clear to the wife and show her how she can adjust to them.

IN A NUTSHELL

So, dear friends, if you want a lasting and stable relationship, go easy on your mobile phone, Facebook and the in-laws. Yes, the in-laws!

PART IV

A DIRECT WORD OF ADVICE

Friend: Do you think advising is a thankless job?

Writer: On the contrary, everything I advise comes back with a thanks.

A Word from the Author

I decided to write this book when I realized that most males would be able to solve their marital issues if they could decipher how the female mind works. I've tried to do that, and now a direct word with all the concerned parties in a marriage would be in order. That is what this final section is dedicated to.

However, before getting down to serious business, let me tell you, in a lighter vein, what men have always been wishing for.

PRENUPTIAL BOND—IF WISHES WERE HORSES

Prenuptial bonds are the flavour of the season but I have rarely seen them making a difference. A bond of a different kind that can save your marriage, IF she agrees to sign on the dotted line:

- Always ask for what you want—subtle hints don't work, strong hints don't work. Just say it.
- Don't expect us to know what day it is. Mark birthdays and anniversaries on a calendar and remind us a day in advance (and in the morning in question).

- Yes and no will be accepted as perfectly acceptable answers to all kinds of questions.
- You'll come to us with a problem ONLY if you want our help in solving it—just listening and sympathizing will be left to your girlfriends.
- Anything said seven days or more ago will be null and void and inadmissible in arguments.
- If you say 'nothing', when we ask, 'What is wrong?'→it will mean nothing is wrong.
- The toilet seat will be put down without fuss, if it is up. We'll put it up, you put it down. Period.
- Peeing standing is more difficult than shooting at point-blank range. Misses will be accepted.
- Never ask us if you are looking fat. If you think you are—then you are. We won't reply.
- We won't be told to go shopping—it is not a sport and will never be for us.
- When going out, you can't do the following:
    - Ask us to choose your dress at the last moment (we probably chose ours last week).
    - Expect us to appreciate more than seven colours in the spectrum VIBGYOR. Peach is a fruit for us, not a colour.
    - Asking us to choose which pair of shoes out of thirty goes with your dress (we've had only three pairs since childhood, how can we know?).
    - Prevent us from ogling (it is natural that we do).
- Finally, crying is not allowed in front of us. It is blackmail and, therefore, illegal.

27

A Word for the In-laws

> God felt he couldn't be everywhere, so he made a mother.
>
> The devil felt he couldn't be everywhere, so he made a mother-in-law.

When Sally entered the restaurant, Savvy was already lapping up Pammi's story.

'Come on in, Sally. Pammi was telling me what happened when she came to know that her husband was also HIVpositive.' Then turning to Pammi, she asked, 'Then what did you do?'

'Like always, I rushed to my mom for advice,' Pammi said. 'She said, "Don't worry. I am not dead yet. If they did this to you, we will make their lives so miserable that they will ask, with folded hands, for your forgiveness."'

'How would that help?' Sally asked.

'Nothing can help my situation. They have ruined my life. As Mom says, "Now the aim of your life is to make sure that they pay the price." My mother has thought of everything, like always. She always plans immaculately, considering all pros and cons. I've talked to her every day since I got married, and told her everything that happens in my in-laws' house. She advises me on what to do.'

'Is it right to tell her everything?' queried Sally.

'Of course! If we can't take our mothers into confidence, who can we? I tell her everything. She has much more experience of these things. After all, she has fought pitched battles with three sisters-in-law and two brothers-in-law before she succeeded in extricating my father from his family. She had planned something similar for me, before this problem cropped up. You know what my mom did? She went to their house and pounced on my mother-in-law the moment she opened the door. She gave her a piece of her mind right there at the front door, with the whole neighbourhood listening. My mother-in-law lost all her haughtiness and requested my mom with folded hands to come in and talk peacefully but my mom didn't pay heed. She shouted the whole story—impotent, adulterer, HIV, everything, right there in front of everybody.'

Sally gasped with disbelief.

Pammi continued as Savvy looked at her, transfixed. 'Then, she told me to pack up my things and move out of that house pronto. My mother-in-law was embarrassed because of the neighbours peering from their terraces. She didn't even come to my room when my mom and I were packing. Seizing the opportunity, my mom told me to pack all his original documents, degrees, certificates and even his laptop along.'

'What good would that do?' asked Sally.

'Mom says the more trouble you can make for the enemy the better. Let him run from pillar to post to get all the originals. Moreover, the laptop was a brilliant idea of my mom. The lawyer whom we contacted as soon as we reached home said that this laptop could provide plenty of fuel for the forthcoming battle.'

'You are so lucky,' gushed Savvy. 'Your mother is readily available for taking up the cudgels on your behalf. My mother is so far away that I can consult her only on very important matters by calling on the neighbour's phone. One advice she always gives me is that I should get my husband in my control, by hook or by crook. She says, "The husband should either be so besotted by your beauty or so afraid of you that he would readily follow you against the wishes of the whole family." The first approach has not been entirely successful, so I am trying the second one. Now he does seem somewhat scared, so I think this second route is working.'

'What about you? What does your mother advise?' Pammi turned to Sally, who was silently sipping her coffee. 'Where does your mom stay?'

'Just a few minutes' drive from our home.'

'You're so lucky!' exclaimed Savvy. 'Then you must be meeting her on a daily basis and taking her advice.'

'Not really! My husband and I go together once a fortnight.'

'Don't you get along with your mother?'

'On the contrary, we are like close friends.' she said. 'In fact, she is one of the reasons that my marriage is fine.'

After a pause, Sally continued, 'I told you about our initial skirmishes and that twice I had rushed to my mom in a huff. What I did not elaborate was how the matter had got resolved. I was kind of embarrassed as to how you would evaluate my mom's actions and my bowing to her wishes. Today, I realize how vital my mom's actions were for our marriage and I have no hesitation in telling you the grisly details.'

All eyes focused on Sally's face. 'The first time I reached my mother's place, she must have sensed my mood and gauged why I was visiting alone. She didn't say anything except asking calmly, "So when is Susheelji coming for dinner?" Her no-nonsense attitude told me that she was not interested in knowing about my skirmishes. It is not that she was not interested about my life and well-being. Normally, whenever we met, she would ask many questions about my in-laws' lifestyle and food habits. But that day she sent me a clear message that I should have come with my husband. I had no choice but to sheepishly call Susheel and invite him for dinner.'

'Oh my, what a letdown! What did he do?' enquired Pammi.

'He also came with lot of scepticism, thinking that maybe he would be chastised or advised about our skirmish. But he soon realized that Mom was oblivious of our fight. He felt really relieved and believed that it was I who had acted so maturely. At home, he thanked me for this and then we made up by apologizing to each other, followed by some great love . . .' She giggled.

'Then what happened?' asked Savvy.

'Well! The same thing happened once more and again my

mom didn't offer to hear my woes and I got a feeling that she would be very unhappy if I told her about our fight. This time, Susheel came more readily when I asked him over, convinced that I don't divulge unpleasant things about him to my mother. He told me in so many words how he appreciated this and promised me that in future he would patiently hear and address all my complaints, as I had nobody else in whom I could confide. I believe this has strengthened my marriage no end, because he has started acting as my guardian and even takes a position against his family if he finds them acting unfairly with me at any point. This is one thing he had never done before and never would have, if it weren't for my mother's wisdom. She gave a clear message to me and indirectly to him that our lives were our business and that we have to find solutions to our problems ourselves.'

'Didn't you feel forsaken by her attitude?' asked Pammi.

'Well, I did. After our first fight I had wept, believing that my mother was indifferent to my needs. Now I thank her for her wisdom, for I realize how difficult it must have been for her to keep from asking about what was wrong. This system of fortnightly visits was her idea. Now, everybody knows that I go there twice a month and my mother-in-law is happy that I don't keep rushing off to my mother's house. This way, my parents also kind of celebrate that visit with special dishes and festivities and even Susheel looks forward to the visit. When my brothers get married, my bhabhi too will appreciate that I interfere so little in their lives.'

Shravan's hand sprang up to clap but his involuntary action was checked by a loudly blurted 'Wow!' Then he embarrassingly added, 'Ahmm . . . This vada tastes great.'

Daiv looked at his plate and smiled, for Shravan was eating idlis.

Pammi looked vague. She was thinking of how her brother and his wife were already making her feel unwelcome in her mother's home.

~

Dear parents,

I know most of you are proud of the sacrifices that you have made for the studies/well-being/career/ success of your wards. When it comes to doing something that will ensure lifelong happiness for them, will you be found wanting? I can hear your resounding 'No!'

That crucial juncture is the marriage of your child. Your actions in the first two years of their marriage will define their happiness quotient.

What do you have to do?

NOTHING!

Yes, you've read correctly! It is not what you do for the relationship of your children that will decide their happiness. It is what you feel like doing but desist from doing that will decide their happiness—when you do something for the relationship of newlyweds, irrespective of how well-meaning the gesture is, it will be considered an infringement of the couples' privacy by one or both partners.

As parents, the foremost thing you should do is not meddle in the newlyweds' day-to-day affairs. Mothers, hand over the reins of your son, if they were in your hands, willingly and happily to your daughter-in-law. She has the same right on your son as you have on your husband. And the only way you were able to strike a balance with your husband was in total privacy. Those of you who were not accorded that privacy, as was common in conservative families of the previous generation, are still groping for an equilibrium. Let that not happen with your child.

Second, and more important, I need to address the mothers of the wife. All said and done, India is still mainly a patriarchal society and the bride still moves to the groom's home after marriage. Till this changes, try to remember that your daughter has got married now and has a life of her own, and the less you interfere in it, the happier she'll be.

You overlook the fact that when your daughter communicates with you, she only tells you about selected incidents. This is akin to showing highlights of a day-long cricket match in two minutes, so it appears as if each ball results in a six or a wicket. There may have been a number of other caring incidents that were not highlighted but comprised the majority of the day.

If at all you advise, gear your advice towards strengthening the marriage, not extracting a pound of flesh, nor seeking an eye for an eye. You're probably listening to only one side of the story, and your advice should be to settle differences between themselves as far as possible. Even your best-intentioned advice can be aggravating, just because it is coming from you.

Human reactions, like all reactions, follow a set of rules. As in chemical reactions, two elements meet and react and the reaction goes on until an equilibrium is reached and a new compound is formed that is vastly different from any of the constituent elements. There can be catalysts or co-enzymes that can affect the reaction, but these catalysts cannot really enter the equation and remain unchanged at the end of the equation. If they enter the equation, even slightly, not only is the new compound formed unstable but it will also be vastly different from the original compound. As a parent, don't enter the equation or enter as a catalyst.

The worst thing parents can do is to take up cudgels on behalf of their child and directly confront the in-laws, as Pammi's mom did. It will spell disaster by polarizing the issue so much that any chance of normalcy is obliterated.

Sally's mother on the other hand, was the wisest. Her actions acted as a distant catalyst, to hasten the return to peace in the couple's relationship. They also communicated to the husband that the responsibility of listening and caring for Sally now lay on his shoulders. Sally's mom's policy of minimum interference helped develop mutual caring and understanding between the newlyweds.

IN A NUTSHELL

Realize that you, the parent, have now become the proverbial foreign hand in the lives of the newlyweds. Lay off and see your child's marriage flourish. Amen!

28

A Word for the Husband

The atmosphere of the restaurant was suffused as each woman present had a load that needed to be taken off her chest. Pammi and Savvy seemed to be still collecting their thoughts, so for a change Sally decided to open the conversation.

'Today, I really snapped at my husband.' This was new, and Pammi and Savvy were curious.

'Why?' asked Pammi. 'What did he do?'

'Nothing. Actually, it was not his fault at all. He had just asked me for a cup of coffee, while I was beginning to cook dinner. I was already tired because of my tedious project and upset with my mother-in-law who has been very edgy this past week because of my sister-in-law's marital discord. She asked me to shut down my computer and quickly make dinner for her son, who was tired after working in the office all these long hours. I felt resentful, thinking if he has been working then what have I been doing since morning—playing computer games? I dumped this irritation on him.'

WHY MEN CAN NEVER WIN:

- You put a woman on a pedestal to protect her from the rat race→you're an MCP
  - You make her work and you manage the household→you're a sissy
- You mention how nice she looks→it is sexual harassment
  - If you say nothing→it is male indifference
- You cry→you're a wimp
  - If you don't→you're an insensitive jerk
- You make a decision without consulting her→you're a chauvinist
  - She makes a decision without consulting you→she is a liberated lady
- You ask her to do something she doesn't enjoy→it is domination
  - She asks you→it is a favour
- You like her to shave her legs→you're a sexist
  - You don't→you are unromantic
- You try to keep yourself in shape→ you're vain
  - You don't→you are a slob

TAKE YOUR PICK

'What did he do?'

'Poor thing slunk away and made his coffee in the microwave upstairs.'

'Good!' said Pammi. 'These men should be taught these lessons occasionally, otherwise they start taking you for granted.'

'But I felt very sorry for him. I vented my frustration of not being considered an equal by my mother-in-law on him. He even offered to rub my shoulders and forehead at night to ease my tiredness. I really felt very guilty.'

'You start feeling guilty too quickly. I don't have any such compunction regarding opponents.' Pammi was categorical. 'My husband has done a big wrong and I am determined to teach the whole family a lesson. Last week I lodged the FIR in the dowry cell and the police came for them. I informed the media too. Though the whole family remained in the police station only for a few hours, the media castigated my MIL as she is the acting secretary of this cell against atrocities on women. What crazy surnames they appended to her—"Miss Jekyl and Hyde", "The vixen in sheep's clothing" and what not. Now she will never be able to show her face to the world.'

'Yes, I read that, but didn't you tell us that they never demanded any dowry, and even your reception was jointly funded by your parents and your in-laws? Then why?' Blurted Sally.

'This is the only way I can send them to jail. Marrying off their HIV positive son to me, despite knowing everything, is not an offence in the eyes of law. So let them face the consequences of their actions, even if I have to be devious. Not just that, I've also told all my husband's friends and colleagues that he is HIV positive. They have ruined my life, so I have ruined theirs—quid pro quo.' Pammi clapped her hands.

'Bloody bitch!' thought Joginder. Shravan, too, was flabbergasted. 'Would Maya do something this underhand?'

'No!' he muttered without conviction. He could hear a much louder 'Definitely!' in his head.

Savvy was propelled to launch into her story. 'I, too, have pretty much fixed up my Mr Know-all.' She sipped her cold coffee with the straw at the corner of her lips, just as she had seen that vengeful bahu do in her favourite TV serial. 'He used to tell me that he knew everything about my activities and threatened to send me off to his home in the village, if I didn't desist from talking and laughing with others. Just because he is an introvert, he wants everybody to sulk in solitude. Yesterday, when he threatened me, I told him that I cared two hoots about his threats. He got infuriated and shouted that I was a slut from a low-grade family. I got mad and in a fit of rage I told him that the child was not his and that I was leaving him as he was incapable of satisfying me. And also that I am going to tell the whole world that he is impotent.'

Sally noticed that the words were borrowed ad verbatim from Jassi, so was her tone.

All her listeners were aghast. 'Won't you regret this? Your husband is already so suspicious,' commented Sally.

'I am no fool. I have taken a firm commitment from Rehaan that he will elope with me and his child. And, in case of any eventuality, the landlord has already consented to marry me as he also believes that the child is his.

'I had not imagined my husband's reaction to my statement. You know what? The guy slumped to the ground, shattered. He stuttered, "Don't ever say such things! All husbands and wives fight but don't ever say such things. Don't. Ever." He must have felt threatened, scared of being branded as impotent. Then he started placating me. It was very funny. For the first time in my life, I was fuming and he was trying to appease me, despite my harsh statement.' Savvy was laughing uncontrollably.

'He doesn't know me. I know how to squeeze him dry. Now he will stay in my fist forever and do what I tell him to. He'd better.' She twirled a strand of her hair, the way Kamolika, her favourite TV vamp, did, to the tune of the background strain of 'Nikaaaa'.

~

My dear friend, I have written the whole book addressed to you to remove strife from your marriage. For this, you—the husband—have to take the lead by investing in your marriage and nurturing it with care.

Take marriage seriously. Don't enter it frivolously, as if it is a computer game where you can reboot the game by the push of a button. Also, do not enter this institution under the influence of testosterone surging in your loins. Getting married for the sole purpose of sex is like going to a college for the sole purpose of having some fun. Think of marriage as a lifelong commitment.

You need to gain respect in the relationship. For this, be just and fair. Don't be greedy. Don't just think of what you can grab from the marriage or from the girl's side. Don't expect the wife to be a beast of burden who will take care of your household all alone while juggling with a full-time job to add to the household income. Either take over the responsibility of earning and let her manage the home exclusively, or share the household chores with her when she is sharing your role of provider.

Be mindful to project a true image of yourself in her mind before the marriage. By all means, be on your best possible behaviour and play down some of your avoidable negatives. But don't depict such a lofty image so that you find yourself unable to fit into your own portrayal.

After marriage, don the mantle of the master of the house. To be considered the senior partner, you would have to be the more mature one. Accept that women are taking over some male-designated jobs and doing them very well. Laud and encourage them. Also accept that women are rebelling against the very concept of adjusting because she's bought into the belief that adjustment is a sign of weakness. Lead by example. Instead of competing with her non-adjusting nature, show that you will voluntarily make bigger adjustments in life. This would suggest that adjusting in married life is a sign of strength, not weakness.

Adjustment can come in the following ways:

- Sharing of household work, especially if the wife is working.
- Moulding your parents (specially your mother's) attitude to accept the daughter-in-law's role as another breadwinner who has to be accorded the same respect and consideration as you are given. This may be a bit tricky.
- For a housewife, the parents have to be made to understand that the wife has her own aspirations and plans about life, which have to be respected. Also, try to ensure that the wife, if not working at a job, is gainfully engaged in some other constructive activity, which can range from fine arts to culinary art, depending exclusively on her taste and choice.

- Adopt the role of a mentor and explain to your wife her duties as well as rights in the house. This would help her gel with the family as a whole.
- Plan a perspective about future with her, irrespective of whether she is working or not, so that she can envision her role in the future of your joint life.

Even after doing all this, understand that women are very different from men. As they say, the female of the human species may or may not be deadlier but she sure is more complicated.

LASTLY, RESPECT HER

The lady of the house is the stabilizing factor in a family. Since time immemorial, we have worshipped the female deity as the benefactor of the human race despite accepting that the power lies with the figurehead, the male deity.

Unfortunately, our worship has now become more ritualistic and we've relegated the female to a secondary (or even tertiary) status in the house. This is what has brought the downfall of the institution of marriage.

Agreed, now the so-called liberated woman is rocking the boat for the reverse reasons and is decimating the institution of marriage further. But the only way out of this 'strike-counter-strike' is to reinstate the respect for the lady of the house unilaterally and unconditionally. This gesture, if genuine, will be admired and reciprocated in equal measure. A marriage in which there is mutual respect and admiration can never go off track.

~

Finally, no amount of advice or counselling will really be able to crack the code that will win over the specific partner that you have been paired with. Try to learn her perspective as much as possible. This takes time.

Until you've figured out her perspective, walk a tightrope somewhere between appeasement and a non-caring attitude. Here 'wit' is your only balancing pole that helps you stay on the rope. When I was a newlywed, I kept my fingers crossed and prayed to God and so should you. When you are praying, ask that God takes care to pair you with a Saloni, not a Savvy or Pammi.

IN A NUTSHELL

Marriage, as they say, is the biggest gamble of life and the dice are rolled in heaven. Respect what the gods have destined for you.

29

Catharsis—a Word from the Wife

For a relationship of two, the patience of one is a must.

The restaurant Rendezvous had been her favourite destination but today she was trudging along as if her feet refused to take her there. She would not have come today, had she not heard the interview yesterday.

It was, after all, Independence Day. The market was deserted, reflecting her sombre mood. Apart from some eateries, all shutters were down.

She entered the restaurant and as was expected, there was nobody there except the three gents, whose presence she had always resented. Despite her anonymity, she had always been uncomfortable with their eavesdropping. Today, however, she was relieved to see them there.

She hesitated for a moment. Should she turn back? She really wanted to. 'No, I have to go in,' she thought. She had to. She owed this to her friends. She took a deep breath and walked in.

Dr Daiv was startled to see her approach his table instead of her own.

'May I sit down?' she asked.

Daiv was so startled that he almost knocked his coffee off the table as he spluttered, 'Yes... yes. Yes, please.'

'Today, I have come to have a word with you. All of you.' She looked up towards the other two, beckoning them over to their table.

Shravan and Joginder exchanged startled glances but did as told. 'I have come only to talk to you all today. I've been forced to come here because of Dr Daiv's interview yesterday.'

Two pairs of eyes turned towards Daiv. They had obviously missed the interview.

'Well, I am a writer and . . .' Daiv answered the querying eyebrows, '. . . I had given an interview regarding my new book on marital relations, especially addressed to the male.'

'What was your closing comment yesterday?'

Daiv fidgeted in his seat, 'Well, actually I was commenting on this new trend of women becoming a cause of strain in a marriage and a pain for the husband and in-laws.'

'That is much more mildly put than what you said yesterday.' Saloni's tone was matter of fact, rather than accusing, Daiv nodded in agreement.

'Yes, I vociferously pointed out that some of these so-called liberated women are bringing unimaginable misery to the lives of their husbands and in-laws by their connivance and unreasonable attitudes.' Daiv shrugged as if defending his comment.

'Okay! Let it go.' Saloni nodded grudgingly because his statement still did not reflect the bitterness of his remarks at the interview. 'Those comments disturbed me no end. Not that your comments were wrong. But they were incomplete and I didn't want that picture to colour your readers' minds, especially women.'

'I have mentioned right on the cover that the book is specifically meant for males and forbidden for . . .'

'Chances are that many wives or 'would-be' wives will read it for this reason. That is why what I am going to tell you is so important. But first can we have a cup of coffee please? I am exhausted.'

'Should I get coffee prepared for others also?' asked Joginder hesitant, pointing towards the door.

'No!' she sighed. 'No one is coming. No one!'

Saloni got up and hurried towards the toilet but failed to hide the tears welling up in her eyes.

~

When she came back, they all settled down to their coffee. Saloni closed her eyes to collect her thoughts. 'I know you all have been eavesdropping on our conversations for a while for reasons of your own—Dr Daiv for writing his book and you two maybe to learn about women.'

Two embarrassed, red faces mumbled something incoherent.

'I resented this intrusion but today I feel that maybe it had a purpose.' Saloni took a deep breath. 'When Dr Daiv talked about the damage modern women are inflicting on men, I realized that he is seeing only one side of the story. I am not saying whose fault it is. I agree that in today's marriages, most of the strain is, indeed, contributed by women.' She sipped her coffee.

Daiv felt a load lift a load off his shoulders as he heard Saloni's comment.

Saloni continued. 'I wanted to draw your attention to another very important aspect.' She paused as if thinking about what to say next. 'Whenever there is a stressful situation, both partners become unhappy, irrespective of who is its perpetrator and who is at the receiving end. Life is not a TV soap serial, where in one scene the vamp-daughter-in-law makes life hell for the in-laws and the husband and in the next scene, she is sitting in a club enjoying her success. In fact, the very idea that a conceited daughter-in-law conspires for the sole purpose of causing suffering is too far-fetched.

'Women in real life may have misplaced notions about in-laws and marriage but they fight only because they really believe,whether rightly or wrongly, that they are the victims. Once they are convinced that they have been wronged, they do retaliate in whichever way they know. It may be fair or foul. It may even be outright deceitful but their anguish is the only motivating factor.

'These women don't just make life hell for their husbands or in-laws but for themselves, too. In fact, they are the worst hit because in the end they are the unhappiest of all. They are not to be hated but pitied.' Saloni fell silent, as if unable to go on. Her face had pain written all over it.

After a prolonged silence, Daiv decided to intervene. 'Aren't your friends deliberately and unjustifiably causing pain to their husbands and in-laws and from all accounts getting away with it while others are paying the price?'

Saloni smiled wryly. 'You think they have got away with it? Let me enlighten you, Doctor: Pammi was fighting because she believed that her husband had been cheating on her and as a result gave her HIV. One day she called me at home. She had a heavy load on her chest and she wanted to tell someone who would not judge her. We met at a nearby restaurant.

'She told me she had gone to Dr Gupta, who is also her friend. He informed her that the tests had confirmed that it was she who got the infection first, maybe even before marriage, and that she had now passed the virus to her husband, not the other way round. She was hysterical with guilt. I tried to console her but she was wracked with guilt. She just didn't know how she could face all those people in front of whom she had labelled her innocent husband characterless. Above all, she just didn't have the courage to meet her husband. She told me to apologize to her husband from her side.'

'I tried to reason with her but my words could not penetrate the dark clouds that had enveloped her soul.' A tear slid down her moist eye. 'The next day, I got the news that she had committed suicide. Her guilt was too much to bear.'

A hushed silence fell over the place. For the men, it was as if a well-known friend had passed away.

Daiv was the first to recover, 'Savvy must be shattered. She considered Pammi her mentor.'

The tear-streaked face of Saloni broke into an ironical smile. 'Yes, she would have been shattered had she got the news.'

Three pairs of eyes asked for an explanation. 'Her own plan to use her sexuality to come out of the drudgery of her household chores has misfired, even worse. The pregnancy that she wanted to use to triple advantage became the proverbial millstone around her neck. As the tongues got wagging, her affairs started tumbling out of the closet.

'Her husband was the first to rebuke her, which was expected. The landlord, whose house she had dreamt of inheriting turns out to be the father of three sons working in Mumbai and Bangalore. He quickly pronounced her as characterless and washed his hands off her and the child. Her prince in shining armour, who had her believe that he would take her to Dubai if anything went wrong, simply vanished.'

'Then where is she now?' Joginder spoke for the first time. He had always believed that if his wife was to ever become evil, she would resemble Savvy.

'Her in-laws sent her back to her parents with an unwanted pregnancy and the stigma of being loose. The disgraced parents abandoned her for fear of the stigma affecting her sisters. When I last talked to her, she had been left in an abandoned hut on the outskirts of the village to fend for herself. Now, in this pregnant state, she is all alone with no one to help her and without basic amenities like electricity or even drinking water. Even her phone is dead now.'

The atmosphere by this time was so heavy that every person's breathing could be heard clearly. The air-conditioner suddenly coughed and came to life as if trying to lift the pall of gloom. 'These women have burnt much more than their fingers while trying to burn their marriages.' she added.

Saloni looked at Daiv. 'Fighting nature is not the way to gain equality and independence. In our zeal to do whatever a man can do, we have not only burdened ourselves with double the tasks but have also relegated our original tasks of homemaker and child-bearer. Worse still, while emulating the male, we have also imbibed their weaknesses like intolerance and solving problems via aggressive confrontation. Hence the overtly rebellious attitude. Fearing compromise will be manipulated as was in the past, women refuse to adjust to the new life. I believe this intolerant attitude is the core of marital discord.

'This refusal to see logic and get swayed by the hype and hyperbole of others is a surefire recipe for marital disaster. This is what has caused the tragedy of my two friends and this is what I want you to warn women about.'

Saloni slumped exhausted in her chair, as if the mission had been accomplished. She had surprised herself with her capacity to talk. Her silence initiated a cascade of thoughts in each listener's mind.

~

Daiv started scribbling on his pad:

'The last word—for the wife'

Just then Joginder broke the silence, 'I am Joginder Singh. My father sent you here to make me realize how conniving women of today are. He believed that I was a joru ka ghulam who, unlike him, doesn't see the need to beat my wife. Witnessing all that has happened has opened my eyes to the reality that my wife is indeed very good. I have been neglecting and mistreating her. I have decided to apologize to her and make our lives harmonious and happy.'

Shravan nodded as if on cue. 'Very true. I, too, have gained invaluable insight. I was on the verge of sacrificing all my values and relations that I hold sacred, in the lure of a modern wife who would add to my status in life. I was so mesmerized by her white skin that I could not think straight. Thanks to you all, I was prevented from committing a ghastly mistake. I have quit my job and broken my engagement to that socialite. I am returning to my native town in Bihar. There I will start life afresh on the plot of land that we have. I'll try to find someone who holds my values dear, as a life partner. I thank you for coming here today from the core of my heart.' He bowed to Saloni in a silent pranam.

IN A NUTSHELL

The young waiter sitting on the stool was thinking, 'One thing is for sure. When I marry, I will be a husband with a spine . . .' Then he looked skywards and said, 'God willing.' Maybe he realized that this is not always in our hands.

30

The Last Word from the Author—For the Wife

On our first wedding anniversary, my mother presented us with a TV. She said, 'The TV is for the husband, the remote control is for the wife.'

Dear lady reader,

I know, despite my forbidding you, or is it because of it, some of you—the inquisitive ones—will surely have read this book. Remember what Eve did when forbidden to eat the apple in Paradise, and that was God speaking. Then what chance did I, a mere mortal, stand to stop you from reading this. In fact, I am glad you are reading this because you are the most important factor in the success of a marriage, much more important than the male.

However, if anything in these pages infuriated you, I apologize and hope that my hard-hitting approach will lead to some soul-searching. In any case, you will feel vindicated with my next book, titled *Slap Your Husband—With love*.

~

Daiv's gaze fell on the dustbin. The torn manuscript of his book, *Romance Your Wife — It Could be Your Marriage-Saver* stared back at him mockingly. He looked at the table and the heading of the last chapter of his new manuscript, *Learn to Slap Your Wife?,* jumped out at him. He had finished the chapter just the day before.

He started going through the chapter titled, 'Live-in Relationships—The Only Solution'.

'After deliberating for long, I have come to the conclusion that for the metro-male, live-in relationships (LIR) seem to be the only solution out of this rat-hole called "marriage" . . .'

- The best point about LIR is that it takes care of males' exploitation at the hand of the female . . .
- The Western world has tried this experiment with varying degrees of success. It is time that the Indian male wakes up to its possibilities and insists on it . . .
- In the beginning most women and their parents will oppose it. But if the male lobby stands as one on this issue, they would have to succumb and accept it . . .

Yesterday night, after finishing this chapter, he had felt like a saviour of male-kind. He had envisioned himself as a philosopher and a solution-giver along the lines of Karl Marx, who had liberated the oppressed classes. At that time, he had felt proud of his solution and the wisdom that he was going to impart to oppressed men.

Today, he wasn't so sure. The more he read his own words, the more extremist his views sounded even to himself. If this, indeed, was a solution, then it was definitely a flawed one, because it looked at only one side of the story. Today's encounter had definitely added a new dimension. The shrill cry of this new perspective was demanding to be addressed.

At long last he shook his head, tore his last chapter and tossed it into the wastepaper basket where his romantic ideas lay buried.

He took a fresh pad and started writing the last chapter afresh.

~

The last word—for the wife

This piece is addressed to the modern wife because whatever I tell the husband has scant meaning till you two work in tandem to make your marriage a success. If marriage, as an institution, has survived this long, it is because of the woman. You have not received your due recognition for this role. Men have exploited you, in the past, in most instances.

What has he gained from this exploitation and domination? If anything, he has a heavier load of worries on his head, resulting in hypertension, more heart attacks, more strokes and a shorter lifespan.

As roles get altered, there is a blurring of boundaries. You have started doing conventionally male-designated jobs and are doing them pretty well, as you by nature are more adaptable. Men are trying to do some of the jobs that were designated to women, but they are slower to adapt, as always. This has resulted in this new-found stress in our marriages—the stress of dominance and competition. Unfortunately, while staking the claim of equality, you also staked claim to his attitude and in the process lost your own strength of compatibility and tolerance.

One thing is sure. Marriage as an institution is very relevant today. It needs to be catered to and protected, otherwise this oasis of tranquillity will wither in front of our eyes. The alternatives all have one problem—they are not equitable. Take the example of live-in-relationships, which don't do justice to women. Call me old-fashioned, but at the end of an LIR, if the woman is eight years older and saddled with a child and no support, it is very unjust to her, despite the Supreme Court granting her alimony.

The problem is not in this institution but in attitudes dictating that one has to dominate or manipulate to gain from a relationship. It is a sad commentary of the times we live in. This attitude of 'take-take' and expect the other partner to 'give-give' was initially indulged in by the male. Now, when women have the chance, they've seized the opportunity but are committing the same mistake of trying to 'take-take' from the marriage.

Please don't. I don't mean for you succumb to male dominance or exploitation. All I am asking is that just because you can, don't become the exploiter. Be just.

As Sally very wisely says, the perpetrator of torture does not sleep easy.

We need to enter this institution with complete faith.

~

Plan for a married life—not divorce

For a long time, marriage could be defined as commitment to a relationship. When a person was said to be ready for marriage, it meant he was ready for the commitment and the responsibility that came with it.

With changing times, the mindset regarding the roles in marriage has also changed. Today, more and more people enter marriage thinking, 'Let us try out this arrangement', with a cynical suspicion that it might NOT work.

Having a plan B might be a good entrepreneurial strategy but when applied to marriage, it definitely shows a lack of

PRENUPTIAL AGREEMENTS

In 1980, research from three universities started following the cases of 2000 couples for twelve years. They found that men and women who had thought of divorce were nine times more likely to get divorced by the end of the study. Simply thinking about divorce, or contemplating what you will do in case of divorce, makes you vulnerable to it. Think what elaborately planning for it, as in prenuptial agreements, can do to your marriage.

commitment to Plan A. Marriage is built on trust and goodwill. It is your attitude that is of paramount importance. Only if you enter the bond with faith and optimism will you be able to absorb the jolt and turbulence of the post-honeymoon phase, the proverbial second year (or it could even be the second half of the first year).

If you enter marriage with trepidation and scepticism, your chances of tripping escalate. Which is why prenuptial bonds and agreements are not a good idea. They shout from the rooftop that you are entering the contract with suspicion.

~

Dear ladies—either accept or don't accept: decide one way

Today's gen-next considers life and marriage as a shopping mall, where you can take your trolley and choose what you want and what you don't. So the hubby taking over the responsibility of earning is added to the cart but his dominance in money matters is left on the shelf. The independence of a unit family is picked up from the shelf but the responsibility of bringing up children on your own is thrown out of the cart.

This is not how life operates. It's a package deal. In Package A you might get a twenty-inch TV + OTG + A/C + Scooter + two B/R apartment + eight hours of office for five days a week.

If you want that Optra Chevrolet car, then you might need to pick Package B, in which you either have to forego the TV and live in a single-room apartment with just a fan or take

Package C in which you have to put in twelve hours a day for six-and-a-half days a week.

Similarly, in marriage when you are looking for

1. Freedom +
2. Independence from in-laws +
3. The chance to pursue your hobbies the package will have to include
4. Not agreeing to having an arranged marriage +
5. Moving out of the boy's parents house and starting afresh (rather than the customary shifting of the woman to the man's house) +
6. Laying off claims to his ancestral property or business just as you have done to your parents'.

And, when funds are needed, say for a fresh business, both parents are approached equally (or neither is approached).

Now the choice is yours but you can choose only one.

A) You would abide by the prevalent norms and live according to the traditional system in the boy's houses. or

B) You would outright refuse to marry in accordance with the system of the girl shifting to the groom's house and insist on setting up a separate house with equal financial contributions at the very outset.

What you can't do is marry in the customary way, shift to the groom's house, enjoy the financial security provided by his parents but raise a stink regarding male dominance or in-laws interfering in your marriage. This will not only make your in-laws' life stressful but will also spoil your own life.

Regarding the shopping list of choosing a husband: assess the qualities that you expect from a husband: he should be handsome but shouldn't look at another woman, dashing but listen to all your nonsense meekly, an earner of big money but spend all his evening and holidays with you, a great romantic but a practical planner. The list is endless. Over-expectation?

Unfortunately, these qualities are too many to fit a single human. So, unless you want to be saddled with five husbands, like Draupadi, please tone down your expectations or else you will always feel that life has dealt you the short straw, at least in some department.

~

DONT UNDERMINE YOUR HUSBAND

You can't rise in stature by dwarfing your husband's image in front of others. By showing your husband in a poor light, you only lower your own status because people see you two as a single unit. If he is actually not so well off, then a corollary of this is that you as a part of the couple are not well off. If he is dumb, your couple is only 50 per cent wise (considering that you have excelled by proving yourself to be 100 per cent wise).

Also, when you lower his image, you lower his expectations of himself as a husband. He will become a lesser partner than he actually is. He will become less caring, less chivalrous and less responsible because he believes that only this much is expected from him. Expectations are a double-edged sword. You can neither have too much nor too little.

The worst part is—what have you belittled him for? Earning a few brownie points from insignificant outsiders?

Lastly, the very logic behind the reasoning of 'They have exploited us for so long, now it is our turn' is flawed. If you start breaking a mosque for every temple broken in the past or kill one of a certain community because his forefathers killed one of your community, then there would be nobody left in the end. Likewise in marriage. Enter it with an open mind, a positive attitude and a smile. Deal with it on a day-to-day basis, realizing that it is also not easy for the male. Acknowledge and reciprocate good deeds and voice your disagreement against any nonsense that comes your way. Chances are, your reward will be a joyful marriage and an indebted husband and as a result a happy and contented you.

This is what bliss is made of.

Epilogue

When the game of love is played right, both partners win.

I just wanted to share some good news with my readers. My wife came back to me after she read my book, *Learn to Slap Your Wife*. Actually, after I read my own book with an open mind and realized her going away was more my fault, I requested her to reconcile and come back.

—Daiv

P.S.: Please note the words 'with an open mind'. That is what is needed to turn a readable or an interesting book into a relation-saver. Try it.

A Note on the Author

Dr Sunil Vaid specializes in Paediatrics. He belongs to a family of vaids, traditional ayurvedic healers. He is also a motivational speaker and the author of six published books.

His dream: to quit his busy medical practice one day, and write full-time.

A Note on the Type

Garamond is the name given to a group of old-style serif typefaces named after the punch-cutter Claude Garamont (latinized as garamondus). It is considered to be among the most legible and readable serif typefaces for use in print applications and one of the most eco-friendly major fonts when it comes to ink usage.